CHARLOTTE S. CUSHMAN AS MEG MERRILIES

This picture of Charlotte Cushman is taken from the *Stage and its Stars,* published by Gebbie and Company in Philadelphia about 1895.

SIR WALTER SCOTT'S NOVELS ON THE STAGE

BY

HENRY ADELBERT WHITE

ARCHON BOOKS

1973

Library of Congress Cataloging in Publication Data

White, Henry Adelbert, 1880-
    Sir Walter Scott's novels on the stage.

    Original ed. issued as v. 76 of Yale studies in English.
    Originally presented as the author's thesis, Yale, 1924.
    Bibliography: p.
    1. Scott, Sir Walter, bart, 1771-1832. 2. Theater—Great
Britain—History. I. Title. II. Series: Yale studies in English,
v. 76.
PR5343.D7W5   1973   823'.7   72-10751
ISBN 0-208-01140-4

[Yale Studies in English, vol. 76]

CONTENTS

I. INTRODUCTION

Though the author of the Waverley novels had a hankering for many years to write a successful piece for the stage, he at last settled down in the conviction that his 'turn was not dramatic.' Of his five attempts at play-construction, only two reached the stage in anything like acceptable presentations. Introducing his *House of Aspen* in Edinburgh in 1829, the playbills timidly ventured the suggestion that the play afforded 'the admirers of the celebrated author an opportunity to test its fitness for the stage.' The acting roused a mild enthusiasm for six nights. Of *Auchindrane,* another sketch that had a brief run, Genest said wisely, 'It is a well-written poem, but not a good play—too much is said, and too little done.'[1]

Sir Walter Scott, however, knew the conditions that make successful nights in the playhouse. He followed the fortunes of the Royal Theatre of Edinburgh for many years, acting as one of the committee of managers, and nominating Henry Siddons for the position of active agent of the owners. He chose many of the plays that enjoyed more than ephemeral fame, such as Maturin's tragedies, and the literary dramas of his friend Joanna Baillie, to whom he gave valuable assistance in producing the *Family Legend.* For many years he found leisure to act as patron of ambitious young dramatists.* Eventually his fame crossed the ocean to New York, from which centre a presumptuous young lady forwarded her choicest composition (giving Scott the honor of paying the postage), with the modest request that the great English poet would do well to compose a prologue and epilogue, secure a copyright, and for-

---

[1] *Some Account of the English Stage* 10. 245; Dibdin, p. 328; Lockhart, *Life of Scott* 2. 327, 393, 475.

* Indicates that a further comment will be found in the appendix.

ward to her the benefits of a production at Drury Lane. Scott balked at this ambitious contract, and yet he did almost as much, in effect, if not in kind, for several of the dramatists of Scotland.

The Waverley romances came out at the right moment in a period of transition. By the time they began to swarm from the press, melodrama had firmly entrenched itself, after waging a lively contest with the conservative critics. In 1812, according to H. B. Baker, 'There was a positive dearth of dramatists, if we except melodramatists, who were plentiful enough.'[2] Plays with songs interspersed, musical interludes, and a variety of scenic effects, were by no means unfamiliar before 1810; but the vogue increased after this date so rapidly that the older 'legitimate' dramas soon fell into the class of occasional productions. Sentimental comedy gave way, after a further stubborn resistance, and even Goldsmith and Sheridan lost their vogue on many stages.

Thomas Holcroft's *Tale of Mystery* introduced the melodrama of characteristic French influence into England in 1802. By 1812, 'melodramatick' effects in drama were often mentioned. These were understood to include musical numbers, highly intensified scenes of contrast, surprise, and spectacle, and play-endings that called for no end of pageantry. For almost a generation critics and play-managers quarreled over the scope of the term 'melodrama.' From time to time the battle raged between the patent theatres and the numerous minor houses that sprang up all over London. The unlicensed halls and small places, of which more than twenty existed at some time in the decade just previous to 1825, resorted to the name *burletta* for an undefined, but extensive, group of types and modes of acting dramas. During these formative years of transition, it was quite to the advantage of the minor houses to have as much divergence

---

[2] *Our Old Actors*, p. 145.

of opinion and of plays as could reasonably be offered. Once the two patent theatres joined forces long enough to attempt to get Parliament to define *burletta* as 'a piece of verse accompanied by music.' Both the patrons and the unlicensed theatres opposed all such limitations, and no comprehensive agreement ever was reached.

Sheridan Knowles once remarked to Edward Fitzball, a maker of varied melodramatic plays, that *Macbeth* is a melodrama. Fitzball at once eagerly rushed to the conclusion that Shakespeare's tragedy is, therefore, not 'legitimate' in the definition advanced by the patent theatres, and so could be offered on any stage. Indeed, the unlicensed playhouses usually found some way of outwitting their older rivals. If the managers had not relied on the safe assistance of the playgoers themselves, they never would have dared to be so defiant of Drury Lane and Covent Garden. As it was, however, the unlicensed Surrey Theatre, during the management of the great Elliston, offered the same *Macbeth* as a 'grand ballet of action and music.' Yet the performance as such differed from the traditional ones only in that a few omissions were made from the text, and a few specialties and musical numbers were added as interludes. Another playhouse engaged some musicians to scrape now and then on their fiddles, so that a legitimate drama could be claimed as a genuine musical play. One programme went so far as to describe the *Beggar's Opera* as 'a burletta melodrama.'

In retaliation, the licensed theatres eventually copied the methods first used in such houses as the Surrey and the Adelphi. For a time it was a game of tit for tat. Bunn of Drury Lane abandoned most of the older forms of drama by 1839, and competed thereafter with the minor houses by introducing tight-rope walkers, sleight-of-hand performers, and even Van Amberg, the lion-tamer.

Nautical and other entertainments offered added varieties for the delight of crowded pits. Next followed the introduction of horses at Astley's Theatre shortly after 1800.

Blue Beard, one of the 'horse plays,' in 1811 ran for forty-four nights.   The critics fumed and stormed, but the public insisted that the horses must continue on the stage.   'So should the hordes of folly commence their triumphal register,' said one infuriated spectator, 'from the open flight of common-sense on this memorable night, when a whole troupe of horses first made their appearance in character at Covent Garden.'[3]

Likewise the musical settings of dramas won their place only after subborn resistance by the conservatives.   Ballads were thought to lower the tone of the drama.   Genest spoke of melodrama as 'an unjustifiable species,' which he also called 'a mixture of dialogue and dumb-show, accompanied by music.'   Now and then a critic continued to snipe at this form till after 1850.   'The introduction of music,' said one reviewer in Edinburgh, 'has induced gross and grievous violations of nature,' which he believed could be proved 'by a critical examination of all the modern dramas that have been rendered operatic.'[4]

Taking these elements as the basis of the study in the chapters that are to follow, I shall extend the definition of melodrama to include a wide range of new and startling effects on the stage.   Audiences in the North always doted on Highland pictures, with an assortment of glens, lochs, mountain-views, and narrow defiles which every playhouse, no matter how small, possessed in original painted scenery. The word *Gothic* often appears to describe interiors of halls, chapels, rooms, and single pieces of furniture.   In several plays, actors crossed torrents of real water on the stage in full view of applauding spectators.   The horses had their

---

[3] Dutton Cook, *On the Stage* 2. 305, and other pages. See also Adams, *Dictionary of the Drama,* p. 227; Percy Fitzgerald, *History of the English Stage* 2, chap. 3; Clement Scott, *Drama of Yesterday and To-day,* p. 481; W. S. Dye, Jr., *Melodrama from 1800 to 1840,* p. 5.

[4] *Theatre,* Edinburgh, Feb. 1, 1852.

part in bearing the warriors in numerous battles, while in most of the Scotch dramas the tartaned legions of the Highlanders, marching in their clans to the favorite airs of the pibroch, inspired competent scene-painters to vivify a host of canvases.

All these elements appear in the majority of the versions drawn from the poems and romances of Sir Walter Scott. One might spend a deal of time in carefully comparing the dramas with the novels and the metrical lays. Within the limits of the present study, however, I am forced to confine myself to some of the main characteristics; for otherwise a treatment, now altogether too extended, might well run to twice the length of this monograph.

Seventy-five different texts have been read with some degree of attention. One can hope to trace only the chief developments, with sufficient criticism and illustration to make the main thesis fairly comprehensive and clear. I have, therefore, decided to confine my present study to the novels, leaving the poems for future consideration. Some of the specific points of comparison are those mentioned below:

1. Faithfulness of the transcripts with regard to the original story as told by Scott.

2. Relationships among the several versions of the same novel.

3. Some of the conditions that affected the production and the success of the dramatic versions.

4. Incidental mention of the chief actors in the typical plays.

5. Criticism of some of the dramas as suitable for the acting of skilled artists.

6. Finally, an estimate of the main elements of melodrama that are common to most of the transcripts.

Some of the reviewers of the prolific adaptations from the romances of Scott sharply disagreed among themselves as to the merits of many of the transcripts. I have often been impressed by the seeming lack of agreement as to the judging of melodrama, and by the absence of anything that might be called recognized criteria. The conservatives always failed to do justice to the newer dramatic and musical effects. Again, the newer dramatists often failed to understand what was real, and what was merely evanescent in taste.

These and other conditions make dramatic estimates hazardous, and somewhat problematical. If the reviewers disagreed with regard to a certain performance or text of a play, I have endeavored to quote at least one typical example from each school of criticism. When some scored a play, and others lauded it to the heavens, the conditions of the performance, such as number of times, variety of the scenes, and names of the actors, have been taken as indicative of success or failure. Now and then excellent dramas failed because they fell to the lot of bungling actors. Not a few musical plays, on the other hand, won a notable triumph because of the songs or the acting, though they had no literary and little real dramatic merit. If the text of the play is still available, this has been studied to show its connection with the scenes of the original novel, and to form some estimate of its literary merit. In many cases, literary and dramatic excellences are not easily separable or comparable. Some good dramas, perhaps, made poor acting plays. Altogether, considering the variety of interests and elements, I have hoped to show how Scott reached the stage, and under what conditions his novels indirectly influenced the course of melodrama in the nineteenth century.

Most of the chief sources of the historical material will be acknowledged in the notes and bibliography. I owe a debt of gratitude to Professor George Henry Nettleton of Yale, for first suggesting the subject of versions of Scott on the stage. During the course of the preparation and revision of my account, he has offered valuable advice, which is most gratefully acknowledged. Whatever shortness of vision or deficiencies of critical treatment may be discovered in the following chapters should be charged to the pupil, and not to the teacher who has inspired him to undertake the subject. Professor Albert S. Cook, editor of the *Yale Studies in English,* has also offered kindly advice, and detailed criticism of the manuscript, while it has been preparing for the press.

II. GUY MANNERING

'Though Sir Walter Scott abstained strictly from any mention of the Waverley novels, he did not scruple to talk, and that with great zest, of the plays which had been founded upon some of them, and the characters as there represented.' Lockhart thus quotes J. L. Adolphus, a German critic who spent a month at Abbotsford in 1823, and who afterward wrote his conjectures as to the authorship of the Waverley novels in a series of letters to Richard Heber. Only once during the month did Scott even casually allude to his novels. Yet he often 'dwelt with extreme delight' on a number of the plays drawn from his romances, as he returned again and again to mention some scene 'with all the fresh and disinterested enjoyment of a common spectator.' Among many other illuminating comments, Adolphus gives this opinion: 'I do not know a more interesting circumstance in the history of the Waverley novels than the pleasure which their illustrious author received, as it were on the rebound, from those creations of his own mind which had so largely increased the enjoyment of all the civilized world.'[1]

In view of this generous enthusiasm of Scott for some of the plays that he often called his 'literary godchildren,' one does not marvel that the great author stepped aside from the beaten path to assist Daniel Terry, his friend of many years, in making a version of *Guy Mannering,* which was the first of a long line of transcripts from the Waverley romances. From the night of the first performances at Covent Garden, on March 12, 1816, Scott began to call similar attempts to dramatize his novels the art of 'Terry-fying.' After a number of such transformations had been accomplished, Scott once remarked, 'I believe my muse would be Terry-fyed into treading the stage even if I wrote a sermon.'

---

[1] Quoted by Lockhart, *Life of Scott* 2. 333.

Besides contributing the song, *Lullaby of an Indian Chief,* Scott helped select the dialogue and adjust the characterization of the main persons of the drama.[2]

OUTLINE OF THE TERRY AND SCOTT PLAY

As literature, the Terry drama falls somewhat below the standard of the best dramatic versions drawn from the Waverley novels. Yet the initial run was rather long for the age, this being due partly to the excellent music of Bishop, and the novelty of seeing a Scott romance in stage-clothes. Not until Lockhart published his *Life* in 1837, did the public learn that Scott had any hand in the composition of this first *Guy Mannering.**

Journals like the *Theatrical Inquisitor* warmed up more than usual to the merits of the melodrama. It was pronounced 'extremely well written,' the vocal selections being 'infinitely superior to the generality of musical comedies.'[3] Fifteen years later John Genest echoed this sentiment, though he was set against such productions.[4]

By omitting much of the material of the first dozen chapters or more, Terry secured the impression of unity and dramatic effectiveness. Other judicious changes heightened the interest for playgoers. Thus Meg and Dominie Sampson share the honors of the stage. Bailie Mucklethrift, a deliberate and practical ironmonger with an eye to business; Mrs. MacCandlish, the typical keeper of an inn; the two pairs of lovers; and even the tribe of Meg, all appear true to the originals in Scott.

Many little changes in the setting and plot, however, add to the vividness of the entire drama. Glossin, for instance, though not in need of funds, is a harder man to bargain with when Lucy begs him to be generous in his demands upon

[2] Lockhart 1. 404, 421; 2. 11, 13, 78, 306, 333, 393, 618, 628.
[3] 8. 231.
[4] 8. 550.

the estate. All he will do to relieve her anxiety is to hint that she might marry him. Julia Mannering is the sister, not the daughter, of Guy Mannering. The lake no longer is a part of the estate of Arthur Mervin, but belongs to Woodbourne, the park of the Colonel. Brown comes across the water in the early evening to attract the fair Julia by his fluting.

Meg herself appears less frequently, but with ever cumulating power in the drama. She gradually assumes the lead; and, to maintain her supremacy, a number of slight adjustments are made in the plot. Dominie Sampson, for example, does not seek Meg at her hut, but she goes forth and meets him in the way, forcing him to accompany her, and at last to summon help from the house at Woodbourne. In the final scene, she dies in the presence of the entire company at the cave of Glossin, and not alone with the clergyman and lawyer, as shown in the romance. Dirk and Glossin do not die violently, but live to become amenable to the procedure of justice.

When the curtain ascends in the first act, we behold the usual alehouse group, with their glees and rude joking. Not long afterwards, Mannering appears at the inn, and takes Glossin down a peg by intimating broadly that he knows a little about the estate at Ellangowan. The highest point of interest in the first act is the generous declaration of Dominie Sampson that he will never forsake Lucy Bertram, even though he can no longer serve her house as a hired attendant.

The Dominie, in the second act, precipitates an awkward situation, when he chances to run across Brown while prowling about late at night in the library of the Mannerings in search of a rare tome. Hearing Sampson approach, the ladies have draped their young visitor in the robes of a Brahmin, and have tried to conceal Brown behind a large harp, which the Dominie overturns in his awkwardness, bringing the master of the house from his own apartment.

Brown escapes through a window to the lawn outside, and the Dominie is led out by a servant, at the suggestion of Guy Mannering.

From the first appearance of Meg later in the second act, she dominates the entire action. Dandy Dinmont has already mentioned her as 'known as a witch all over these parts.' Likewise the young men of her Bohemian tribe, though they fear and respect her will, believe that her best days have gone for ever. Two of the bolder ones are discussing whether they must refuse to assist Dirk Hatteraick because Meg has ordered them to desist. One of them says in feigned contempt, 'Why, she doats; she's no more what she was, or ought to be: she's turned tender-hearted, and swears she'll hinder us from lifting a finger against the lad of Ellangowan, and that, if we attempt to keep him from his own, we but fight against fate.' The promise of gifts from Hatteraick still dangles before their imagination, firing their cupidity; while the members of the tribe urge as a pretext the ancient grudge against the house of Lucy and Henry Bertram, because the old laird broke up the gypsy camp at Derncleuch.

Dinmont and Brown, as Henry is still known, have arrived at the rustic encampment along the brow of the cliff overlooking the bay and the pirate boat lying at anchor. They are about to fall into the ambush set at the instigation of Dirk, who seeks once again to abduct Henry. Meg darts from behind a tent, advances a few paces, and stands leaning on her forked stick, while she surveys every line in the countenance of the young man with Dandy Dinmont. Henry mistakes her for a common fortune-teller, though his companion has mentioned her as 'the ruler and terror of them all.'

> 'My good woman,' he at last exclaims, 'do you know me, that you look at me so hard?'
> 'Better than you know yourself.'
> 'Aye, aye; that is, you'll tell my future fortune.'

'Yes, because I know your past.'

Spurning his offer of money, she continues in her most sententious tone,

'Offer it not. If, with a simple spell, I cannot recall times which you have long forgotten, hold me the miserablest impostor. Hear me, hear me, Henry—Henry Bertram!'

'Henry Bertram! Sure, I have heard that name; but when and where—'

'Hark! Hark! to the sound of other days! Listen and let your heart awake.'

While the gypsy girl, who recently served the travelers with food, sings a plaintive air, old scenes, faces, and events revive in the memory of young Bertram. After convincing him that Ellangowan should indeed be his own, Meg announces that changes now impend. By this moment, the treacherous gypsy lad has clambered up the rocky cliff, and Meg, lest he shall overhear, adopts the methods of the common fortune-teller in her warning to Henry. Looking into the palm of the heir to all the near-by estates, Meg exclaims that 'the fortunes past' have been 'wandering and woe, and danger, and crosses in friendship and in love.' Yet for the future are promised 'honor, wealth, prosperity, love rewarded, and friendship re-united!' For the present, however, 'there's a trace, which speaks of danger, of captivity perchance; but not of death.' Meg then whispers a warning to Dinmont to act resolutely, if his group is attacked by the band of Dirk, after which she vanishes without warning into the darkness.

Gabriel, the gypsy lad who offered to guide them, seeks to lead Dinmont and Henry into the hands of the conspirators that lie in wait at the foot of the cliff. On the rocky eminence above, Meg now once more appears, surveying calmly the scene below. At the proper moment, she calls to her tribesmen, 'Children, obey me, and depart.' Aided by a few of the gypsies who are faithful to the travelers, Dandy and Bertram now secure and bind Dirk as a prisoner. Now finally in full control of events, Meg bursts out in prophetic confidence: 'From one peril I have preserved young Bertram. His greatest and last is still to come. From that too will I protect him; for I was born to raise the house of Ellangowan from its ruins.'

In a short time, however, Sebastian bears word that Glossin has connived to assist Dirk to escape from arrest, and that both design to meet once more toward evening in the cavern along the sea, not far distant from the rude home of Meg at Derncleuch. Their plan is to separate Henry from the honest Dinmont, and to rush the young man aboard the lugger waiting for them in the bay, with Holland as their intended destination.

Meanwhile Dominie Sampson meets Julia and Lucy, who are taking a walk, while Miss Mannering seeks to interest her companion in the merits of the Colonel. Sampson appears to be still marveling because his 'vestments have been renovated miraculously.' The good man does not realize that his solicitous friends at Woodbourne have abstracted his ancient threadbare garments during the night, and have substituted for them a complete new suit. While he is still 'prodigiously' amazed that the climate of Scotland seems so favorable to preserve his clothing, Meg suddenly darts from behind some tree or bush, and confronts the befuddled Dominie in the road.

'Woman, I conjure thee!' cries Sampson in confused alarm, pouring forth a torrent of Latin scraps, amended by rude translations. Meg imperiously cuts him short by making him take a nip from her flask. In utter confusion of mind and language, the Dominie more than ever mixes his epithets. He announces that he will remember Meg's commands 'most pernicious; that is, most pertinaciously.' He calls her 'most accursed,' which phrase he at once amends to 'most accurate'; and at last promises to 'hie me nimbly, most fascinosus; I would say fascinating.'

Meg orders him to summon at once the party at Mannering's home, for all must join with her at the cave along the shore, 'or the heir of Ellangowan may perish for ever.' Unless her plans are driven astray,

> 'Bertram's right and Bertram's might
> Meet on Ellangowan height.'

Though rather 'oblivious,' indeed, as he himself remarks, and as digressive as ever, the Dominie at last makes Mannering and the ladies understand that armed men are needed at the old home of Meg at Derncleuch. Following the Colonel and some servants, Sampson rushes out, discharging a gun accidentally as he leaves the house.

All the main persons of the drama are marshaled at the seashore for the closing events. Here the play gathers up parts from several chapters, and weaves them cleverly together, to make a compressed and theatrical climax. There are no Pleydell, no burning of the buildings at the town, no arrest of Bertram, no murder of Glossin and suicide of Dirk Hatteraick, no Hazzlewood wishing to marry Lucy; but the essentials of the tale, otherwise, are carefully treasured, and brought into the definite focus of interest.

Bertram and Dinmont have been secreted within the recesses of the cavern. Dirk, Glossin, and Meg enter in turn. The two conspirators, fearing her power, and strength of arm, turn to taunts, boasting, and threats. Meg increases in confidence, spurred on by their open confession of past wickedness and impending designs. When the party within is well prepared, she proclaims that Dirk will leave this world by means of hemp. 'It is sown, it is grown, and hackled and twisted. Did I not tell you that the boy would return in spite of you? Did I not say the old fire would burn down to a spark, and then blaze up again?'

As she concludes this final prophecy, Meg throws a bit of hemp on the embers of the fire, which blazes into new life, lighting the cavern to the roof. Bertram rushes forward and seizes the hands of Glossin, while Dandy Dinmont wrenches a sword from Hatteraick; but the latter quickly draws a pistol, and Meg herself falls mortally wounded.

At this instant Mannering rushes in with his party, completing the arrest of the two confederates.

Little remains, except for Dominie Sampson to welcome to his arms his long-lost 'little pupil'; for Meg in her dying moments to bid them proclaim Henry as the real lord of Ellangowan; and for Julia to convey more than a mere hint that the Colonel and the heir are hereafter to be friends and 'brothers'; and for Dandy Dinmont, having been warmly praised for fidelity and courage, to let himself go far enough to kiss Lucy Bertram on the cheek. In utter amazement, Sampson caps the scene with his favorite exclamation, 'prodigious!' Then the characters arrange themselves in a final tableau, with Lucy and the Colonel in the centre, while all join in the 'Finale and Chorus.'

THE SONGS OF THE TERRY DRAMA

Altogether fourteen lyrics are interspersed throughout the first *Guy Mannering* play, being divided among convivial or general songs, solos, duets, and choruses. For this and similar productions, the name 'musical play' was often used in contemporary criticisms and printed dramas. They do not parallel very closely the ballad or comic operas of that time and later. The lyrics themselves never rise above mediocrity; yet some of them reveal an easy gracefulness, a turn of sentiment, or a droll situation that gave a vocalist a chance to make a hit. No modern reader of the printed Terry adaptation could doubt that the excellent music of Henry R. Bishop accounted for much of the popularity of the songs from 1816 to 1850. Bishop, a man of classical training and taste in music, was successively composer to both the patent theatres. A few of his songs and airs have lived into the twentieth century.

Much in the mode of the Elizabethan glees, the initial song at the inn of Mrs. MacCandlish celebrates the joys of winter. Two or three pensive ballads, the darlings of contemporary melodrama, are given to Lucy and her brother.

Thus Lucy expresses her sad memories and regret, when she is forced to leave the old home at Ellangowan. The topical ballad is represented by Dominie Sampson's 'A good fat hen, and away she goes.'   This has little connection with the narrative of the drama, but it gives the Dominie full license to reveal his 'prodigious' awkwardness, in a way that seldom failed to captivate the audiences, and proved utterly 'facetious,' as Sampson himself often said of other things.

Terry and Scott chose a lyric from the poems of Joanna Baillie for two gypsy men and a woman to sing as a trio. Some of the lines are

> The chough and the crow to roost have gone,
>   The owl sits in the tree;
> The hush'd wind wails with feeble moan,
>   Like infant charity.

Scott contributed the *Lullaby* as sung by Lucy Bertram, and also, years before, by Meg Merrilies in happier days. Meg again revives the smouldering memories of Henry by having a gypsy girl croon the old melody, now that she herself no longer has a voice for singing.   In the representations, however, Meg often took the lines as her best solo. Charlotte Cushman, the great American actress (to be mentioned at length a little later) always made a tremendous impression when she sang this sentimental lyric.

> Oh! hark thee, young Henry,
>   Thy sire is a knight,
> Thy mother a lady,
>   So lovely and bright.
> The hills and the dales,
>   From the towers which we see,
> They all shall belong,
>   My dear Henry, to thee.
> Oh, rest thee, babe; rest thee, babe;
>   Sleep on till day.
> Oh, rest thee, babe; rest thee, babe;
>   Sleep while you may.

When all the perils and uncertainties are overpast, Miss Mannering, Miss Bertram, and Henry join in a trio, while the chorus by the entire company welcomes once more the rightful heir to Ellangowan.

> For there's nae luck about the house,
>   There's nae luck ava';
>   There's little pleasure in this house,
>   When your smiles are awa'.

BRIEF STAGE-HISTORY OF THE FIRST GUY MANNERING

For the first production in 1816, Covent Garden trained one of the most capable casts. As the Dominie, Liston rose to great eminence, so that later at both the patent houses he continued to draw immense crowds. As Dinmont, Emery brought out another of his rustic impersonations which ruled as favorites for more than two decades. Miss Stephens introduced herself as an unusually charming young vocalist, and Mrs. Yates, first to create the difficult part of Meg, long was pronounced only second to the greatest in this rôle.

Soon this drama was winning its way in all the chief dramatic centres, such as Bath, Liverpool, Dundee, Glasgow, Edinburgh, and New York. One of the first performances occurred in America, where large crowds applauded the Dominie and Meg long before audiences of Edinburgh had seen them in the playhouse. Corbett Ryder made a tour of some of the northern cities during the first season, but evidently he did not reach the Scotch capital. After a tardy start in Edinburgh, however, *Guy Mannering* never failed to call forth applause for many years, with the chief revivals in 1851, 1855, 1859, and 1866. Some of the later performances in London fell in 1818, 1823, 1830, 1847, 1854, 1871, and 1883. More than twenty revivals succeeded in New York alone, with Charles Kean as a most popular Henry Bertram, as he was also in Liverpool, London, and Edinburgh at several different times. Joshua R. Anderson, Mr. and Mrs. Joseph Woods, and Henry Compton were other favorites in later days.   Charles Mackay led as Dominie Sampson.

Of the score of trained actresses who inspired at least some temporary enthusiasm, one may name Mrs. Renaud, Mrs. Yates, Mrs. Alfred Bunn, Mrs. William West, Mrs. Henry Siddons, Mrs. Egerton, and, in later days, Mrs. Waller and Madame Janauschek.   Of all those who at some time or other added Meg to their repertoires, Mrs. Egerton probably ranked next to the great Charlotte Cushman. William Oxberry, a very seasoned dramatist and critic, remarked once that he hated to think of being forced to determine which of these two actresses was the more talented. Edward Ball (who as Fitzball wrote many dramas) reported the tradition · that some considered Mrs. Egerton as Meg almost equal to the great Siddons as Lady Macbeth.[5]   Yet all contemporary accounts, on both sides of the Atlantic, seem to agree that Charlotte Cushman outranked them all as the gypsy sibyl.

Several favorite singers of the nineteenth century tried their art in the different rôles of the Mannering musical drama.   Among the famous tenors, John Braham perhaps attained the widest and most enduring regard, though he often failed miserably as an actor.   Indeed, Walter Scott himself spoke of Braham as 'a beast of an actor, though an angel of a singer.'[6]   Sims Reeves, pronounced by many the most finished vocal performer of his age in England, tried a part or two in the Mannering play, but won his greatest fame in other parts, only a few of which were taken from the Scott romances.   The Seguin Opera Company, different troupes managed by Joseph Woods and by Mr. and Mrs. John Wood, and the Harrison-Pyne singers, all kept alive

---

[5] *Thirty-Five Years of a Dramatic Author's Life* 1. 95.   See also Adams, *Dictionary of the Drama*, p. 320; Marston, *Our Recent Actors*, p. 114.

[6] Lockhart 2. 68; Adams, p. 199.

the best of this and other Scott dramas on both sides of the Atlantic. Harcourt Bland, who also was an author, vocal teacher, and lecturer on plays, maintained at Glasgow for years a consistent lead in a variety of characters, including Guy Mannering. Miss Stephens continued to add to her list of rôles, until she included Diana Vernon, Effie Deans, Isabella (of the *Antiquary*), and Rowena.[7]

Passing over a host of minor but very worthy performers in *Guy Mannering,* we now come to the great Macready and Joseph Jefferson the first (grandfather of the J. J. of Rip Van Winkle note). Both these gentlemen won considerable early fame in these parts. Liston for two decades proved a continued favorite as the Dominie, Wamba, Nicol Jarvie, Captain Dalgetty, and Jonathan Oldbuck, in one or another of the dramatizations of Scott.[8] Henry Compton always brought out the 'touching effect of devotion to his pupil' as shown by Sampson, and evidently above all others revealed 'a soul of pathos in things absurd.'[9]

Since Nancy Sykes, Meg Merrilies, and Lady Macbeth are the characters most often cited as revealing the genius of Charlotte Cushman at its climax, one might well study at length some of the traits of her peculiar interpretation of the gypsy prophetess. Nothing illustrates the conditions of the producing of melodrama more to advantage. For more than thirty years, this great American actress reverted again and again to the parts in which she won her early triumphs. Thus Meg Merrilies became one of her first, and also one of her last, great impersonations.

Some of the more important dates and places of her acting may be cited as typical of the immense number. After losing the range of her voice while attempting too ambitious operatic rôles in the St. Charles Opera House of New

[7] *Dict. Nat. Biog.* 54. 169.
[8] *Ibid.* 33. 239.
[9] Marston, *Our Recent Actors,* p. 114.

Orleans—then the second largest in America—Miss Cushman was advised to take up a speaking part in drama. Having been offered a contract by the manager of the Bowery
Theatre in New York, she appeared first as Helen Macgregor on September 13, 1836, after having already appeared
in the character of Lucy Bertram, in 1833, with the Joseph
Woods Company of Boston. Her biographers[10] seem to
believe that she acted as Meg in May, 1837, but it must have
been a year or two before she became known in this difficult
part. She certainly came into prominence while appearing
in 1839 with John Braham in New York City, at which time
she acted as understudy to Mrs. Chippendale during the
latter's illness.·

Some of her notable triumphs occurred at the Broadway
in 1849, Niblo's a year later, at the Broadway again in
1852 and 1855, then at the Winter Garden in 1860, at
Tripler Hall in 1871 with Wallack, and at last for her farewell performance in 1874.

Across the ocean some of her great victories were won
in Liverpool and Birmingham, where she created a 'furore'
in 1846; at the Surrey, London, in 1848; the Prince's
Theatre, Glasgow, 1855, when she was accompanied in the
cast by her sister Susan; and at the Haymarket, London, in
1854.[11]

Testimony in great abundance comes down to us from
her biographers, associates, and the dramatic critics of the
period. John Braham, he of the golden voice, acting as
Henry Bertram in the New York production of 1839 or
1840, in which she gained lasting fame, was among the very
first to pay tribute to her intuition and realism as Meg—a

---

[10] Besides her biographers, see Hutton, *Plays and Players*, p. 228;
Brown, *New York Stage* 3. 39; Coleman, *Fifty Years* 2. 383.

[11] See Brown 1. 243; 3. 39, 110 for details. Others may be found
by consulting the index. See Hutton, p. 228. Hereafter, in the footnotes, the title of a book already cited will usually not be repeated,
but merely the name of the author, and the reference, will be
given.

realism sufficient to make 'a cold chill run all over me,' as Braham later exclaimed.[12]

Clara Clement, one of her biographers, asserted that Miss Cushman awoke suddenly to her profound impression of the solitude and pathos of the old gypsy woman.[12] One intense scene of the drama reveals the key to this complete understanding. Meg's disapproval of the gypsies who seek to aid Hatteraick is well known by her tribe. Yet some of the youths hesitate to bend to her imperious will. A bolder gypsy than the others says lightly, 'Why, she doats. She's no more what she was, or ought to be; she's turned tender-hearted.'[13] From this as the starting-point, Miss Cushman must have grown to realize the many discordant elements in the life and actions of Meg herself. From this first 'powerful influence,' the eminent actress, says another biographer, 'gave herself with her usual energy, and flashed at once upon the stage in the startling, weird, and terrible manner which we all so well remember.'[14]

Inspired by a fine understanding of Meg, then, Charlotte Cushman allowed her conception of the gypsy's imperial sway to mount gradually toward the grand climax of sacrifice for the sake of the young lord of the house of Ellangowan. Six times the sibyl flits out of the shadows of nowhere, or arises from beside the roadway, to confront Dinmont and Henry, Dominie Sampson, Dirk Hatteraick, or the young folk of the wandering tribe. From each of these sudden meetings greater and greater interest arises, with the mystery deepening, until one can behold at every turn the old and broken gypsy woman in full command of all whom she would have obey her fiats. Acting changes into real life itself. No doubt, Meg Merrilies was Charlotte Cushman, and Charlotte Cushman was Meg Merrilies. Audiences now and then may have come to question her

[12] Clement, *Life of Charlotte Cushman*, pp. 14, 15, 81, 96.
[13] Act 2, scene 3, in *Modern Standard Drama* 77. 38.
[14] Stebbins, *Charlotte Cushman*, p. 147.

powers as an artist, but evidently all who saw her as Meg went out convinced that this is a real personage in Scott's novel, in Terry's play, and, above all, in the acting of Charlotte Cushman. We are told that it was uncanny, magical, and reasonable beyond reason, despite all contradictions and difficulties that may have appeared at first.

During some of the tensest moments of the drama, both character and actress arose to summits of utter realism. There is the pathos of the forsaken and tottering ancient prophetess, and yet there is also the iron will that never acknowledges more than a temporary defeat. Already Meg seems like a disincarnated spirit. Her meeting with Henry Bertram, when she reveals to him that his name was never Brown; the telling of his fortune, 'honour, wealth, prosperity, love rewarded, and friendship re-united'; her determination at the cost of even her life to protect Henry from the greatest and last peril; her braving of Dirk and his rowdy companions; and, above all, her prophecy—stand forth as great touches of the drama. Perhaps the climax of the interest occurs when Meg stands on the cliff, overlooking two parties below—Dirk and his crew, ready to take Bertram aboard the lugger; and Dinmont and Henry, with a few guides, proceeding into the trap ahead. From the eminence Meg surveys the two groups, and calls to her people, 'Gypsies, strike not at your peril! Children, obey me, and depart.' Perhaps the climax of the interest in Meg herself occurs when she sends word to Guy Mannering, and foretells her own imminent death. 'That you tell him not to forget Meg Merrilies, but to build up the old walls in the glen for her sake, and let those that live there be too good to fear beings of another world; for, if ever the dead come back among the living, I will be seen in that glen many a night after these crazed bones are whitened in the mouldering grave.'[15]

[15] The quotations are from the American edition of Charlotte Cushman's time. At some points the wording differs from that of the English texts.

'Like Scott himself,' wrote Marston, 'she had made out of the forlorn woman—with her fealty to the house of Ellangowan, with her passionate, almost maternal love for its heir, her fixed resolution to restore him, her weird insight into the future, including her own fate—a union of the terrible, the pathetic, and the mysterious which was truly tragic.'[16]

Doubtless Charlotte Cushman added somewhat to the original conception of Meg in the novel. Terry's drama unifies and adds some material. Yet Scott again and again added little touches to describe Meg more fully, and make her seem a human being, though considerably disordered in mind. In chapter 28, Scott himself informs us of Meg's apparent madness, 'And yet it is more like the wildness of energy than of madness.' In chapters 2, 4, 8, 27, and 53, he also describes Meg at some length, giving us a picture of how she might appear on the stage. 'The mixture of insanity and wild pathos with which she spoke these last words, with her right arm bare and extended, her left bent and shrouded beneath the dark red drapery of her mantle, might have been a study worthy of our Siddons herself.'

When one compares these definite pictures of the novel with the statements of those who witnessed the acting of Charlotte Cushman, he is led to believe that the eminent actress studied Scott's text faithfully. She must have contributed much of her own personal feeling and interpretation, as a matter of course; and hence many have seen in her production a Meg that is quite different from the conception of her in the novel. 'It has been said (we think hypercritically),' remarks H. L., who prepared the text for the New York edition, 'that the Meg Merrilies of Miss Cushman, great as it is admitted to be, is not that of Sir Walter Scott. If it is her own creation, the greater the genius of the artist. From her first entrance from the

---

[16] *Our Recent Actors* 2. 81. See also Robbins, *Twelve Great Actresses,* p. 357.

gypsy tent to her last death-throe, the character is never for a moment lost sight of: appearance, dress, gait, gesture, intonation of the voice, all are in perfect keeping. It stands out like Spagnoletto's figures, in bold broad lights and shadows, and with a power of life and truth that only life itself can be its parallel.'[17]

Henry Morley, one must notice, thought the acting of Charlotte Cushman finally became somewhat strained. The larger effects came from the tone, poise, and stage-manner, more than from the words that the actress was speaking.[18] James E. Murdock, the American actor and elocutionist, wrote in depreciation of Miss Cushman's 'intensely prosaic nature,' and of her 'fierce personality in that dramatic nondescript, Meg Merrilies.' Mr. Murdock also believed that this actress allowed 'an imperious wilfulness' to take the place of 'imagination all compact.'[19] From his brief remarks one may fairly conclude that he overlooks the merit in Miss Cushman of having chosen the part which best suited her temperament, manner, and rather masculine stage-presence. Should this be called a defect of genius, or a proof of it?

In all fairness, however, one must admit that Miss Cushman herself late in life expressed a definite preference for her acting of Lady Macbeth. She even disparaged her Meg. 'Yes,' Marston reports her as saying a bit testily, 'with an outlandish dress and a trick or two, I can bring more money to the theatre than when I give the public my life's blood in my finest creations.'[20]

Several further quotations from contemporary criticism reveal that the dress, make-up, and manner contributed a large share to the peculiar effect of her acting and speech.

[17] *Modern Standard Drama,* vol. 77, introduction, speaking of the production at the Old Broadway Theatre, New York, 1849.

[18] *Journal of a London Play-Goer,* p. 80, after seeing Miss Cushman at the Haymarket Theatre, London, 1854.

[19] *Stage,* p. 239.

[20] *Our Recent Actors* 2. 81.

Banyham presents to us a clear picture of her on the stage in Glasgow. Darting noiselessly from the gypsy tent, she did not appear fully in the moonlight till she straightened up and stood motionless, 'with her large lustrous eyes, o'ershadowed by her white eyebrows, gazing on Henry Bertram. One bare, gaunt, wrinkled arm was outstretched, and a skinny finger pointed to him—she supporting herself on the bough of a tree.' Gradually the impression deepened, until Meg became 'a weird presence dominating the dark woods and cavernous hills, an inspired prophetess, an avenging fury.'[21]

Gradually from here and there all the various items of her nondescript costumes were accumulated. Finally, her dress was fashioned from different colors and odd patches, but these were arranged according to rude ideas of precision and taste. At the Broadway Theatre in 1849, Charlotte Cushman's apparel consisted of a brown cloth petticoat and body, torn old red cloak, torn pieces of plaid, and old russet sandals. After a time, her face also came to have a regular set of lines, placed as Miss Cushman herself said where she 'just felt' they ought to be. When she leaned mysteriously on the forked staff or sapling that she often carried, looking intently without speaking at some object or person, her entire manner seemed to hint that she could indeed penetrate the spaces invisible to ordinary sight.[22]

Compare with this account the picture that is used as a frontispiece of our present study, and with the description by Scott in chapter 8 of the novel. In all three one may observe a certain harmony of conception and arrangement. When Meg Merrilies, at the end of the line of thirty gypsies that were leaving Derncleuch, confronted the laird of Ellangowan, who had just dispossessed them, she appeared in Scott's account of her as follows:

---

[21] *Glasgow Stage*, p. 149.
[22] Mrs. Catherine Reingolds-Winslow, *Yesterdays with Actors*, p. 21.

'We have noticed, that there was in her general attire, or rather in her mode of adjusting it, somewhat of a foreign costume, artfully adopted perhaps for the purpose of adding to the effect of her spells and predictions, or perhaps from some traditional notions respecting the dress of her ancestors. On this occasion, she had a large piece of red cotton cloth rolled about her head in the form of a turban, from beneath which her dark eyes flashed with uncommon lustre. Her long and tangled black hair fell in elf-locks from the folds of this singular head-gear. Her attitude was that of a sibyl in frenzy, and she stretched out, in her right hand, a sapling bough, which seemed just pulled.'

Many thought Charlotte Cushman's Nancy Sykes her most realistic creation, Lady Macbeth her most artistic, and Meg Merrilies her most theatrical and pathetic. In the devotion of the old nurse to the house of Ellangowan, her maternal solicitude for the life and fortunes of Henry Bertram, and the deep pathos of her loneliness in the impersonation of Meg, the great Cushman may have revealed some of the solitude, anxiety, and tenderness of her own celibate life.

Next after Miss Cushman, some of the patrons of the drama called Emma Waller a noble and affecting Meg; for 'her delineation was wild, fearful, and startling. She gave it all of Charlotte Cushman's powerful impulses, but blended with it a feeling of pathos that killed the whirlwind of passion, and smothered the ruggedness of its features.'[23]

OTHER MANNERING PLAYS IN ENGLISH

One effective dramatization of a Waverley novel almost invariably encouraged new playwrights to try their own luck with imitations or with variant transcripts. *Guy Mannering* heads the list of early adaptations, though only Terry's musical play, and one or two others, came to any considerable vogue.

[23] Brown 1. 409; 3. 117.

Either an entirely new adaptation, or at least a generous revamping of the first Waverley drama, appeared on the stage at the Park Theatre, New York, in the spring of 1818. No account is extant, save the contemporary notices in connection with the preliminary advertising in the newspapers. The musical numbers described indicate that they were unlike those of the Terry musical play, which had been produced two years previously in New York.[24] Since two of the original New York cast are mentioned for this second drama, one might reasonably infer that the first *Guy Mannering* had been revamped, or imitated, in the meantime.

During the second decade of the century, Hodgson's *Juvenile Drama* condensed and simplified several of the dramatizations, for the use of children's playhouses. Directions for producing on a parlor or miniature stage usually accompanied each piece. *Guy Mannering* is represented in the series by a shortened form of Terry's version, with the difficult parts curtailed, the wording made more suitable to children, and the scenery rendered somewhat meagre. The cavern of Meg, for instance, becomes a stretch of shore along the bay near Ellangowan.

THE WITCH OF DERNCLEUCH

For a leader of the August programme in 1821, the English Opera House offered a play by 'Mr. Blancham,' who immediately was recognized as J. Robinson Planché, author of the *Vampire,* and numerous dramatic pieces of almost every type. In the absence of any published text, one must now rely on the critics to determine how closely this new version followed the novel, and the first drama based on it. Lucy Bertram disappears altogether, but Julia Mannering is restored as the daughter, not the sister, of the Colonel. Young Hazzlewood again appears as a suitor, but Brown is preferred, as in Scott, by the lady he admires.

[24] *Evening Post* of day before the first production; Brown 1. 114.

Charles is wounded when Dirk and his gang attack the Mannering estate, not in a skirmish along the country road. Dandy Dinmont first enters the action at the burning of the Custom House and Jail at Portanferry. Planché contributed one wholly original scene that shows Hatteraick and a smuggler companion discussing in detail the various rogueries practised on the family at Ellangowan. Yet two highly effective scenes, both of the novel and of some of the other dramatic versions, do not appear in the work of Planché. One describes the initial appearance of Meg when Dinmont and Bertram sup at the gypsy camp above the rugged shore; the other pictures the attack made on them by the cohorts of Hatteraick.

Evidently the Lyceum Theatre drew some 'unceremonious drafts' on the music of Henry Bishop, including the gypsy glees, which made such a tremendous hit when the original piece by Terry held the boards at Covent Garden. Yet the overture was 'composed anew,' with additions also of some sentimental songs of mediocre merit, set to the notes written by William Reeve. An account of a later performance in Dublin mentions some of the titles of these, or at least of similar lyrics; such as, 'When the youth was kneeling, His passions revealing,' 'Tho' twined round my heart, dear,' and 'It is the hour to lovers worth.'

In Dublin the spectacular burning of Portanferry Jail was described as 'the finest and most sublime scenery and scenic machinery that we ever witnessed.' Yet the dialogue did not please, and the critics called on Samuel Beazley, a favorite reviser of plays, to fuse the best of the work of Planché with parts of the original Terry drama. The latter, however, found a permanent place in the hearts of the audiences, when singers like John Braham and Miss Stephens personally received something like an ovation in the rôles of Henry and Lucy, when they appeared in Dublin.[25]

[25] *London Times,* July 31, 1821; *Drama,* Dublin, pp. 132, 139, undated.

THE GIPSY OF DERNCLEUCH

Never willing to be outdone by rival playhouses, Sadler's Wells next brought forward Douglas Jerrold's *Gipsy of Derncleuch,* on August 21, 1821, three weeks after the English Opera House had introduced another Mannering melodrama. Phelps as the Colonel, and Mrs. Egerton in her old favorite impersonation of Meg, aroused much favorable notice, as she did later in Dublin and elsewhere, in numerous revivals of the Jerrold modification. In broad outline, Jerrold followed an excellent French musical play, then 'performing in Paris with the greatest success,' according to announcements of the London programme. Though Jerrold adhered to Scott in the chief details of the action, his play is distinctly disappointing to the modern reader. It is a case of following the letter, and losing the inner reality and literary charm.

Meg, for instance, has degenerated into a common fortune-teller and witch, quite unlike the character in the novel and the other plays. Dominie Sampson has likewise become a shell of his former self—a mere caricature of his old awkwardness and pedantry. Even the lovers are pale creatures of sentiment and convention.

Yet the Jerrold transcript won its share of applause in London, Edinburgh, and especially in Dublin. North of the Tweed, it was the acting of Mackay as the Dominie, of Mrs. Renaud as Meg, and of Miss Stephens in her favorite part as Lucy, that won the greatest interest. The critics, nevertheless, spoke harshly of the irrelevant songs in both the Jerrold and Terry plays. In Ireland, however, the musical parts, notably the sentimental solos, called forth abundant favorable comment. This was due to the love of the Irish for opera, irrespective of any strict adherence to the story or the sentiment of Scott's novels. Temporarily the Jerrold imitation eclipsed all others in Great Britain; yet, eventually, it fell into oblivion, while the Terry drama continued to maintain a steady interest.[26]

[26] *Dublin Univ. Mag.,* May, 1851.

With the opening of the autumn season in the theatres, the Coburg ventured to claim its share of patronage by revamping the Jerrold piece, and calling it *Dirk Hatteraick, the Dutch Smuggler.* One review spoke of the new work as a 'Grand Legendary Melodrama,' without offering any definite information as to the meaning of the phrase as thus applied.[27] Lucy and Dinmont no longer had parts. According to the secondary title, *The Sorceress of Derncleuch,* one infers that Dirk shared with Meg the interest of the production. Obviously, the Dutch smuggler was brought into the spotlight for the purpose of giving T. P. Cooke another chance to show himself as 'the best sailor, out of all sight and hearing, that ever trod the stage.'[28]

Eight or ten subsequent modifications of *Guy Mannering* call for no particular comment. All had their brief day on the boards. Some of the most popular ones appeared after 1850. The only good additional version before then was a 'popular burletta,' as the playbills announced a musical play, at the St. James Theatre in 1838, with the manager, John Braham, as Henry Bertram, and Madame Sala as Meg Merrilies.

Thirteen years afterward, the same house used parts of the novel for the marionettes. Henry Leslie, in Glasgow in 1873, revived an older version, or made an original one, which attracted only temporary notice. Francis C. Burnand wrote one of his clever travesties, entitled *Here's Another Guy Mannering,* which was followed by Robert Reece's *Guy Mannering in a New Guise.* Dion Boucicault tried to bring Meg once more into the limelight with his *Spae Wife,* at the Elephant and Castle in 1866. During the next season, William Wyndham varied from the plot of the novel so much that Edinburgh audiences gave his drama a cold reception.

Finally, in America, Robert W. Chambers attempted to fan into flame the dying embers of enthusiasm for Meg and

---

her stage-companions. Though praised as a good entertainment, his play at Daly's in New York, 1897, departed essentially from the narrative and spirit of the original, and in this respect was censured by some of the critics. Yet the acting of Ada Rehan as Meg, Tyrone Power as the Dominie, and Mrs. G. H. Gilbert as Mrs. MacCandlish, notably for her Scotch jig, received some encomiums.[29]

SCOTT ON THE FOREIGN STAGE

Scott always had a prodigious following in France, where his novels formed the basis of numerous adaptations in drama and opera; and the vogue of his works extended into Germany and even into Russia.

Of a number of German dramas drawn from the Waverley novels, one of the most interesting is a 'Schauspiel,' written by William von Gersdorf, and printed in Liegnitz in 1818. The title is *Meg Merrilies, die Zigeunerin,* but details of representation are lacking. So many of the incidents of the novel are used that the impression one gets is rather unfavorable. Some changes are made to suit the persons to German ideas of rank. Thus the poor befuddled Dominie is a 'Magistrate'; honest Dandie Dinmont is created 'bailiff of the Royal domains of Charlieshope,' Lucy is 'Lucie Bertram von Ellangowan.' Sir Robert Hazzlewood's son, Karl, is paired off with Lucy Bertram. Glossin, made rather a figure, urges Sir Robert to punish Brown for wounding Hazzlewood's son. Though still wearing a mantle of prophecy, Meg has lost much of her imperial sway over her subjects. One also misses the humor of the Dominie and his awkwardness, but finds instead additional touches of sentiment in the characterization of the lovers.

Two operatic versions gained permanent fame in France. A *Sorcière; ou, l'Orphelin Ecossais,* composed by Victor and Frédéric, opened at the Gaieté late in the spring of

[29] *Drama Register,* 1852, p. 21; Clarence, *'Stage' Cyclopædia,* pp. 288, 422; Adams, p. 221; *N. Y. Evening Post,* March 13, 1897; letter from Mr. Chambers.

1821.[30]   During the first season it ran forty-nine nights, and during the second, eighteen.   The *Pandore,* one of the chief theatre-journals, called this piece an 'encyclopædia' of almost 'everything that has been in a thousand and one melodramas.'[31]   Some of the elements stressed are disguise of the main characters, a dash of the supernatural, many sentimental songs both on and off the stage, a considerable number of people on the boards at once, and several high emotional climaxes.

Much of the original material, however, is borrowed from Scott.   The dramatic exposition is clear, the traits of character are precisely shown, and the scenery is picturesque. Mannering here too has become a lord, Glossin a sheriff with a valet, Hatteraick a lieutenant; and Lucy, in the absence of a girl companion, is in charge of a typical French 'gouvernante.'   Meg retains much of her original fire, and the Dominie much of his absurdity, which is best shown in the scene of his accidental discharging of the musket. Curiously enough, Julia Mannering is provided with a second suitor, whom the Colonel disapproves; yet at one point the young miss is trying to get the recognized lover to bear a message for her to the rival.

Another Gallic libretto, from the prolific hand of A. Eugène Scribe, was set to music by Adrien F. Boieldieu, the acknowledged leader of the French school of light opera. From *Guy Mannering* come the name Brown and the motive of the lost heir; but the chief incidents of the plot come from the mystery of the White Lady of Avenel, as described in the *Monastery.* with touches from the *Abbot* and two or three other Waverley novels.   Called *Dame Blanche,* this operatic play appeared in Paris in December of 1825, and as the *White Lady,* in partial translation, at Covent Garden two seasons later.

[31] Stage names for Victor J. H. Brahain-Ducange and Frédéric Dupetit-Méré.
[31] For May 4, 1821.

III. ROB ROY

Waverley, the earliest of the romances by Sir Walter Scott, attracted no adapter till several of the other works had lived their day upon the stage. It is not relevant to consider the causes of this neglect. Somewhat less than two years elapsed between *Guy Mannering,* the second novel of the series, and *Rob Roy,* the sixth. Since the latter brought out rounds of applause on many stages, it will next be considered in detail. Some of the minor dramatizations of the remaining novels, in the meantime, will be reserved for later chapters. These include the *Antiquary, Old Mortality,* and *Black Dwarf.* The latter two, as if they had been composed by another hand, appeared in a new series, entitled *Tales of my Landlord.* Scott could not withdraw the familiar evidences of his genius, however, and so the disguise was easily detected. Though few knew absolutely before 1826 that he was indeed the author of the two series, everybody suspected it, and several critics ventured to ascribe all the novels to the 'Great Unknown,' or the 'Wizard of the North,' which were two of the phrases frequently applied to Scott. Yet not even Joanna Baillie and Charles Mackay, two of his intimate acquaintances, knew the secret from the lips of the celebrated man himself.[1]

What claims has *Rob Roy* as a drama? The musical version by Pocock and Davy saved the Royal Theatre of Edinburgh from bankruptcy, awakened the embers of enthusiasm for drama in Scotland, brought Mackay to the zenith of his fame as a comic actor, and drew forth hearty praise from Scott himself. As recently as 1904, John Coleman testified that *Rob Roy*—next to a few of the Shakespearean tragedies, *School for Scandal,* and *East Lynne*—for many years outstripped all other dramas in Scotland.[2]

[1] Carhart, *Life and Work of Joanna Baillie,* p. 35; Lockhart 2. 563.
[2] *Fifty Years of an Actor's Life* 2. 365.

The Pocock Musical Drama

Even before Isaac Pocock and John Davy composed a *Rob Roy* for London, an early transcript had appeared at the Pantheon Theatre in Edinburgh, within a fortnight after the original came from the press on the final day of December, 1817. Haste in composition and low adaptability to an audience seem to have damned this play. Everything was tried to make the scenery and acting above the average, and 'several fashionables graced the boxes' to show their interest; yet somehow the piece lived for only a few nights.[3]

Nearly two months elapsed before Pocock's *Rob Roy Macgregor; or, Auld Lang Syne* went into rehearsal at Covent Garden. Here, too, no expense was spared on furnishings or drop-scenes. Beginning on March 18, 1818, the performance continued for thirty-two evenings, an unusual number for the period. Later in the season it began a new series, which intermittently proceeded at Covent Garden, until the rival patent theatre engaged the acting rights in July, 1821, for a revival on a rather splendid scale.

Even a cursory reading of the drama shows that Pocock followed the original story. A large part of the first chapter is, however, omitted. As the curtain rises, we view the inevitable inn, with Owen, Francis Osbaldistone, and a certain Mr. Campbell, deep in conference. While Francis has remained at the Hall in England, letters designed for him have mysteriously failed to arrive. He has, therefore, not learned of the impending financial crash of the house of Osbaldistone, through the plots of Rashleigh, Frank's cousin and rival for the affections of Diana Vernon. In the following scene, Sir Frederick Vernon, disguised as Father Vaughan, is leaving Osbaldistone Hall, having received assurances from his daughter that Frank is trustworthy. As the latter enters the library, Sir Frederick is going out through a secret panel in the wall. Soon afterward, Diana

---

[3] Dibdin, *Annals,* p. 338.

sends Frank to Scotland, with certain letters, which he is pledged not to open till ten days before the bills of the Osbaldistones finally become payable.

The drama next introduces the temperamental Bailie Jarvie in his house in Glasgow. The mysterious Campbell now appears to warn Frank against meeting Rashleigh in the streets of the town. Frank soon discovers that Campbell is the Highland chieftain, Rob Roy, when he appears at the Tolbooth, where the Dougal creature presides, and where Owen of the firm has been imprisoned by some unknown persons. Though the nature and intentions of Campbell remain somewhat unrevealed, Frank soon learns the details of the embarrassment of the house of Osbaldistone, and also something further of the schemes of his cousin against himself, Diana, Sir Frederick, and the cause of the Highlanders.

More of the designs of Rashleigh appear fully developed in the second act. Campbell comes from nowhere to rush between Frank and his cousin, as they are preparing to fight it out in the public park of Glasgow. Again, the scene shifts to England, where Sir Frederick informs Francis that the odious cousin has turned traitor to the Roman Catholic interests as well as to the rest, since Diana still refuses to become his bride. Letters arrive by messenger, a man who might be the elusive Highlander himself in one of his many disguises. Induced by these important missives and by several further reasons, Sir Frederick and Diana decide to visit the Highlands.

Now, in the second act, we are introduced to a motley array of English and Scotch persons at the inn kept by Jean M'Alpine. We notice successively Frank and Dougal, Captain Thornton of the English company that is seeking Rob Roy and others of the Highland clans, with several attendants, and finally Nicol Jarvie himself, who enlivens this act with two of his drollest adventures. 'Hawks are abroad' is the gist of a message from Campbell to Frank.

The English soldiers and the group of Scotch travelers do not look upon each other with any degree of toleration. Francis and one of the soldiers enter into a quarrel, which precipitates the following lively scene, as described in the language of the drama:

> Galbraith. No, we want naither your company nor your pranty; and, if ye be pretty men, draw (unsheathing his sword, while Frank and a Scotch companion do likewise).
>
> MacStuart. Ay, traw!
>
> Bailie (starting up). Draw! I'm neither a pretty man, nor have I ony thing to draw; but, by the soul of my faither, the Deacon, I's no tak a blow without gieing a thrust. (He runs to the fire, and seizes a red-hot poker.) So that he that likes it, has it.
>
> Dougal. Her nainsel has eaten the town-pread o' Glasgo', and she'll feught for Nicol Bailie Sharvie at Aberfoil—troth will she. Och, neish!
>
> MacStuart. Haud, haud! The quarrel's no mortal, and the gentlemen's hae given raisonable satiswhaction.
>
> Bailie. I'm glad to hear't.
>
> Galbraith. Weel, weel, as the gentlemen have shown themselves men of honor—
>
> MacStuart. Men o' honor! Who ta teevil ever saw men o' honor feught wi' a fire-brand before. Figh! my braw new plaidie smells like a singit sheep's head.
>
> Bailie. Let that be nae hindrance to gude fellowship; there's aye a plaister for the broken head. If I've burnt ye're plaidie, I can mend it with a new ane. I'm a weaver.
>
> Galbraith. A weaver! Pah!
>
> MacStuart. Well, Sir, the neist time that ye'll feucht, let it be wi' a swoord, like a Christian, and no wi' a red-het poker, like a wild Indian sawage.
>
> Bailie. My conscience! a man maun dae his best. I was obliged to grip at the first thing that came my way; and, as I'm a Bailie, I wadna desire a better.[4]

Shortly afterward, a new quarrel arises, during which the English captain, on finding Rob's letter in Frank's pocket,

---

[4] The quotation is from the edition published by French during the 'fifties in New York. The different texts vary somewhat in language, especially in the Scotch dialect.

places Frank under arrest. Bailie Jarvie becomes so loud in his protestations that he also is taken into custody.

As the group proceeds toward the Highlands, with Frank and his two companions still under military guard, the Macgregor flashes into view on an eminence, enters into a broil with the officers, and at last is securely bound by order of the captain. The march proceeds further into the Highlands, despite the protests of Frank and the warnings of Rob Roy.

Suddenly a woman of the Meg Merrilies type appears before them, blocking the pathway of the English troops. With the aid of her stalwart sons and a resolute band of neighbors, she holds the entire company at bay. When the rallying clansmen begin to appear from behind almost every rock, and the fire gets too hot for the English, command is given to retreat. While the company retires in disorder, all the prisoners escape in different directions.

Bailie Jarvie forgets his caution once more. In his eagerness to come off quickly, he scrambles down a cliff, misses his footing, and lands in a small thorn-tree, where he dangles till Dougal happens that way to release him from this threatening position by cutting off the tails of the Bailie's coat, greatly to the discomfiture of the owner himself.

Shortly afterward Francis appears from another direction, and the following dialogue ensues:

> Bailie. My conscience.
> Frank. Somewhat damaged, I perceive; but I heartily rejoice the case is no worse.
> Bailie. Thank ye, thank ye. The case is nothing to boast of. They say a friend sticks as close as a blister; I wish I had found it so. (Putting himself to rights.) When I came up to this cursed country—forgive me for swearing—on no one's errand but yours, Mr. Osbaldistone, d'ye think it was fair, when my foot slipped, and I hung by the loins to the branch of the ragged thorn, to leave me dangling like a regimental target, set up for ball practice, and never once try to help me down.
> Frank. My good sir, recollect the impossibility of my afford-

ing you relief, without assistance. How were you able to extricate yourself?

   Bailie. Me extricate! I should have been there a twelve
month if it hadn't been for the Dougal creature. He cut off
the tails of my coat, and clapped me on my legs again, as clean
as if I had never been off them.[5]

Charles Mackay in this scene always called forth rounds
of applause by his droll impersonation of the Bailie.

When the English captain falls into the hands of the
Highland clansmen, Helen Macgregor informs him that Rob
Roy must be freed within twelve hours at most. Meanwhile
the Campbell has escaped, however, and, when the call
'Gregarch' resounds among the rocks and glens, he rushes
into the group once more, ready to take his place if a battle
against the English is impending. One by one further
details of the treachery of Rashleigh appear, until the Highlanders are convinced that he intends to betray them, as well
as the Roman Catholics and the house of Osbaldistone.

Religious and personal ties no longer prevent the Macgregor and his party from the will to engage the forces of
the English crown. Realizing now that the conflict may be
postponed no longer, and that Rashleigh has little further
claim to his friendship, the Highland chieftain exclaims,
'May the fiend help me, if this good blade and his heart are
not well acquainted.'

From this climax of the action, four stirring scenes bring
the plot to a highly theatrical close. Sir Frederick and his
daughter overtake Francis alone in the rocky mountain-
defiles. For the third time, Diana warns her admirer that
'a gulph of absolute perdition' is yawning between them.
On this point the novel is somewhat obscure, but the drama
makes it certain that the fair lady, though she dislikes
Rashleigh Osbaldistone, believes that differences in religion
between herself and Frank prevent any thoughts of marriage.

---

[5] From the New York edition of 1818, p. 48. This quotation shows
how the Bailie's dialect was revised for American hearers.

Toward the close of the drama, Rob Roy appears in dejection at a roadside inn. He realizes as never before that necessity, rather than deliberate choice, has forced him to lead the life of a hunted animal among the hills that he loves next to his kinsmen and his family. He has come also to realize that his sons must inevitably follow in the same course which he has taught them to begin.

Yet the bold clansman has not lost his spirit or his firm resolution. In exact contrast, Rashleigh and a fellow plotter are shown cringing and panic-stricken, because all attempts to secure the packet which rightfully belongs to Francis have come to nought.

All the main characters are now marshaled toward the rocky cave not far from the scene of the battle that impends. Frank, who has arrived first of the group, is informed by Helen Macgregor that Diana and her father are on the way. Outside, the clans are heard gathering in the moonlight. Helen detains Rob Roy long enough to bid him an affectionate farewell. Francis has previously offered the Macgregors his protection, if the outcome of the engagement is fortunate, for the family of Rob Roy might find a welcome shelter in France.

When Sir Frederick and Diana enter the cave, Rashleigh emerges from the inner recesses where he has lain concealed, and commands some of the soldiers to arrest Frank and his party. Having overheard the main details of the plot, however, Dougal has warned Rob Roy, who now returns just in time to save his English friends. While trying to gain an unfair advantage over his antagonist, Rashleigh falls to the ground; but Dougal rushes in to bear him off the scene before the Highlander's claymore can 'taste his blood.'

Thus we observe that the salient features of the novel are reported. Much tedious detail of the first and the last chapters, however, has been wisely excluded from the drama by Pocock. Diana is not so attractive as Scott makes her seem, but her father plays a more important part than he does in the novel. Genest rebuked Pocock for 'the one gross and unpardonable blunder—he has reduced the interesting and spirited Diana Vernon to a mere singing girl.'[6] Jarvie is somewhat exaggerated, Dougal much suppressed, Rashleigh made a deeper villain, Rob a more consistent hero, and Francis much to be admired, in the acting drama that soon won tremendous favor on many stages.

Besides mere faithfulness to the original story, Pocock and Davy's *Rob Roy* has three major claims to favorable notice. Rob Roy appears as a great national type, the proscribed Scots Highlander, who is driven by necessity and the designs of English enemies to lead the life of a generous freebooter. He never deserts a friend, and never breaks his word. Only the heroic, the noble, and the generous traits remain, along with the elemental conceptions of duty to the clan and the national honor.

It is essentially a drama of loyalties. Almost every bush and stone hides a Highlander ready to rise at the cry of 'Gregarch.' Bailie Jarvie and his friends gather about Rob as the centre of their clan, and Rob himself undertakes the knightly adventure of assisting Francis. His generous impulses lead him to brave famine, capture, even death itself, for his newer friends, whose fortunes at their best could gain little of personal reward for the Highlander himself.

Unquestionably the second prominent influence is the group of the Bailie and Dougal. The latter, with his barbarous 'she's,' his quaint fits and starts, his almost dog-like fidelity to his friends, is a truthful type. So is Nicol Jarvie, discounting some exaggeration. One might find him in the walks of Glasgow—not every week, to be sure, but more than once in a twelve-month. Both Scott and Pocock recognized the Bailie as a complex character, a bundle of contradictions and humors, with his officiousness, pedantry, and love of exaggeration in display. We are highly diverted by his claims to relationship among clansmen, by his pride

6. 687.

in being a remote connection of Rob Roy's, and by his utter petulance toward Rob, when the chief departs from the path marked out by his mentor.

It is equally true, in the third place, that the lyrics and setting of the drama share in making it a triumph. Covent Garden provided a number of new drops to represent northern scenery. The text mentions several picturesque views, including a wild Highland landscape, 'the romantic pass bordering the loch,' various displays of rocky summits, endless files of Highlanders in the dress of their various clans, and a cavern, finally, for the meeting of the main characters.[7] The painters of some of these scenes copied actual descriptions from the novel. Everything tended to increase the interest in the grandeur of the mountains.

Some of the music by Davy had been used for an older *Rob Roy* fifteen years before. While borrowing several popular Scotch airs, this musical play does not always consider the occasion. Thus Frank, rather out of keeping at the inn, with English soldiers about, sings 'Should acquaintance be forgot.' Using a lyric from Wordsworth, 'A famous man was Robin Hood,' Major Galbraith keeps more faithfully to the real sentiment of the gathering. Frank and Diana charmed the audiences with their solos and duets. Remembering the bewitching girl at the Hall, Frank sings, 'O my luve is like a red, red rose.' The elusive Diana playfully introduces the air of 'A highland lad my love was born.' At the time that she informs Frank that a 'gulph' lies between them, Diana concludes their interview with the plaintive song, 'Forlorn and broken hearted, I weep my last adieu.' Though this is not really her own sentiment at the time, it must have taken well with the playgoers. In the text printed in London, the grand finale is, 'Pardon the bold

[7] The Oxberry edition, London, 1820, has been used for the description of the scenery. One published by Huie in Edinburgh, 1823, differs from this somewhat in wording and in much of the scenery, though in no significant detail or degree.

outlaw, Rob Roy Macgregor, O.' In the Scotch text. Diana herself sings the closing number, 'Duncan Gray came here to woo.'

THE POCOCK DRAMA IN ENGLAND

When the work of Pocock appeared on the stage for the first night in March, 1818, W. C. Macready impersonated the title-character. For fifteen years or more, he continued to act Rob Roy with varying success. In August, 1829, at the Haymarket, he was very pathetic in the words 'I did not think that mortal man would see a tear in the Macgregor's eye.'[8] Once Macready himself recorded this in his diary: 'I acted tonight with spirit and in a manly tone, better perhaps than ordinarily, in the part of Rob Roy.' Later he admitted that this play helped him to break 'the malignant charm that seemed to weigh upon me, and contract my sphere of action,'[9] though once he made Bunn agree not to force him to act in Rob Roy.

John Liston, the first Bailie at Covent Garden, took a place second only to that of Mackay for many years in frequent revivals. Mrs. Egerton as Helen, and Miss Catherine Stephens as Diana, likewise received applause whenever they appeared in England and Scotland, where Miss Stephens raised her part to the highest rank.

Drury Lane staged a revival in 1821, when Mackay came down from Edinburgh on special contract, and Mrs. Egerton returned, after a triumphant tour in northern cities.[10] Sir Walter Scott himself may have been right, however, in his prediction that the audience in London might not enjoy Mackay, since the English might not recognize in him a faithful Scots portrait.[11] Though never as much appreciated in London as in Edinburgh, he prolonged his stay

[8] *Dramatic Magazine,* 1829, p. 197.
[9] For Jan. 22, 1833; *Diary* 1. 7, and also 1. 163.
[10] Oxberry 3. 127.
[11] Lockhart 2. 230.

in 1821 for a few nights.* By July he had returned to
Scotland, and Macready had then given way to Daniel Terry
as Rob Roy when the Queen came to a special performance
at Drury Lane.

After 1823 several playhouses used the Pocock comedy,
or some of the imitations, for numerous revivals. Accordingly, the Haymarket in 1835, the Princess a decade later,
the Olympic in 1843 and 1852, Astley's the following season,
and the Royal Theatre in Covent Garden, brought out appreciated restorations. John Henry Anderson, like Scott
familiarly called the Wizard of the North, combined his
show of legerdemain with certain parts of *Rob Roy,* to make
up a full evening, with himself as 'the vociferating hero.'
As an entertainer, Anderson was a prince; as an actor he
was grotesque in the opinion of the judicious, though he had
a large following among the laity. 'He explodes his asides
defiantly into the faces of people who are not to hear them,'
remarked a writer for the *Times,* 'and looks as if he could
thresh the other *dramatis personae* all around, without much
fatigue to his muscles.' Night after night, nevertheless,
during his management at Covent Garden in 1856, the 'full'
sign was displayed outside long before the time of commencing the performance. The engagement continued in
unabated vogue until early in March, when, after a night
of disorder incident to a *bal masqué*, Anderson commanded
the lights to be turned low as a sign for the crowd to dis-
perse. Shortly afterward fire was reported, and by daybreak of March 5 the playhouse had been reduced to a pile
of embers.

Drury Lane in 1867 engaged the eminent tenor, Sims
Reeves, for a new production of the operatic *Rob Roy*.
The singer broke his contract at the last moment, however,
giving illness as the excuse; but Manager Chatterton won
damages of fifteen hundred pounds from him in a court of
law.[12] During the same year, William Harrison took the

[12] Stirling, *Old Drury Lane* 1. 278.

part abandoned by Sims Reeves. Thomas Powrie, who for years acted chief parts in Dundee, once came down to London, there to receive every mark of appreciation from large audiences.

Scores of revivals were arranged in the British Isles. Farren won ovations whenever he appeared as the Bailie in Bath, and later at different points when he appeared as Isaac of York, Sir Henry Lee, and Jonathan Oldbuck. Morley spoke of him as 'one of the most finished actors by whom the stage has been adorned during the past century.'[13] Frederick Warde carried off the honors as Rob for many nights at Bath. In 1820 he left for Dublin, after terminating his engagement with a gala performance, which was patronized by the fashionable set of that popular watering-place.[14] He was joined in Ireland by Cobham, Williams, Mrs. Vaughan, and other well known theatrical folk. The *Drama* spoke of Warde as a 'romantic and feudal chieftain,' who divided honors with 'his little fellow laborer,' Cobham, in the part of Rashleigh.[15] Some five or six years afterward, Oxberry reported that 'Cobham's exit through the gate, and Warde's reproach to Rashleigh, are spoken of yet.'[16]

Different towns applauded their favorites for many years. John Cook won a royal patent for his new theatre in Liverpool, after he had produced *Rob Roy* so well that the public demanded that he be so favored, though he had been apprehended at first for bringing on a play without a license. J. Bronson Howard at Bath, Liverpool, and other cities, in 1881 and 1884, won a generous hearing for an American actor. Mackay, Gourlay, and Farren led all others as the Bailie.* Though Macready and John Henry Anderson were

[13] Quoted by Adams, p. 493.
[14] Genest 9. 74.
[15] 1821, p. 52.
[16] 5. 257.

favorite Robs, Corbett Ryder excelled all others in his day, and likewise M'Neill, his son-in-law, became 'the best of his time' in the part of Rob.   Murray was a good Rob in Scotland, and Terry was 'no bad for an Englishman.'

AMERICAN NIGHTS WITH ROB ROY

No fewer than twenty-five references mention Rob Roy dramas in American theatres.   First at the Park, June 8, 1819, the Pocock version was seen fully eight months before it reached Edinburgh.   Charles Mathews, one of the actor-friends of Scott, appeared as the Bailie in 1826.   The Lafayette Theatre in the autumn produced this drama with elaborate scenery and augmented orchestra, when Burroughs as Rob, and especially Somerville, as the Dougal Creature, received 'very emphatic applause.'   Macready impersonated Rob during the next season.   Mrs. John R. Duff, during the same year, made a profound impression as Helen Macgregor, when she acted so well that Hyatt, a veteran actor, burst into tears, and 'the entire audience exhibited the same unmistakable evidence of deep emotion.'   Nine years later, 1836, J. B. Booth made a good Highlander at the Chatham Garden.   John R. Scott appeared at the National early in the same year, and Charlotte Cushman as Helen Macgregor at the Bowery in September.   H. Wallack, Keene, Williams, Madame Ponisi, Mrs. Entwistle, and Mrs. Stowe, made favorable impressions before 1860.   J. W. Wallack appeared with Mrs. Duff as early as 1837; later in England he joined forces with the Wizard of the North, John Henry Anderson who won a great following in New York also in the 'fifties. Niblo's produced the original play in 1859, 'with great care and completely new scenes and dresses.'   Now and then revivals were arranged until as late as 1875.[17]   Altogether

[17] N. Y. *Evening Post,* June 10, 1818; Sept. 12, 1836; Ireland 1. 44, 336, 497, 530; 2. 241; also Ireland's *Mrs. Duff,* p. 77.

these men, in the aggregate, appeared for more than two thousand times.

Rob Roy at Home in Scotland

James C. Dibdin assures us that *Rob Roy* became 'the most memorable and important piece ever put on the Theatre Royal boards.' Year after year managers brought it forward, whenever other dramas failed to awaken the interest of their patrons. So this Pocock version came to be known as a 'managerial sheet-anchor.' No similar play won so many distinctions: it saved the fortunes of the playhouse; it attracted a galaxy of good actors; it drew more audiences than any other drama in Scotland, with but two or three exceptions; it led to the founding of the Scots Theatre Fund; and it aroused the enthusiasm of Scott beyond any similar piece at the Royal Theatre.[18]

Yet the northern capital hesitated to receive the work of Pocock, for some reason now difficult to explain. It was once supposed that Corbett Ryder first introduced a Rob Roy play into Scotland. Lawson, on the contrary, has proved that William H. Murray of the Royal brought into action the Pocock, or a similar transcript, at Glasgow, some eight nights before the Ryder players acted in Perth on June 18, 1818.[19] Yet another eight months elapsed before Edinburgh audiences saw any Rob Roy drama.

At Perth the performances continued for sixteen nights, which at the time was a record there for continuous length of run. This marked the beginning of Ryder's great successes in many towns, with Williams as a Dougal, and Mackay as a Bailie that never were equalled by other players. Before his retirement in 1853, Mackay had enacted this part for more than eleven hundred nights. No similar record exists in all Scotland.

Ryder continued in the original for three or four years,

[18] *Annals*, p. 286.
[19] *Scots Stage*, pp. 154, 169, 223.

and then brought out variations of his own in March, 1823, at the Caledonian, Edinburgh, and in December of the same year a third version. By this time his playbills were heralding the two hundred and fifty-third night of his acting as the Scotch chieftain. By 1829 the same company was announcing the five hundredth performance, to which Ryder added not fewer than fifty more by 1836, when he retired. In acting the part, he never had a competitor. His conception of the Highlander was romantic, stern but kindly, and full of little suggestions of a better Rob than most of Rob's enemies gave him credit for being.[20]

A Fortune for the Royal of Edinburgh

Eleven months intervened from the first performance at Covent Garden to the first, on February 15, 1819, at the Theatre Royal, Edinburgh. No English law or Scotch custom then forbade the using of a play at once, after it had opened a run in London. For three or four years, however, the Waverley dramas made their way but slowly on the boards in Edinburgh, largely, perhaps, because of a certain prejudice against playacting. After 1819 the case was altered: English texts were soon carried northward; imitations were also in considerable demand in swift succession.

Thus two classes of adaptations came into vogue in the North. One of them followed the English text rather closely, with certain verbal changes and new scenery; the other pruned, combined, or expanded the existing forms, with here and there some additions from the corresponding novel. A bit later a few original versions came into being. As seen in the Scotch playhouse, the version by Pocock and Davy illustrates the first class. All the scenery was painted

[20] Dibdin's *Annals,* pp. 253, 337, 343. Dibdin could not decide how much Ryder changed the Pocock text for his other versions. No contemporary notes throw light on the subject. See also Calcraft's article in the *Dublin Univ. Magazine,* May, 1851.

anew. Some of the drops showed the usual Highland backgrounds, with cataracts, rugged passes, and mountain views. The Theatre Royal added some glimpses of the haunts of the Bailie in Glasgow, including the Public Walk, where Frank and his cousin were interrupted by Rob Roy while they sought to settle some old accounts, and also the jail over which Dougal presided as turnkey. Some stage-directions were curtailed, modified, or rejected altogether. The language of Dougal was corrected at times, and some of the other dialect was modified. Greater stress seems to have been laid on certain songs, a few new ones being introduced, and some old popular airs being revived apparently as encores.

For forty-one nights of the initial run, the public continued to jam the playhouse. Since the Irish singer, Miss O'Neill, had appeared several years previously, no crowds like these had been known in the Royal. The audience at the close of the season demanded that Mackay should again appear as the Bailie for his benefit-performance. It was contrary to custom to use an active play on such occasions; and the manager with difficulty persuaded the public to allow Mackay to act as Dominie Sampson in a revival of *Guy Mannering*. All the ready funds of the Royal at the time were in arrest for rent and other bills payable. *Rob Roy* added three thousand pounds to the treasury during the first season, saved the playhouse from receivers, and from time to time for fifty years at least was revived in hours of financial stress.[21]

Mrs. Renaud, well trained in the Meg Merrilies school, achieved a triumph by her Helen Macgregor. In these parts, and later as Elspeth, Lady Douglas, Queen Caroline, and Janet (in the *Two Drovers*), she continued to win applause for two decades.[22] As Dougal John Duff left

---

[21] *Sketch of the Royal*, p. 19 (1859); Dibdin's *Annals*, p. 286.
[22] *Dict. Nat. Biog.* 46. 237.

little to be censured, and most of the minor persons were creditable. Charles Mackay, naturally, was singled out as the 'great and unrivaled attraction.' Like the Bailie a native of Glasgow, this talented comedian knew the Scots dialect 'in its racy perfection.' For years Mackay typified in his Bailie the peculiar 'Scotch feeling of the play.' Sir Walter often witnessed Mackay in the part, of which he spoke many times, showing his inordinate esteem for the man and the artist.

WALTER SCOTT, BAILIE JARVIE, AND CHARLES MACKAY

When the modified *Rob Roy Macgregor* opened at the Royal on February 15, 1819, Scott took a box for his family in the lower tier. As one of the shareholders of the playhouse, he may have witnessed a rehearsal; at any rate, he left his seat during one of the intermissions to remind Manager Murray that Mattie 'must have a mantle with her lanthorn.'[23] At the close of the fruitful season, when Mackay took a benefit, Scott sent the great actor a note for five pounds and a letter by a circuitous route, perhaps by one of his publishers. Lockhart quotes from the copy found in the papers of Scott. After commending Mackay for his skill, and very warmly for his 'private character,' Scott added a bit of caution: 'I pray thee not to let Rob Roy twirl thee around in the ecstasy of joy, in regard to overstepping the limits of nature, which otherwise thou so sedulously preservest in thy admirable portraicture of Bailie Nicol Jarvie.' Scott signed the *nom-de-plume* he was then using to mystify the public—Jedediah Cleishbotham. According to Lockhart, neither Mackay nor Miss Baillie shared the literary secrets of the Great Unknown.[24]

Recognizing from the outset the drama by Pocock as one of his 'literary godchildren,' Sir Walter Scott grew more and

[23] Lockhart 2. 121.
[24] 2. 565.

more enthusiastic as Charles Mackay continued to act Bailie
Nicol Jarvie. He wrote letters at various times to exhort
his friends to attend this play. During the initial run in
Edinburgh, he sent this comment to Terry: 'It was the living
Nicol Jarvie: conceited, pragmatical, cautious, proud of his
connections with Rob Roy, frightened for him at the same
time, and yet extremely desirous of interfering with him as
an adviser. The tone in which he seemed to give him up
for a lost man, after having provoked him into some burst
of Highland violence, "Ah, ah, Rab," was quite inimitable.
I do assure you that I never saw a thing better played.'[25]
To Lord Montagu Scott wrote in similar language, adding
that it was the 'degree of national truth and understanding,
which makes the part equal to anything I have ever seen
upon the stage, and I have seen the best comedians for
forty years.' Yet he feared somewhat that London
audiences might find Jarvie too 'broad a caricature in depict-
ing national peculiarities.'

He rounded out his picture of the acting of Mackay in a
letter to Joanna Baillie, in which he added: 'He is completely the personage of the drama, the purse-proud con-
sequential magistrate, humane and irritable in the same
moment, a true Scotchman in every turn of thought and
action.'[26]

On his own side, Mackay said of Scott at the time of the
dinner given to the actor on his retirement from the stage:
'It is to the pen of the mighty dead that I owe my theatrical
success. Had he never written, I never would have been
noticed as an actor.'[27]

The wizard of the novels and the wizard of the comic
presentations met under rather pathetic circumstances at a
dinner sponsored by Murray in the spring of 1827. This
was the first public appearance of Scott since the failure of

[25] Lockhart 2. 132.
[26] *Ibid.* 2. 229.
[27] Coleman 2. 383.

the publishing houses in which he had for several years been a silent partner. He desired to attend because the dinner was arranged to start a fund for the benefit of retired actors. Both he and Mackay were guests of honor. Lord Beaverbrook, the chairman, had requested permission from Scott to announce the Great Unknown as indeed the author of the Waverley novels. The novelist had replied, 'Do as you like—only don't say much about so old a story.'

This first announcement called forth thunderous applause from the hundred or more literary persons at the dinner. Scott responded to the toast to the author of the novels by admitting that his 'caprice' had hitherto kept him from public acknowledgment, and also by assuming the responsibility for being 'the total and undivided author' of the entire series.[28]

Then he graciously asked Mackay to respond to the next toast. 'I beg leave to propose the health of my friend Bailie Nicol Jarvie,' said Scott, 'and I am sure that, when the author of *Waverley* and *Rob Roy* drinks to Nicol Jarvie, it will be received with the just applause to which this gentleman has always been accustomed: nay, that you will take care that, on the present occasion, it shall be pro-di-gi-ous.'

> *Mackay.* 'My Conscience! My worthy father, the deacon, could never have believed that his son would have sic a compliment paid him by the Great Unknown!'*
> *Scott.* 'The Small Known now, Mr. Bailie.'[29]

LATER REVIVALS IN EDINBURGH

Scores of times the Pocock melodrama entertained large crowds in all the dramatic centres of England and America. Many actors became famous through their connection with this and other Waverley plays, but only a few of the productions in Edinburgh need be mentioned as typical of the

[28] Lockhart 2. 563.
[29] *Ibid.* 2. 565.

entire range. Calcraft extended an éngagement at the
Royal to more than eighty nights between February of 1820
and the next winter.   During his temporary illness in March,
the place of Calcraft as Rob was ably taken by Daniel
Terry, who was imported from London.   Duff as Dougal
continued to be called for during many seasons.[30]   For
the visit of George IV in 1822, *Rob Roy* once again was
brought out as a trump-card, to the great amusement of the
monarch who had 'commanded' this play.   The King
laughed loudest over the predicament of the Bailie when he
lost an essential part of his coat, and also over Mattie's
phrase, 'nane of your Lunnon tricks,' while he seemed to
take no offense at the allusion to his father and himself as
Old and Young Nick.[31]

By March, 1837, William H. Murray had reached the two
hundred and eighty-fifth performance, to which his company added at least a hundred others before he retired in
1851.[32]   Mackay was coaxed from his retirement again and
again for a 'last' or 'positively the last' evening, till in 1852
at Glasgow he reached the eleven hundred and thirty-fourth
performance, at which time Murray also came out of private
life once more to act as Major Galbraith, with Glover as
Rob.[33]   Early in this season, a revival in Edinburgh called
for one hundred and seventy persons on the stage at different
times during the evening, with seventy in one of the combats,
and twenty-eight in the Highland fling.

RIVAL PLAY BY GEORGE SOANE

Two weeks after the original drama began its career at
Covent Garden, George Soane rushed a bad imitation upon
the boards at Drury Lane on March 25, 1818.   This distorted version, called *Rob Roy, the Gregarch,* survived only

[30] Dibdin, p. 283.
[31] Lockhart 2. 289.
[32] *Ibid.* 2. 121, footnote; *Sketch of the Royal,* p. 19.
[33] Dibdin, pp. 432, 466, 484; *Theatre,* 1851-2, p. 133.

till the sixth night. Though the scenery and cast attracted some favorable comment, the reviewers lifted up a united cry in censure of the text itself.

Blackwood announced the effort as 'a hoax on the public, a bait to draw a full house the first night—"a springe to catch woodcocks"—and it succeeded, no doubt, to the infinite satisfaction of the "Noblemen and Gentlemen" who condescended to manage the theatre.'[34] Never quite generous in his criticism of the average musical drama, Genest thus freed his mind in regard to Soane's adaptation: 'So many changes are made that one is disappointed and consequently disgusted.'[35] Years later, Dutton Cook, almost always kindly toward old plays, spoke of 'Soane's bungling adaptation.'[36]

Both the narrative and the sentiment of the novel are dwarfed out of all reason. To begin with, the Bailie is a pale caricature of the original kinsman of Rob Roy. Dougal is a mere shell of his 'ain self,' and Francis is merely mentioned in the text. Instead of being once more the noble and spirited wife of the Highland chieftain, Helen Macgregor has been transformed into his mother, and a quite different sort of virago without a heart. As the worst travesty of all on Scott, Rob himself has lost a foolish heart to the sentimental Diana Vernon, who is no more than a simpering and pale Southron.

Soane might be characterized as a play-mechanic, one who followed real hits with sentimental or revised transcripts from a novel for the patrons of a minor playhouse. *Rob Roy, the Gregarch,* being a fair example of Soane's work, needs a bit of attention: for the narrative shows many turns from the pathway of the novel.

From the initial scene, Rob and Diana are two conventional, thwarted lovers, forbidden at first by Helen Mac-

[34] 3. 82.
[35] 8. 643.
[36] *Hours with the Players*, p. 27.

gregor and Sir Frederick to marry. Diana is virtually betrothed to Rashleigh, a man suited to her by creed and family interests. In a raid on the home of the Vernons, Rob carries off his beloved to the northern fastnesses. His mother, Helen, is a revised edition of the wife of Macgregor in the novel and the older dramas only in that she fights off the pursuers who come to reclaim Diana for her father. At home Rob Roy soon becomes effeminate: neither the clan, nor the combat, nor the chase in the Highlands, pleases him after his union with Diana Vernon. He refuses to leave his wife even for a day or two, though Helen tries repeatedly to rouse him to his old interests..

At last the mother becomes infuriated. She now invokes curses to fall on both the son and his wife. Very conveniently, too, she recollects that some of the Vernons killed her husband. Rashleigh now takes advantage of the Macgregor's inactivity, and makes a raid on the Highland clans. From an old wizard, living in a secret cave, Helen obtains a potent liquor, designed to put Diana into her last sleep. She forces Diana to drink this; but soon afterward Helen is struck by a thunderbolt, as a punishment for her treachery. Thus ends the second act with a melodramatic flourish.

Dougal is at hand, however, to rescue the sleeping Diana, after he visits the obscure abode of the wizard, and learns that the draught was only a sleeping potion. Diana soon awakens. Meanwhile, the chief has been abducted by his old enemies. Rashleigh heaps every type of insult upon Rob Roy, finally inciting him to combat by calling him too craven to fight. With much of his old vigor, Rob seizes a claymore, rushes upon his challenger, and pierces Rashleigh to the heart. Now, in all melodramatic swiftness, the English captain arrives, bearing a complete pardon for the Highland outlaw. Nothing is left except for Diana once more to rush into Rob's arms, while the final curtain descends to slow music.

This drama was printed shortly after it was first produced,

but Drury Lane secured, to replace it, the acting version of
Pocock's musical play in 1821.

SOME UNIMPORTANT LATER DRAMAS

Astley's brought out *Gregarch, the Highland Watchword,*
in 1831, followed the next year by an opera in Paris composed by Duport and de Forges, with music by Frederick
von Flotow.[37] Both the Royal and the Adelphi in Edinburgh produced elaborate versions in 1851, with some
favorite actors engaged for each, including Powrie for Rob,
Gourlay for the Bailie, and Mungal as the 'Dougal Crature.'
Later works by Arthur Shirley, J. R. Park, and others, were
produced in England. Henry B. Smith wrote the words, and
Reginald de Koven the music, for a late musical play bearing
only a very remote connection to Scott, in that the chief
character is Robin Oig, son of the great Rob Roy.[38]

Robbing Roy, a travesty on the Soane version by Francis
C. Burnand, attained more than common fame for a burlesque
at the Gaiety, London, in 1879, after which it ran in Dundee
and other towns, and again once more in London ten years
later.[39] It was too ephemeral for printing.

Burnand deliberately keeps the Soane 'hoax' in the foreground; but does not mention the older play. The Scots
chieftain has now lost much of his boldness and most of his
companions. He has finally become a rather ordinary hen-
pecked husband, and Diana a rather ordinary shrew. Rob's
kilts have become altogether too cold for him. He no longer
commands, but is heckled and taunted, while he moves the
audience to laughter by his cringing and his shivering.
Rashleigh, too, in his turn has become the sort of villain that
one might see in some of the cheap vaudeville houses of the
period.[40]

[37] Details of the production are lacking.
[38] *Theatre,* Edinburgh, 1851-2, p. 136; Clarence, p. 385.
[39] Brown 3. 385. It was printed in Chicago in 1894.
[40] Boyd, p. 88; *Theatre,* May 1, 1889.

This travesty by Burnand was the first of a long list of similar affairs by the same author and men like Reece, the Brough Brothers, Plowman, and Henry J. Byron. *Robbing Roy* introduces us to the bewildering realm of puns, twists of phrases, and equivocal meanings, such as an age that produced *Alice in Wonderland* loved to contemplate.

IV. THE HEART OF MIDLOTHIAN

Within six months after *Rob Roy,* another of the *Tales of my Landlord* came from the press in June of 1818. Not a few critical readers had predicted that the cunning of the unknown hand very soon was sure to fail; but the new *Heart of Midlothian*—as the publishers and Scott finally named this novel—immediately conquered all temporary opposition, except for that of some few who might have shared the aversion of one maiden gentlewoman that refused to countenance 'those low creatures, the cow feeders' of Midlothian.

Neither Pocock nor Terry this time brought out the first transcript. The honor fell to Thomas J. Dibdin, known widely as a versatile compiler, and as author of a dramatic version of the *Lady of the Lake,* and finally as the sponsor of at least five additional adaptations from Scott. Fourteen variations of *Midlothian* followed at intervals after the piece of Dibdin won great favor, but no single one ever came to any renown. Again Terry tried his hand after Dibdin, yet his drama ran only a few evenings. Soane once more concocted one of his notorious imitations; and two or three foreign playwrights made operatic productions that won some contemporary applause. Edinburgh revisers, as usual with them, busied themselves with redactions and modifications, adding new excerpts from Scott, and making some new scenery. George Dibdin Pitt compiled a literary, and rather unconvincing, sequel to the story of the lost child of Effie and George Robertson. Brough Brothers made a sprightly burlesque.

For the first six months this novel lay as fallow ground to the dramatic gleaners. It was not till December 31, 1818, that Sarah Egerton invited the prolific Dibdin to make a play for her to act in the part of Madge Wildfire.* The task of compilation was completed within a week, and on the thirteenth day—one is tempted to remark that Dibdin was often lucky—the Surrey Theatre brought out his *Heart of Midlothian; or, The Lily of St. Leonard's.* Its run of one hundred and seventy nights in nine months seems to have established a record for the time in melodrama for length of continuous acting.   Genest informs us that the house was crowded on the eighty-fifth night, the 'full' sign being occasionally displayed even afterward.   From the author we learn that the average nightly proceeds were only a little below a hundred pounds during the first year.[1]

The critics unanimously showered both the play and the acting with heartiest praises.   One periodical described the drama as 'a truly excellent, pathetic, and interesting piece.'[2] For once Genest threw off much of his reserve when he pronounced the entire production commendable, especially the scenes in which Madge protects Jeanie at the roadside barn, and the interview between the Scotch lass and the Queen in London.[3]   Oxberry outdid himself in a lengthy review, in which he exclaimed, 'It is a piece which may fairly be stated to be the best adaptation ever made from a novel.'[4]

The printed text of 1819 shows hardly any element of effective characterization lacking.   One notices particularly the excellent contrasts between the Deans sisters, Robertson and Dumbiedikes, Madge and her mother, old Margery, David Deans and the callous officers of the law.

Mrs. Egerton in Madge certainly rose to the climax of her fame as a melodramatic actress, though some believed that her creation of the wild woman of the rocks in *Midlothian* resembled not a little her brilliant Meg Merrilies of some two years earlier.   Though cast considerably into the shadow, some of the minor characters are individual and realistic.   For comedy, the deliberate Dumbiedikes, in his conservatism to the last thought and the last coin, made a

---

[1] Dibdin, *Reminiscences,* pp. 71, 176, and preface to London edition, 1819.

[2] *Theatre,* Feb. 20, 1821.

[3] 9. 67.

[4] *Dramatic Biographies* 4. 239.

great opportunity for Fitzwilliam, who took the original characterization, and made a style for other great masters, like Liston and Mackay.

For seven long years, the Scots laird has worn a beaten path to the door of David Deans, without having arrived within conscience of a proposal to Jeanie. Dibdin enlarged some of the hints of the novel, making Dumbiedikes into a ridiculous and jealous lover. He is infinitely droll throughout. When the laird finds that a man is meeting Jean at Muschat's Cairn, he comes near actually believing that he has indeed postponed a proposal too long. Yet he hesitates as to whether this is the opportune time. Later, when Jean has refused his offer of a large loan, Dumbiedikes reveals his state of mind in a conversation with Saddletree in regard to the going of the Scotch lassie to London.

> Dumbiedikes. Neighbor, I'd go myself, but my poney knows but two ways: that's from my house to this house [the Deans cottage] and from this house to my house. That's all.
>
> Saddletree. Then away home, and fetch the thirty pounds.
>
> D. Twenty; I said twenty. You know that, neighbor.
>
> S. At first, but afterward you said thirty.
>
> D. Did I? That must have been when Jeanie gave me a look. Oh, dear, how sorry I am, because, if I said so, I must do it. Oh, Jeanie, Jeanie! Should you not think the tears in Jeanie's eye looked like beautiful drops of—water (Sniveling).
>
> S. Yes, and he who cannot be melted (as Counsellor Brazennose says) by the tears of a woman, has a little too much of the *fortiter in re* about him.
>
> D. Forty! I didn't say forty. I don't know what you have about you, but, if I had thirty pounds about me, and as much more, I'd give it over and over again, to kiss away the tear from—Oh, Jeanie, Jeanie! What a fool you make me make of myself.

The crazed and romantic Madge remains well in the background, until the action of the drama is sufficiently advanced for her to come into the open as a protector of Jeanie. She appears at times as a harmless lunatic woman, buffeted about by the caprice of fate. As such she often comes under the suspicion of the officers of the law, from whom she cleverly escapes by feigning she is worse in mind than she really is. Many in Midlothian look upon her and her mother as two evil geniuses, and Jeanie herself at times shares the common suspicions. Dibdin emphasizes all this, in order to bring out the climax more forcefully, when Madge is shown to be the protector, not only of Jeanie Deans, but of several others as well, most of whom have never looked upon Madge as their friend.

At many points she appears to be a reminiscence of Meg Merrilies. Both the reviewers and the playgoers, evidently, understood her to be a reincarnation of the nurse of Henry Bertram; and, hence, they looked to her to play a similar rôle in regard to protecting the heroine of the drama. Like Meg this sibyl comes at tense moments to shield her favorites from impending harm: to save Jeanie from the roughness of the officers who are also bent on seeking Robertson at Muschat's Cairn; to warn her of the presence of robbers on the road to London, while Jeanie is going to interview the Queen; and, at last, to shield several of them from the unwonted violence of her own mother, who is the one that has stolen the missing child of Effie and George Robertson. Madge provides Jean with important links in the revelation, watches over her along the way, and then comes into the courtroom, at last, to offer testimony as a witness.

Robertson's part is made even more probable in the play than it is in some portions of the romance by Scott. George has constantly to avoid the officers, to keep from coming into the open until the lost infant is found, and to keep the faith of Jeanie. The Scotch lassie herself can hardly avoid thinking of Robertson with aversion. Not knowing that George and her sister are really married, Jean refuses the loan he offers for her trip to London, taking instead the twenty-five pounds finally tendered by Dumbiedikes.

Dibdin was familiar with the best of the old tragicomedies. He knew the trend of melodrama in his age like almost no other playwright. Many changes in fortune, mistaken identity, wrong interpretation of motives, 'circumstantial evidence' that eventually proves inconclusive, all, in turn, keep the suspense alive till the final scene in the courtroom. The author shows uncommon skill in handling the star-parts of Jean and Madge, notably in the journey to London, and in the mystery incident to the disappearance of Effie's child. He uses much of the language of the novel, introducing only the great scenes, and keeping free from irrelevant incidents. All three acts concentrate the interest on the events in Midlothian, with commendable suppression of the Edinburgh scenes, save for the details of the imprisonment of Effie in the Tolbooth, and the refusal of Jean to tell a lie on the witness-stand, even to save a beloved sister.

The painter Wilson made several drop-canvases for the initial performance at the Surrey Theatre. Erskine contributed some of the incidental music, and adapted some of the songs. Emphasis is laid on the cryptic remarks of Madge. Some of the important pieces of scenery showed the rustic cottage of the Deans family, 'the romantic scene of the Crags' in the moonlight, the cell of Effie in the Tolbooth, the London road with the barn where Madge protected Jean from marauders, and the city itself, including the audience-room of Queen Caroline at Westminster.[5]

Several revivals of this first *Heart of Midlothian* are mentioned in the dramatic annals of the period. Miss Copeland eventually replaced Mrs. Egerton, making Madge Wildfire 'as pretty as Ophelia,' and Miss Taylor became 'one of the most perfect characters we ever saw acted.'[6] When the Queen requested the play for July 7, 1821, the original cast was largely restored. During the same summer, Mrs. Egerton transferred her players to Drury Lane, at which centre she joined forces with the great Mackay. Some playgoers admired the latter in Dumbiedikes fully as much as in Bailie Nicol Jarvie. When Mackay at last returned to his regular

[5] According to the text printed in London in 1819.
[6] *London Magazine* 2. 442.

station in Edinburgh, Fitzwilliam became an admirable sub-
stitute.   Mrs. Brooks as Margerie, the mad mother of Meg,
Madame Vestris* and Mrs. Orger as Jean, followed by Mrs.
Glass at Drury Lane in 1822, with Cooper as an impressive
Duke of Argyle, all gained public favor at every perform-
ance.[7]

Version by Daniel Terry

Terry lost many of his opportunities as a maker of plays,
and failed in the management of the Haymarket Theatre, in
which Scott encouraged him by advice and loans of money.
His forte was acting, and no comedian was more sincere as
an artist.   Genest quotes from the *Dramatic Mirror:* 'No
actor on the stage had less trick than Terry: his conception
of all his various characters was invariably just and happy;
his words were never slubbered over in haste; his emphasis
was always accurately laid; his action was never redundant,
but always appropriate, and well suited to the matter he had
to deliver.'[8]

Lockhart again quotes from the correspondence of Scott
to Terry before the Midlothian dramas appeared.   He first
thought of making a tragedy and at last 'a neat *comédie
bourgeoise*' from the novel.   Disinclination and illness pre-
vented Scott from touching up the manuscript, for 'my
corrections would have smelled as cruelly of the lamp as
the Bishop of Grenada's homily did of the apoplexy.'   Yet
he offered Terry congratulations on assuming the management of the Haymarket, counseled him to keep his 'time
fully occupied,' and wished that the author might succeed
as well as Murray, who had cleared three thousand pounds
from *Rob Roy* in Edinburgh.   That he was still willing to
help his friend is shown by the final offer: 'Write to me if

[7] *Ibid.* 9. 94, 152.
[8] 9. 468.

I can do aught about the play—though I fear not. Much will depend on Dumbiedikes, in whom Liston will be strong.'[9]

Terry made considerable of the Edinburgh scenes, including the Porteus riots in full realism of action, during which Robertson, disguised as Madge, rescues Dumbiedikes from the mob. Madge—not her mother—secretes the babe in a vault of the castle. This touch the *London Magazine* pronounced truly absurd,[10] while *Blackwood* bitterly censured the 'unwarranted liberties' of omitting the journey of Jean to London, and of having her promise to marry Dumbiedikes if he will assist in getting Effie released from prison. Surely, this is not the puritanical lass of Walter Scott's narrative, who now appears as a 'pretty mincing London miss.'[11] The laird of Dumbiedikes is a veritable caricature of his former self, though the spirit of the novel is maintained, in that he is still a tight-fist, who has kept a just account of the 4595 trips to the home of David Deans without attaining the courage to propose to Jean. His jealousy is too absurd, and too highly exaggerated. Effie is made too remorseful, too conscious of having done a great wrong, instead of having entered unwisely into a secret marriage with George Robertson.

Three commendable portions show the escape of Jean from the officers at the Cairn, the mob and burning of the jail in Edinburgh, and the comedy of the laird of Dumbiedikes.

Bishop of Covent Garden provided the music for the lyrics, which *Blackwood* said were ascribed to Walter Scott himself.[12] The songs crooned by Madge in her wild moments, and the plaintive farewell of Effie, 'I'm wearing

---

[9] Lockhart 2. 131.

[10] April, 1819.

[11] 5. 320.

[12] No further proof of this statement has been found. Besides the copy of Terry's manuscript which Scott had, there must have been at least one other, for the play was produced in London on the evening before Scott sent his copy back to Terry.

awa, Jean,' with words adapted from Burns, were highly
commended by the reviewers. For the first run, which
lasted for fifteen nights, beginning on April 17, 1819, the
painters at Covent Garden produced some views of Edinburgh, showing the background of the riots, and three views
showing London as seen by the Scotch lass on her
visit to Queen Caroline. Terry in the part of Deans,
Miss Stephens as Effie, and Mrs. Yates as Jean, were well
up to their usual standard, but Liston notably fell off, contrary to the prediction of Scott that he would be good in
Dumbiedikes. Nothing definite is said by contemporaries
as to the acting of Mrs. Charles Kemble as Madge, and of
Macready as George Robertson, a part greatly extended
from the original conception of Scott.[13]

When the drama arrived at Birmingham in 1822, one
of the critics said contemptuously: 'Were it possible to suppose Walter Scott deserving of punishment, what could we
wish him worse than to see his matchless novels as they are
at present dramatized?'[14]   One should not be too hard on
Terry, however; for William Wyndham said that 'the
novelties of the season' included the Terry drama, a successful tragedy by Shiel, called *Evadne,* and a horribly blood-
curdling tragedy by Maturin, 'at which the indignant theatre
full of people rose in horror and fairly howled it off the
stage.'[15]

MODIFICATIONS FURTHER MODIFIED

Without money for the permission, or even so much often
as a 'by your leave,' the playhouses of Scotland, and sometimes even those of London, borrowed as a whole or in part
some of the popular successes. Patrons of the drama were
never certain just whose play was being produced. Besides

[13] *Blackwood* 5. 320; *Theatre Magazine* 4. 94; Genest 9. 94, 152;
Dict. Nat. Biog. 62. 291.
[14] Birmingham *Theatre Looker-on,* Oct. 14, 1822.
[15] *Annals of Covent Garden* 1. 381.

Soane, the chief authors of conglomerate dramas were Dimond, Bunn, and Murray and Calcraft in the northern towns.

Dimond, 'in a most judicious manner,' compounded parts of the Dibdin and the Terry transcripts, with the original addition of some items from the novel, and an entirely new concluding scene.[16] Audiences at Bath spoke 'the highest encomiums' in 1819, when this version appeared there with special costuming, fifteen pieces of new scenes, and excellent acting by the whole cast. Nine years later, it was again favorably received, with Woulds on both occasions as a realistic Dumbiedikes.

When this adaptation reached Edinburgh in November, 1822, Calcraft acted as Robertson, and Mrs. Henry Siddons was 'particularly admired' in the rôle of the heroine. Scott, on attending the play, received the customary ovation, though (as Lockhart always insists) not as the author of the novels, but as the poet, judge, and patron of the theatre.[17]

Before the Dimond modification reached Scotland, however, at least three different transcripts had already been seen in the theatres of Edinburgh. On February 1, 1819, a drama with the Dibdin title opened at the Pantheon, but lasted for only eight nights. This in the original, or, more probably, in a modified form, ran at the Royal from December 9 to 21. In February another revamping, or an entirely new version, continued for thirty-eight nights, with crowded houses. Tom Dibdin himself thought that this successful drama was his own, but he also believed that it ran for a time at the Adelphi, a condition which seems doubtful. Mrs. Henry Siddons, who became famous for her Jeanie Deans, had witnessed the original Dibdin play in London, and it is quite possible that she brought a transcript back to Edinburgh. Calcraft, Murray, or some of the other 'play carpenters,' as Scott once called such gentlemen

[16] Genest 9. 68, 445.
[17] 2. 121.

of the craft of play-revisers, may have had a hand or at least 'a main finger' in the various Edinburgh modifications.[18]

That the version of Dibdin, revised by Dimond, came to be regarded as the standard text, seems evident from the comment by the critic in Edinburgh in 1822. 'We do not think any one of the tales,' said this writer, 'have [*sic*] been so successfully fitted for theatrical representation, as the one now under review.'[19]

Yet William H. Murray of the Royal brought out another version of *Midlothian* in March, 1824. One notice gave him 'the principal merit of constructing this play, which is as excellent as Terry's is despicable.'

Some of these five or six early adaptations continued to run now and then on both continents: Miss Aitkin won fame as Madge in Glasgow, and Charlotte Cushman in Boston; Mrs. Alsopp as Jeanie in London and Perth, and Mrs. Duff at the Lafayette, New York.[20]

Most peculiar of the early digressions from the beaten path of *Midlothian* is the *Whistler*, a literary drama, written by George Dibdin Pitt, and played for a time in 1833 at the Victoria, London. The playbill described it as 'founded on some unpublished chapters of the novel.' Many changes indeed have been wrought by time in the district of Midlothian. Lady and Sir George Staunton (Effie and George Robertson) have been made wealthy by the death of the old barrister. Their first child was never found. Jeanie

---

[18] The *Caledonian Mercury,* Feb. 1, 1819, praises the play and the acting, but is reticent as to who made the drama. James C. Dibdin is quite positive that Tom Dibdin was in error when he supposed his original was first produced at the Pantheon, and then later transferred to the Royal. Yet the *Mercury* note implied that a modified form was indeed brought from the Pantheon to the rival house. Further evidence seems unobtainable at present. See T. J. Dibdin's *Reminiscences* 2. 74, and J. C. Dibdin's *Annals*, p. 294.

[19] *Dramatic Review* 1. 145.

[20] *Dramatic Review* 8. 40; Banyham, *Glasgow Stage,* p. 105; Lawson, *Scots Stage,* p. 262; Ireland 1. 57.

for years has been Mrs. Parson Butler.   After a time, a wild, nomadic youth appears in the community.   Having grown up without the chastening influences of a real home, he has learned to roam about aimlessly in waste and rugged places.   At last this youth, known as the Whistler, learns that he is the missing child; but he is too romantic, honorable, and sensitive to notify his parents.   Our last glimpse of him shows a wild, reckless, and despairing young man at the top of an eminence, from which he finally leaps into the darkness of the crags below the cliff.

For the sake of varying the idea of a maniac, Pitt introduced a second madman named Sandy Saunderson, in which part he himself acted to the Whistler by Miss MacCartney.

Later Distortions of Midlothian

After the middle of the century, a half dozen additional distortions of the novel gained some repute on a number of stages on both sides of the Atlantic.   Only two of these merit any direct comment: *Jeanie Deans*, by Dion Boucicault, and *Effie Deans*, by George Shepherd.

Boucicault, a truly eminent actor, also had a hand in the composition or revision of nearly four hundred dramatic pieces.   Laurence Hutton mentions thirty of the 'leading' works by this man, among which is the Midlothian drama.[21] It had a run of fifty-four evenings at Laura Keene's Varieties, New York, early in 1860, and afterward in rotation visited four additional theatres from then to 1874. When Boucicault returned to England, he renamed the piece the *Trial of Effie Deans*, for further production at Astley's in 1863.   In the original New York cast were Fechter (the artist whom Dickens loved and helped) as Deans, Laura Keene as Effie, Mrs. Boucicault as Jeanie, and the author himself as Counsel for the Defense.   Pascoe highly commended Mrs. Boucicault for her charming

---

[21] *Plays and Players,* p. 210.

naturalness in the exacting part of the Scotch lassie, who was best of all in the witness-box during the trial.[22] Henry Morley called Boucicault in his part as Counsel 'a bamboozler of juries, who affects an enthusiasm he does not feel,' and the whole play seemed to him a case of 'mock thunder,' almost a burlesque on Scott.[23]

In spite of a few artistic limitations and several startling liberties taken with the narrative of the Great Unknown, Boucicault produced a very effective melodrama. Each of the three acts rises to a marked climax. In the first, it is the arrest of Effie, which is arranged with 'immense dramatic power'; in the second, it is the courtroom-scene, which gave Boucicault his main chance to reveal the unjust effects of 'circumstantial evidence'; in the last, it is the breaking open of the jail by the Porteus rioters. As an original touch to round out the action, Boucicault has Margerie strike down her own daughter, in mistake for Jean, with whom Madge has exchanged cloaks.[24]

While the Boucicault modification was near its acting height in London, George Shepherd rushed out a rival, called *Effie Deans; or, The Lily of St. Leonard's,* at the Surrey Theatre. This title leads one to suppose that Dibdin's original was touched up copiously, to suit the tastes of a later age.[25] Gourlay, a seasoned veteran renowned for his Bailie, made an impressive Dumbiedikes, while Shepherd himself proved a good Duke of Argyle.

Boucicault asserted infringement of his rights by Shepherd, in a letter to the *Times,* threatening 'litigation,' but

[22] *Dramatic List,* quoting *London Times* of Jan. 29, 1863.

[23] *Journal of a London Play-goer,* p. 289.

[24] *Times,* Jan. 29, 1863. 'Old David Deans, who (we suppose in compliment to the Americans before whom the piece was first played) is a teetotaler.'

[25] Morley, p. 289, states that the Boucicault version 'must have been written for an audience lower in taste than that which frequented the Surrey Theatre.'

nothing further apparently was done to stop the acting of the rival success.[26]   On April 21, 1860, Boucicault had complained in the *New York Tribune* that others had stolen his thunder for a play then acting in Philadelphia.

Shepherd's first act begins with the uprising in the jail, shows the hanging of one of the conspirators, and ends with the burning of the Tolbooth.   The second act includes the visit of Jean to Muschat's Cairn, where she is rescued from the impertinent officers by Madge Wildfire.   Though similar to the trial-scene, which was the great hit of the Boucicault play, this portion falls below the other in interest and dramatic tension.[27]   The great feature of the third act is a spectacle or 'sensation' scene, showing a cataract and cascade of real water, with some other picturesque effects, including the rescue of Jeanie by Robertson from Mag Murdochson and her foul crew.   Shepherd finally restored the interview with the Queen in London, and Jean's return to Midlothian with the pardon, just in the nick of time to save Effie from the gallows, which was actually set up in view of the audience.

MIDLOTHIAN IN TRAVESTY

Following in the train of these two legitimate dramas on London stages, Brough Brothers' *Circumstantial Effie Deans* appeared at the St. James Theatre in March of 1863. From an account in the *Athenæum* one learns that the sole purpose was to poke fun at the Boucicault and Shepherd plays.[28]   Much in the manner typical of the Victorian burlesque, Thomas Hailes Lacy published an undated *olla podrida* of all Midlothian plays.   On the title-page it was

[26] Boucicault claimed the rights to 'not only the original dialogue, but also the general arrangement of the incidents which constitute the principal value and success of the new drama.'

[27] The *Athenæum*, Feb. 14, 1863, implies that Shepherd took nothing very essential from the other piece.

[28] *Ibid.*, April 11, 1863; *Theatrical Journal*, April 1, 1863.

called '*The Heart of Midlothian; or, the Sisters of St. Leonard,* a Drama (with unregistered effects) in three acts, adapted from Sir Walter Scott's admired novel, with introductions from T. Dibdin's play, W. Murray's alteration of the same, Eugène Scribe's opera, and Dion Boucicault's conglomeration of the above, Colin Hazzlewood's adjustment and readjustment, J. B. Johnstone's appropriation, and other equally original versions, together with a very small amount of new matter by Thomas Hailes Lacy.'[29]

Besides all these mentioned above, at least one other modification held the boards at the Albion Theatre in 1877, and at the Marylebone, two years afterward. This was credited to George Hamilton.[30]

FRENCH TRANSCRIPTS

One vaudeville piece and at least one opera gained some applause on the French stage. Paul Duport's *Vendéenne,* in which the eminent Madame Rachel made her début, began a run of sixty nights at the Gymnase late in April, 1837. The main interest is derived from the journey of a lass of Vendée to Malmaison to secure a pardon from Empress Josephine for her father, much in the manner of Jeanie Deans.[31]

Apparently the only text now available is a translation into English made by Captain Rafter for the Princess Theatre. It was printed about 1838. Much in the first act resembles the Dibdin play; some of the last, the Terry adaptation. Robertson and Ratcliffe, however, are regular pirates, stealthily evading the customs officers. During the trial, the

---

[29] Johnstone's piece is not identified; Hazzlewood's is printed in volume 850 of Lacy's *Acting Drama;* the others are all described in the present discussion.

[30] Clarence, p. 128.

[31] Dutton Cook, *Hours with the Players,* p. 329; see also F. W. M. Draper, *Rise and Fall of the French Romantic Drama,* p. 34.

Duke of Argyle presides, condemning Effie for refusing to reveal the name of the father of her child. George Robertson eventually proves to be the Duke's own son. Madge, in her crazed imagination, fancies that George is an old lover of hers. She therefore changes her testimony.

For comic relief in the last act, the author introduces some repartee between Ratcliffe and the prisoners under his charge. Argyle delays the execution of Effie for three days, to allow further search for the missing infant. Meanwhile, the sheriff hints to his prisoner that he can arrange it so that Effie may escape from the Tolbooth, but the Scotch lass refuses to agree. Madge takes refuge in the belfry of the church adjoining the jail-yard, and here she sits crooning among the swallows that contend with her for the place. At the close she fires the tower, cuts the bell rope, and makes it into a means of lowering down a basket, in which the long-lost baby is found to be safe. Thus Effie is spared, but Madge is last seen at the window of the flaming tower.

The Opéra Comique, in July, 1833, brought out a *Prison d'Edimbourg,* with text by A. Eugène Scribe and F. A. Eugène de Planard, and with ornate music by Michel de Carafa. Many details of the original novel are lacking: we miss the riots in Edinburgh, the journey of Jean to London, and the comic relief of Dumbiedikes and others. Mad Sarah, as Madge Wildfire is called, has stolen the baby, and now at the close she incites the prisoners to fire the jail. She then perishes, as in the other French version, after letting the baby down in the basket from her burning tower.

In spite of a number of changes from Scott, the affair attained considerable vogue, according to the *Temps*,[32] which pronounced it entirely an artistic success.

---

[32] For July 22, 1833, and the *Moniteur Universel* for the same date. Draper, p. 33, has an interesting discussion of these French operatic melodramas.

A Last Opera

Probably the worthiest of all delayed adaptations of the tale of Jeanie and Effie Deans is the opera with music by Hamish McCunn, and words by the eminent dramatic critic and playwright, Joseph Bennett. This contains four acts and seven tableaux, first staged by T. H. Friend at the Royal Lyceum, Edinburgh, in November of 1894. Though simplified to meet the requirements of an opera, all the essentials of the story are preserved. Several excellent pieces of scenery were painted for the performance. Considerable is made of the songs of Madge Wildfire, all of which are in character.

Midlothian Plays in Retrospect

Thus we have seen that Scott's *Heart of Midlothian* received abundant notice, in all kinds of theatres, from 1818 to 1894 or later. For variety of the versions, it extended its influence somewhat beyond both *Guy Mannering* and *Rob Roy*. Yet the types of theatrical effects remained fairly constant in all three instances.

First came the accurate and faithful transcript by Dibdin, followed by the large modification of Terry. The one drama made a tremendous hit in London and Edinburgh; the other fell almost stillborn into a quick oblivion. Dibdin proved that audiences liked to see Scott 'in his own gallant manner' on the stage, as Charles Dickens remarked when he assisted Fechter to produce a Lammermoor play. Dibdin of all authors succeeded best in reviving the Midlothian types of persons, with good contrasts, dramatic progression, and surprise at the climax of interest. In characterization he was superior. Terry's piece revives the question as to whether Sir Walter Scott lent assistance; but Scott probably never would have sanctioned the 'pretty little mincing London miss,' in place of his puritanical Jeanie Deans.

When William Dimond entered the dramatic lists, combinations began. He seemed possessed of the faculty of taking the best of several plays, and fusing them into an acceptable and popular presentation. With the coming of others, however, the departures from Scott became more apparent and less admirable, though the Edinburgh audiences greatly favored the work of William H. Murray, which probably was based on all previous dramas. Pitt's *Whistler* soon fell into limbo among all the curiously distorted forms that grew out of special pleading, and the making of dramas for particular artists to act. Boucicault's modification exalted the trial-scene, to show the evil effects of a theory and of circumstantial evidence. Shepherd restored the interest to something like the original plot of the novel.

The third stage began with the burlesque of the Brough Brothers. This and Lacy's 'conglomeration' pointed out the absurd features of the plays that left Scott too much in the background. Lacy also called attention to the numerous borrowings back and forth among all previous versions after Dibdin's. Usually the travesties of the Scott dramatizations appeared after the original enthusiasm for such plays had greatly cooled. They were made for a later and less reverent age, when the personal influence of the great Scotsman had declined considerably—an age when the novels were held in less reverence than before 1850.

In the fourth class, two operas appear. One belongs to a time just after the death of the novelist; the other to the extreme end of all presentations. The later was the more faithful rendering, so far as the story itself is concerned.

V. THE BRIDE OF LAMMERMOOR

Before the next great romance came into favor in the playhouse, rumors flew thick and fast that Scott intended to join the ranks of the dramatic authors. Robert Southey urged him to try a new form of composition, 'For I am verily persuaded that in this course you might run as brilliant a career as you have already done in narrative—both prose and rhyme—for, as for believing you have a double in the field—not I.' Scott by this time, however, had given up most of his hope of even assisting Terry; he, therefore, wrote Southey to disclaim any intention of risking his fame by entrusting it to 'low, ill-informed, and conceited actors.'[1]

By this time, furthermore, the playwrights had become more cautious, and somewhat more independent; for they no longer followed the story of the novel slavishly. Opera now gained by leaps and bounds in England, as well as across the Channel. For the first time an operatic version of a Scott narrative long outlived, and far outranked, the corresponding melodramas. This was Donizetti's *Lucia di Lammermoor,* which almost immediately took its place among the great operas of the world. It soon left in the background the many rival dramas sponsored by men like Dibdin, Calcraft, Soane, Simpson, Merivale, and Byron. Of about a score of Lucy plays, the range is from grand opera to broadest travesty; from literal transcripts of men like Calcraft to the wildest vagaries of George Soane; from sentimental melodramas to darkest romantic tragedies. Moreover, Scott's *Bride of Lammermoor* differs from some other romances in that two of the latest transcripts were among the best of all plays drawn from the works of the Wizard of the North. These are the two Ravenswood tragedies—one by Simpson in 1865, the other by Merivale for Irving and Ellen Terry to enact in 1890.

[1] See Lockhart 2. 124, 134, 141.

DIBDIN FIRST AGAIN

Once more the resourceful and alert Tom Dibdin rushed into action before all others with his drama at the Surrey Theatre. He christened it the *Bride of Lammermoor; or, The Spectre at the Fountain,* when the initial run began on June 7, 1819. Six months before, his *Midlothian* had been compiled within seven days, and acted within thirteen, after he had read the novel. This next time he produced two plays in a fortnight, the *Montrose* and the *Lammermoor.*

The scope of this versatile dramatist is revealed by a statement in his *Reminiscences.* He informs us there that his dramatic labors included about two hundred pieces, sixteen of which were extravagantly successful, only ten absolute failures, and over fifty were printed during his lifetime, though not one was taken to the press by the playwright himself. Among his many three-act dramas that were 'misnamed burlettas according to an Act of Parliament,' Dibdin mentions his *Midlothian, Old Mortality, Ivanhoe, Kenilworth,* and *Pirate.* He called his own *Lady of the Lake* and *Montrose* melodramas, for no real reason save that they were produced in the legitimate theatres.[2] Dibdin also composed nearly two thousand songs, many of which long continued to be favorites.*

Montrose and *Lammermoor,* his twin-born dramas, aroused variant opinions among the critics. The first of these, though not up to the usual Dibdin standard, according to the printed text, is an interesting and noble melodrama. *Lammermoor,* which never was published, aroused much censure in the *Theatre* because of liberties taken with the text of Scott; but the *European Magazine* praised it highly. The introduction of a spectre lady, said the *Theatre* reviewer, 'contributes nothing to the plot, but very much to the annoyance of the nerves of the audience.'[3]   Caleb was greatly sub-

[2] *Reminiscences* 2. 148, 176, 338.
[3] *Theatre,* July 10, 1819.

dued to appease some of those who thought the part might seem 'low.' Edgar does not stab himself, but is killed by a domestic. Lucy 'falls a prey to her feelings,' which must mean that she dies in the orthodox manner as described by Scott.[3] Few other changes were made, apparently; for the current *European Magazine* of June, 1819, said, 'Mr. Dibdin has evinced his usual taste and discernment, by giving a faithful outline of the whole story, and flinging into bold relief all those parts which are susceptible of great effect.'

Original Play by Calcraft in Edinburgh

John William Cole, laureate for the Theatre Royal in Edinburgh, came to be known to his friends as Old King Cole, and to the public as J. W. Calcraft, actor and maker of melodramas. Sometimes he revamped a great London success to suit northern tastes and northern scenes. Less frequently he made a play from the ground up. For once, however, in his *Bride of Lammermoor,* he followed the text of Scott so closely that one critic called his work 'slavish.'[4] At first his melodrama failed, because of poor acting and of some difficulties in the management of the production. As issued later in a printed text, his work is much above the ordinary for such pieces.

When the curtain goes up, Sir William Ashton is congratulating himself that the death of the elder Ravenswood has finally put the last of the hated line into his own power. Not long afterward, however, he becomes greatly obligated to Edgar, the son of his old enemy, who has saved him and his daughter Lucy from an infuriated bull. On his side, too, Edgar is put into a new relationship, since he has gone into the open with the avowed intention of shooting his hereditary foeman. Almost at once the note of tragedy appears, when Ravenswood haughtily refuses the advances

---

[4] *Theatrical Observer* 1. 282. The reviewer favored close approximations of the original plots.

made by Sir William. Bucklaw and Craigengelt, boon companions of Edgar, are next introduced; but Edgar is shown breaking away from them for some mysterious reason. Soon it transpires that he has abandoned a proposed trip to France, wishing to remain in the neighborhood where Lucy Ashton may be seen. After coming to terms with Bucklaw a bit later in a duel, Edgar invites this crony to share his humble fortunes at Wolf's Crag. The astonished Caleb, general factotum at the Crag, rehearses the bill of fare, as in the novel, by drawing on a huge imaginary store of provisions. Calcraft apparently did not fear that Caleb might become too 'low'; for he takes full license from all the droll incidents that involve Caleb in the original story.

Sir William and Lucy, in the second act, because of a great storm, take refuge at Wolf's Crag. Edgar, in the meanwhile, has fancied more and more that they might be friends. Lucy, on her side, admires him for his heroism and kindness. Events now move with tragic swiftness, until the lovers plight their troth by breaking a coin at Mermaiden's Well.

From this point, Lady Ashton enters to resume charge of the fortunes of her daughter. She favors Bucklaw, because the Ashtons are in need of money. Calcraft gives Lucy considerable force of character, which she lacks in some Lammermoor plays. The daughter would even resist, were it not that Sir William meekly submits to his wife's pet schemes. Lady Ashton carries forward the wooing; she even incites Bucklaw to a half-hearted proposal. Lucy at once rejects his suit. Caleb is next introduced, to provide the comic contrast just before a grim moment of tragedy. Calcraft puts the absurd butler through all his usual tricks. When the Earl of Athlone visits Wolf's Crag somewhat suddenly, Caleb sallies forth on a foraging hunt, and at last snatches away the dinner which a good woman of the village is cooking at her own turnspit.

In three rapid scenes, the third act brings all events to

a terrible pitch of interest. Lady Ashton's importunities finally wear away the resistance of Lucy. Better than some of the subsequent playwrights, Calcraft shows clearly that the bride of Lammermoor had no real freedom of choice when Bucklaw was selected as her husband. Mainly through guile, Lucy is brought to sign the agreement to marry. She has been persuaded that Edgar is faithless. The lover comes too late, just as she has signed the fatal document.

All the guests and friends retire, leaving Lucy, Edgar, and Lady Ashton alone. Once more the heartless mother manages the scene, while Lucy, in her confusion and heart-sickness, is like putty in her moulding hands. The bride allows Lady Ashton to return the bit of gold which Edgar gave as a pledge of faith. Almost immediately, however, the reaction follows, as she realizes to the full her changed situation in regard to Edgar and her promise to become his wife. Lucy utters a haunting cry, falls limp into the arms of Edgar, and not long afterward expires, having first revealed the treachery practiced against them by her relatives.

The tenseness of the Calcraft melodrama is best shown by a quotation or two from the concluding scenes. After Edgar has returned to find that Lucy has affixed her name to the contract, Ravenswood chides her for her faithlessness, and this dialogue ensues:

> Lucy. Stay! Oh, stay, Rav—Ravenswood—my heart is breaking, and I cannot tell you; but do not leave me thus—a few moments, and all will be over.
>
> Lady Ashton (alarmed at her violence). Lucy, my dearest Lucy!
>
> Lucy. Touch me not, mother. 'Tis now too late. I am beyond all fear. Ravenswood, you know not what I have endured—all united against me—your long silence—my letters intercepted—no friend to aid—no succor—no resource. They have broken my heart; but never, never could they change my love. Ravenswood, forgive, forgive me (falls forward).
>
> Ravenswood. Almighty Heaven! The hand of death is on her pallid cheek. She dies to prove her faith; and I—no, no. 'Tis thou, accursed fiend in human form—thou hast disgraced

the name of mother. Thou, thou, hast destroyed thy child. Speak to me, Lucy, one word to save me from the hell that rages in my bosom. . . .

The violence of Edgar leads to a challenge to engage Sir William Ashton in a duel. Ravenswood, however, rushes on his own sword, with these final words, which end the tragedy:

> Thus I provoke my fate! (falls) 'Tis past! The prediction is fulfilled: the blood of Ravenswood flows in the hall of his ancestors. Accursed race, contemplate, and enjoy your malice. Lucy, I come. In life they severed us, but in death we are united.

On the opening night, May 1, 1821, Calcraft as Edgar of Ravenswood fell somewhat below his usual standard of acting; the man who took the rôle of Bucklaw proved much too great a fop; and even Mrs. Henry Siddons found the part of Lucy somewhat too difficult at first. As Caleb, the great Mackay redeemed the piece from being 'one continued rotation of dull and uninteresting scenes.'[5] Time dealt gently with the lovers of Lammermoor, in respect to appreciation by the audiences, especially since some changes were made in the text of the tragedy. In the autumn of 1821, Calcraft's version came to its own in Edinburgh; afterward a few of the numerous revivals occurred at Bath in 1826; at the Bowery, New York, in 1828; at Dublin during the management of Calcraft in 1842; at Edinburgh again in 1846; at Marylebone in London for a series of evenings in 1846, where Mrs. A. C. Mowatt—fresh from more than two hundred nights with the same play in America—joined with E. L. Davenport for a notable revival; and again in America at Boston in 1853, and at Providence in 1856.[6]

---

[5] *Dramatic Review* I. 133, 141.
[6] Dibdin, p. 297; Ireland I. 565; introduction to edition published, without date, by French, New York; Genest 9. 359; it was also printed as one of the *Waverley Dramas*, Glasgow, 1872.

EARLY MELODRAMA AND OPERAS ABROAD

Almost from the beginning, the novels of Scott attracted translators and librettists in continental Europe. Within two years after the first dramatization pleased large audiences in Paris, three others followed, and gained temporary fame at least. The first of the lot was the *Caleb de Walter Scott,* written by Achille d'Artois and Eugène de Planard for the Théâtre des Nouveautés, with music by Adolphe Adam. Beginning on December 12, 1827, this one-act sketch continued to draw for fifty-two nights, a respectable length for the time in Paris. Great stress falls on the familiar antics of Caleb at Wolf's Crag, in borrowing a roast from the spit of a woman of the village to provide his master with something to entertain unexpected guests. Little is said of the Ashton family; for the master, Lord Douglas, is in love with a sister of an old comrade. The lovers are reunited, and take possession of the Lammermoor estates at the end. This slight affair, translated into English, appeared in St. Petersburg in 1843.[7]

Ducange followed with another of his borrowings from Scott, which he christened *Fiancée de Lammermoor,* and described as 'imitated from the romance of Sir Walter Scott.' Even without any supporting music, it ran for more than fifty nights at the Porte Saint Martin in the spring of 1828. Madame Dorval and Frédéric Lemaître, in the chief parts, were said to be 'very remarkable' in the pathetic scenes.[8] Old Alice and Caleb are both restored to their original place in the action. With commendable regard for French ideals of compression and unity, however, Ashton is made a lord and governor of Lammermoor; Lady Ashton is no longer the mother, but is transformed into the stepmother, of Lucy, whose brother Douglas has been elevated to be Lord Douglas, brother of Lady Ashton; and two

---

[7] *Figaro,* Dec. 13, 1827; Partridge, p. 226.

[8] *Pandore,* March 26, 27, 1828; Partridge, p. 226; Draper, p. 32.

lords of high estate have taken the rôles of those precious adventurers, Bucklaw and Craigengelt. Something is made of King William's victory at the Boyne in 1690, and Ravenswood is incited by the Marquis of Athol to try to kill Ashton, a touch not in the novel. Some Scotch gentlemen quarrel with Edgar at Wolf's Crag, which is attacked and blown up. Edgar and Lucy die in the quicksands or waves near the castle of the Ravenswoods. Except for these variations, the story follows the main outlines of the novel, with some emphasis on the betrothal and the contract, but here Lucy does not kill the bridegroom.

Irlandais is the title of the next piece in French, in two acts, 'imitated from the English' by M. Benjamin, and shown at the Gymnase in September of 1831, with Bouffé in the title rôle, and Despreaux as Henriette, the heroine. During the month it ran for fourteen nights. The story is a badly garbled version of the quarrel between the Ashton and Ravenswood families, or between an English and an Irish lord, bringing out the national characteristics and spirit of each. Both, of course, are in love with Henriette, who prefers the Irish colonel, and who leaves a banknote in his secretary, knowing that he is in need of funds. The Irish lord journeys to her castle to return the money, but there he finds the Englishman ahead of him. The generous Irish colonel, however, would give Henriette up, but the lady herself seems unwilling. Following a noisy quarrel between the two men at the castle, they adjourn to fight a duel, in which the Irishman is beaten. Yet his generous rival, in turn, knowing the goodness of the Colonel's heart, relinquishes all claims to Henriette. Not only that: he also bestows some estates on the happy couple, which had been claimed by the Englishman, much as the Ravenswood estates are held by the Ashtons in Scott's *Lammermoor*.

Of this production, the *Quotidienne,* among other comments, said, 'It is a picture of those religious and political hates that still morally divide England and Ireland. We

find in it the very faithful portraits of those Irish gentlemen that spend their life eating, digesting, and sleeping,
unless they have an epigram to fling at John Bull, or a
trick to play him.   The authors have placed in the play two
other types that seem to be a *contrefaçon* of Scott's Ravenswood and of his faithful Caleb.   A special mention is to be
made of the part of the heroine, some bride of Lammermoor as it were, who has been transplanted from the
romantic into classic nature.'[9]

This is but one illustration of the many that show the
debts of French opera-makers to the works of Walter Scott.
By 1828, more than three years prior to the production of
Irlandais, several critics were frequently mentioning that
Scott continued to vie with Cooper and Byron for honors
in the French playhouses.   The same condition continued,
with only some lessening, for another decade.[10]

LUCIA DI LAMMERMOOR

Greatest of all the European operas related in any degree
to the novels of Walter Scott is the *Lucia di Lammermoor,*
for which Cammarano made a somewhat indifferent libretto,
and Donizetti the music of extremely high calibre.   Everybody knows about *Lucia,* even in our day.   Certain parts
have been sung (notably the celebrated sextet) almost as
often as those of any other opera of the nineteenth century.
An account of the hundreds of performances since 1835
would, in itself, fill the pages of a large volume.   Just as
soon as the *Bride of Lammermoor* became known in France
and Italy, the makers of opera at once saw in the tragic story
the greatest of romantic situations for the stage.   Few plots

[9] For Sept. 14, 1831.   The summary of the plot is from the printed
text.   *Figaro,* Sept. 7, 1831, praised the drama.

[10] For statements of the debt to Scott, see *Courrier des Théâtres,*
Jan. 11, 1828; *National,* Sept., 1830; Partridge, p. 198; Draper, pp.
21-55.   Other quotations appear at later points in the present review
of the dramatization of Scott.

are better adapted to the concise needs of classical opera.
Even though the original rendering of the English into
Italian is faulty at certain points, the libretto is compressed,
simple enough, and harmonious to an uncommon degree.

Much of the credit for the tremendous vogue of *Lucia*
has, however, been given to Gaetano Donizetti.   His musical
setting, not long after the first performance of the opera
at the Teatro Fondo, Naples, September 28, 1835, gained
for the artist a professorship in counterpoint at the local
conservatory of music.[11]

Salvatore Cammarano, in his operatic drama, reduced the
story of *Lammermoor* to three short acts and an epilogue.
Only seven characters appear, out of the thirty in the novel,
and the dozen or more in certain other operas.   The elder
Ashtons drop out altogether; so does the droll Caleb.
Enrico, older brother, acts as guardian of Lucy.   Bucklaw
is renamed Arturo; Bide-the-Bent is Raimento, whose main
business is keeping the peace among the men; and Edgar is
Edgardo.   The minor details of each scene revolve about
one central point of emotional interest.

Though plenty of translations of the original words of
Cammarano are available, for the sake of comparison a
brief summary of the salient details of the plot is here
provided.[12]

Sir Henry Ashton, the brother and guardian of Lucy,
stands in need of funds for the dignity of the house of
Ashton, and for a cover to some treasonable schemes of his
own.   He therefore wishes an alliance between Lucy and
Bucklaw, a foppish but wealthy young adventurer.   Lucy
hears some of the plans through her tutor, Raimento, but
fails to comprehend just how they affect her.   Raimento

[11] Grove I. 716.
[12] An English translation by Natalia Macfarren has also a parallel
Italian text and the original Donizetti music.   *Opera Synopses,* by
J. Walker MacSpadden; Upton, p. 81; Davidson, p. 191; and the
Victrola Book of the Opera, have good summaries of the plot.

points out to Henry that his sister may entertain thoughts of a secret lover, who seems to be the youth that rescued them from a dangerous bull. It soon transpires that Edgar Ravenswood, hated foe of the house of Ashton, is indeed the lover of Lucy. Her brother plans a speedy revenge. Edgar meets Lucy at Mermaiden's Well, to say good-bye before leaving on a dangerous mission abroad. Ere he quits the country, he must have an interview with Henry. In great consternation, Lucy warns him of the dangers of such a meeting. At the close of act one, they pledge their troth by breaking the coin between them, each retaining half as a token.

While the absent lover is in France, Henry intimates to his sister that he expects her to wed Bucklaw. Lucy at last declares that such a union is unsuitable to her, especially since she has made a pledge to Edgar Ravenswood. For a considerable time, she resists all covert hints, persuasions, entreaties, and even open threats. Henry secures aid in having some letters forged, by which they at last convince the bride of Lammermoor that her betrothed loves another in France. Edgar's letters to her, meanwhile, have been intercepted by order of Henry. When she is fully convinced that Edgar is lost to her, she reluctantly consents to marry Bucklaw. This portion of the plot is handled with extraordinary skill.

At the beginning of the third act, Edgar has returned to Lammermoor from his sojourn abroad. He rushes into the hall of the Ashtons just a few moments after Lucy has signed the momentous marriage-covenant. In her confusion, Lucy admits that she has willingly agreed to the contract. Without waiting for her to explain, Edgar believes her faithless to her troth. He tears the document into bits, rushes from the castle, and arranges with Henry, who has followed, to engage in a duel at daybreak. Lucy is now allowed to retire to her apartment, where the bridegroom already awaits her.

Not long afterward, Raimento distractedly rushes into the

hall among the guests, who are making merry, to inform them that Lucy has slain the lord of Bucklaw. While consternation dominates, Lucy herself confirms the report, though she just dimly realizes what has been happening. The bride becomes more and more incoherent in her conversation, frequently summoning Edgar to come and save her, until she finally falls into a deep faint, from which she never rallies.

Meanwhile Edgar has wandered to the burial-plot of the Ravenswoods, and there he loiters while bitter thoughts and revengeful emotions surge in his mind and soul. When he hears the familiar tolling of a bell at the castle, he infers that Lucy has paid the forfeit of trusting her relatives instead of her beloved. Soon a messenger brings word that the bride of Lammermoor is dead. For the first time, Edgar fully realizes that he has unjustly accused his betrothed, for whom he breathes a fervent prayer, adding one for himself that God may forgive his rashness; and then he falls upon the point of his sword. By this time the wedding-guests have found their way to the burial-plot, where they stand about, making impotent gestures of horror and consternation.

To spare the feelings of the audience, this tragic short tableau among the Ravenswood tombs was often omitted.

Though in greatly compressed and abbreviated form, this opera takes all the essentials from Scott, making only those modifications that are needed for clearness, simplicity, or emphasis on some detail not made prominent in the novel. The opening choruses follow the original; so do the interview between Sir William and Ravenswood, the love-scene at Mermaiden's Well, with the duet in which the lovers plight their troth, and, finally, the scene among the tombs.[13]

---

[13] Canning, *Sir Walter Scott studied in Eight Novels*, p. 139, notes the resemblances and differences between Scott and Cammarano. He mentions that the general plan of the novel is similar to that of *Romeo and Juliet*, and that the sense of impending fate links it also with *Macbeth*.

Most of the comedy at Wolf's Crag is omitted, as being unsuited to the tone and bearing of a tragic opera. The main scenes are laid at the Ashton Castle of Lammermoor; the grove where the lovers meet and exchange vows; the apartment of Lucy; the hall of the Castle; and the churchyard.

In the musical score, the basso parts are assigned to Henry and Raymond; the tenor to Edgar, Arthur, and Norman; the soprano or contralto to Lucy and Alice. For the *première,* Donizetti had in mind as principals the great Italian artists, Mme. Persiani and Duprez, both of whom won a triumph in Naples, and later in Paris. Each of the four portions rises to a climax of emotional realization. Some of the great musical settings are: the opening chorus of the band of hunters; the duet of Edgar and Lucy at the Well, ending in their betrothal, with an exchange of tokens; the sextet, *What restrains me? (Chi mi frena?),* as Edgar returns to find his beloved contracted to another, with the following reply by the quartette, *Get thee gone;* the chorus, *Oh, dire misfortune,* when report arrives that Lucy has stabbed the bridegroom; *Farewell to earth,* the poignant solo by Edgar, when he hears that Lucy has expired; and, finally, his *Thou hast spread thy wings to Heaven,* an address to the soul of Lucy, in which Edgar expresses the hope that his soul may join hers in another world.[14]

Probably the mad scene and the celebrated sextet have been sung as often as any selections from opera among English-speaking peoples. They have been used at times by almost all the great concert and operatic artists, including Tetrazzini, Sembrich, Melba, Galli-Curci, Caruso, Amato, Daddi, Journet, De Luca, Bada, and many others in recent years.

Following the prodigious vogue of the opera, a host of editions have been printed in all modern tongues. It would

[14] See Lohee, *Annals of Music in America,* p. 28, or any other standard work on the history of music and opera.

take a page of text to enumerate even the titles of these. Twenty major versions, half with parallel Italian and some other text, are mentioned in six languages alone. In early days excellent translations were made for both Covent Garden and Drury Lane, with parallel Italian and English words. Two later translations of merit are those by Manfredo Maggioni for Covent Garden in 1869, and by Natalia Macfarren for an edition issued in Boston in 1888.[15]

Only a single passage is needed to show the utter simplicity of the words of the libretto, as found in the translation by Maggioni, in a passage which is the most dramatic of the whole opera. This follows the return of Edgar, as he enters the Hall at Lammermoor to claim his bride.

> *Henry.* Ravenswood, within these walls
> Who led thy steps?
> *Edgar.* My fate and my own right;
> I came hither to fetch my bride.
> *Raymond.* Thou must her love forget for ever.
> She's another's.
> *Edgar.* Another's? Ah, no!
> *Raymond.* Look! (Lucy appears.)
> *Edgar.* Thou tremblest—thou art confused.
> Is this thy writing? Answer, answer;
> Is this thy writing?
> *Lucy.* Yes.
> *Edgar.* Take back thy pledge, perfidious heart,
> And mine restore.
> *Lucy.* At least—
> *Edgar.* Restore it quickly.
> Love and heaven thou hast betrayed.
> Cursed be for ever the moment,
> When for thee first sighed my heart.
> Impious race—detested name!
> Yes, I ought to avoid thy snares.
> May the just revenge of heaven
> Be thy destroyer.[16]

[15] Information concerning the number of editions, with a list of the titles (not given here), was supplied by the Music Division of the Library of Congress.

[16] The Maggioni edition was published in London, 1869; the quotation is from p. 31.

Brief Account of Lucia on the Stage

Italian opera slowly gained a hearing in England in the second and third decades of the nineteenth century. Often the best operatic plays of Rome, Milan, and Naples came to the British Isles through the medium of French adaptations, some of which followed Scott only in the barest outlines. By the time of Donizetti's opera, however, the form had become fairly well acclimated in Great Britain, not only in translations, but even in the original Italian.

Outside of Naples the work of Donizetti became current before the middle of the century in places as distant from each other as Berlin and Mexico City. *Lucia* was sung in France in 1837, 1838, and 1846; in London first at the Opera in 1838, at the Princess in 1843 and 1844, at Drury Lane in 1845 and 1848, and finally at Covent Garden in the autumn of the year last mentioned. Sims Reeves, Mlle. Nilsson, and Burdini formed a talented group that took London by storm. In 1848 Reeves began, at Covent Garden, a series of tours that took him eventually to Ireland, Scotland, and America.[17] Next to excel in London were Guiglini and Mlle. Piccolomini at the Lyceum in 1857, when these eminent Italian artists, beyond all others, succeeded in conveying the impression that the mind of Lucy at last gave way as a direct result of the curse heaped upon her by the infuriated Edgar.[18]

To mention only those artists known the world over who have used *Lucia* as a whole, or in certain parts like the sextet, would be to write an outline of the progress of opera, in the nineteenth century. Patti and Melba, for example, established their first great fame through one of the rôles of this opera. Christine Nilsson made a contract with the management of the Academy of Music in New York, which

---

[17] *Theatrical Times,* 2 Dec., 1848, p. 60; Banyham, p. 173; Levey and O'Rorke, p. 125.

[18] Morley, *Journal of a London Play-goer,* p. 175.

called for a salary of a thousand dollars a night, with incidental expenses, and half of the proceeds in excess of three thousand dollars. Clara Louise Kellogg, Sembrich, Campanini, Etelka Gerster, Grisi, Maplesden, Homer, Manzini, Augustus Braham—son of the great tenor—and Madame Schumann-Heink are some of the representative names. In his *New York Stage,* Col. T. Allston Brown cites more than eighty revivals of *Lucia,* including merely the productions of the entire opera.[19]   One of the most recent revivals occurred at the Metropolitan Opera House, February 9, 1924.[20]

ENGLISH AND FRENCH VARIATIONS

Thus far only the original text by Cammarano has been considered, though some of the definite performances mentioned may have used the French or English translations. As early as 1839 it had become the fashion to adapt, amend, and transpose many of the parts of the libretto.   To illustrate some of the typical revisions, one French and two English forms will now be considered in relation to the changes from Scott and from the Italian of Cammarano. These are the *Lucie di Lammermoor* by Alphonse Royer and Gustave Vaës,[21] which was sung at the Renaissance in 1839, and again at the Academy of Music of Paris in 1846; the anonymous English text used at the Princess Theatre in London in 1843; and the revision of the French *Lucie* for a New York opera arranged by George Soane.

Lucie, 'a grand opera in four acts,' follows the main plan of the Italian of Cammarano.   Numerous departures, how-

---

[19] Brown's account of the New York stage in three volumes has an excellent index, which traces most of the transcripts of the Scott novels in New York playhouses.

[20] Even this evening, while I give this chapter a final examination, a selection from *Lucia* is being broadcast from a station in New York City.

[21] Pseudonym for Jean Nicholas Gustave van Nieuwenhuysen.

ever, on almost every page, modify the sentiment and characterization in many little details. The *Temps* commended the corrections, new dialogue, and rewritten recitative by Donizetti, whose original music was used without essential modification. 'The translation is perhaps the best that has been made from the Italian for one of our theatres.'[22]

More revisions still are noticed in the Princess opera.[23] Douglas Ashton takes the place of Henry, and the part was sung by the great Burdini. A peculiar group, in form resembling a Greek chorus, comments on the action, and adds information for the benefit of the opera-goers. Prose, song, recitative, and remarks by the chorus are interspersed almost at random. One form passes into another quickly, whenever a change in emotion occurs. One innovation in the first act is a sword-dance by Douglas to show his desire for revenge against Ravenswood, for his boldness in stealing the heart of an Ashton. Only six main characters appear—Lucy, Edgar, Douglas, Bucklaw, Lockhart (a huntsman friend of Douglas), and Bide-the-Bent.

Several changes greatly affect the second part. It is a forged piece of ring, instead of forged letters, that convinces Lucy of Edgar's lack of faith. Bucklaw, more of a gentleman now than in the novel and variant operas, hesitates to wed Lucy if the maiden is unwilling. The young lady herself deepens the tragedy by hesitating, and by not making her mind clear. Edgar gives Lucy no chance to explain. He furiously snatches the ring from the hand of the bride; and this boorish violence makes the brother follow, and challenge him to a duel. In act second, the celebrated sestettino is retained, beginning with Edgar's defiance of Douglas and accusation of Lucy:

---

[22] For Aug. 11, 1839. The *Moniteur Universel*, however, in contempt designated this as a 'translation made over again,' 'a few pages roughly torn away from one of the most ingenious novels of W. Scott, and as badly sewn together.'

[23] The Princess edition is included in Lacy's *Acting Drama*, Vol. 78.

Ashton, here again behold me,
  Here before thee stands thy foe.
Do not wonder: all was told me;
  Yes, your arts too well I know.
Though her brother vengeance swore,
  Lucy I thought would faithful be.
A constant heart in me I bore;
  'T was, thou false one, true to thee.

The remaining two acts depart in lesser respects from the novel and the original text of Cammarano. The madness of Lucy is increased in violence. After she has slain the bridegroom, she raves about the stage, clutching a gory dagger. Some of the attendants carry her out in a faint, while the awed chorus comments on the terrible events at Lammermoor. Likewise, at the end of the opera, when Edgar has slain himself, the chorus sings in consternation and horror because of the sacrilege of suicide, but in sympathy for the wronged lovers. Even the name of Ashton will be shunned by all honest people henceforth.

George Soane, from 1820 to 1850 or afterward, adapted a lengthy list of celebrated plays and operas. He made drastic changes in many of them, and for such received more than one round of censure from the critics who loved to see the novels little distorted on the boards. Among Soane's many translations from foreign operas, his *Lucy of Lammermoor* ranks high, in spite of his frequent changes in the narrative.

Some of the revisions made by Soane are not injudicious. Henry, for example, informs the guests that his sister hesitates to marry the lord of Bucklaw because of the recent death of Lady Ashton, who is thus at once removed from the list of characters. Lucy is restored as an independent and spirited young lady. She at last agrees to marry Bucklaw when Henry threatens to use his prerogative as guardian to bend her will to his own. No attempts are made to deceive her by forged letters or counterfeit parts of rings. Nor does the bride of Lammermoor slay the unfortunate

Bucklaw on the eve of their marriage.   Little is made of the madness of the heroine, who is reported to be ill in her apartment.   The infuriated Edgar stabs himself within sight of the wedding guests.   Altogether one concludes that Soane made a good acting opera, even though it is a poor interpretation of Walter Scott.[24]

LATER CHANGES FOR CHANGING TASTES

Between 1820 and 1870, the Lucy plays passed through four periods that are typical of changing tastes.   Calcraft, in the first years, illustrates the author who followed Scott closely.   Then came the period of the French and English operatic modifications, typical of which is *Lucia di Lammermoor*.   The third stage is marked by sentimental revisions to suit an age that cared little whether the original text of Scott had direct connection with the play or opera they loved to attend.   Plays by Simpson and Merivale, next to be described, illustrate this third class.   Finally, we notice the travesties and light productions of men like Byron, which complete the distortion of the story in most details.

During the intervening years, a few stragglers are met along the way.   Included in these was a *Fatal Prophecy,* in which old Alice Grey had a chief rôle at the New Brunswick Theatre, London, in 1835.   George Almar made an obscure version for Sadler's Wells before 1865, and Leon Grus made an undated revision, for which the older Ducange operatic play served for a model.[25]   Grus mentions in the preface that Mlle. Nau and Duprez took the chief parts at the Opéra Comique, where the use of the Donizetti music indicates that the opera must have been brought out after 1835, the year when *Lucia* was first sung in Italy.[26]   Mlle.

---

[24] Soane's personal edition was published by Corbyn of New York.

[25] See Adams, p. 204, and *Dramatic Notes,* 1890, p. 119.

[26] The Grus text, however, differs much at times from the older version by Ducange.

Nau afterward appeared at Niblo's in New York in Soane's adaptation.

No trace of these early operatic plays remained on the stage by the time that J. Palgrave Simpson composed his *Master of Ravenswood*. One must always except Donizetti's *Lucia*. All the unpleasant elements had now given way to a gentle romance and pensiveness that permeated the entire Simpson drama. The tragic love of the young pair of Lammermoor holds the centre of attention throughout. Edgar steals his beloved Lucy from the very altar. Pursued by most of the wedding-guests, they make their hazardous way toward Wolf's Crag. Edgar finally takes to swimming, as he hold his precious burden away from the angry tides. Yet he has overlooked the treacherous quicksands, and both lovers go down for ever, while the guests look on in consternation and despair.[27]

Henry Morley found the arrangement at the end rather too mechanical, though he could not help but admire 'the accommodating quicksands that allowed Edgar to stand with Lucy in his arms till he quite finished his theatrical business, and then let them go suddenly down, together with the curtain.'[28]

When the Simpson romantic drama began an extended run at the Lyceum on December 25, 1865, Charles A. Fechter gained additional laurels as the best lover then on the English stage.[29] Little could have been done to improve the cast: for Miss Carlotta LeClercq was Lucy, Mrs. Ternan, after a retirement nine years long, was old Alice Grey, an important character in this drama; S. Emery next to Mackay was the best Caleb Balderstone; and George Jordon was William Ashton. New costumes, and beautiful scenery of the Lammermoor country, made the setting attractive.

[27] Simpson's drama was never printed. The description of the plot is taken from the criticism of the *Times* for Dec. 25, 1865.

[28] *Journal of a London Play-goer*, p. 384.

[29] *Dict. Nat. Biog.* 18. 282; 29. 253.

Charles Dickens assisted his friend, Fechter, in elaborating the stage-arrangements, declaring that he intended 'to put Scott, for once, upon the stage in his own gallant manner.' During the next season, Jordon and Mrs. John Wood combined the Simpson tragedy with an older one by George Almar, and produced the new piece at the Olympic in New York City. Three years afterward, Dickens learned that Fechter and Miss LeClercq were to tour America with the original Simpson drama.* He sent an enthusiastic advance announcement to the editor of the *Atlantic Monthly*, from which the following quotation is taken:

'When the Master of Ravenswood declares his love for Lucy Ashton, and she hers for him; and, when in a burst of rapture, he kisses the skirt of her dress, we feel as tho we touched it with our own lips, to stay our goddess from soaring away into the clouds. And, when they plight their troth, and break the piece of gold, it is we—not Edgar—who quickly exchange our half for the half she was about to hang around his neck, solely because the latter's has for an instant touched the bosom we love deeply.'[30]

HENRY IRVING IN RAVENSWOOD

With elaborate attention to the varied arts of the scene-painter, the costumer, and the stage-manager, Henry Irving and Ellen Terry acted in a *Ravenswood* at the Lyceum for almost a hundred nights from September 20, 1890.[31] Eight years previously, Irving had acquired the original rights to a *Brother and Bride,* the work of Herman C. Merivale, with Sir A. C. Mackenzie as musical composer.

Lucy suffers extreme mental torture because she fancies that Edgar has forsaken her, but she does not go insane. One's interest is focused on the fury of Edgar, which carries the lovers gradually toward their doom. The most effective

[30] For August, 1869; Pemberton, *Dickens and the Stage,* p. 235.
[31] *Dict. Nat. Biog.,* second suppl. vol., p. 617.

part is the concluding tableau, which shows Caleb standing alone by the shore, solitary and broken, while the waves gradually cover up all trace of the treacherous quicksands, into which his beloved master and Lucy have just sunk. One good bit of motivation makes Edgar and Bucklaw fight a duel. The latter is fatally hurt, but reveals that he, too, has been deceived by the Ashtons; and so Edgar and he forgive each other.[32]

Brerton testified that Irving was never seen to better advantage than in certain parts of his *Ravenswood*. The appearance of Edgar on the return from France was terribly convincing. 'He did not bound on the stage in the accepted manner. He tottered on—spent, haggard, and forlorn. On his face were the lines of a year's agony and anxiety. He did not storm or scold. He looked dazed as if he were recovering from a blow. He was a man, a Ravenswood, not an actor.'[33] Though the part of Miss Terry was somewhat curtailed, her acting in the betrothal at Mermaiden's Well, in the contract-scene, and especially at the last when Lucy dies of a broken heart, rose to great heights of sympathetic insight.[34] William Terriss also made an excellent Caleb.[35]

Two Literary Dramas

George H. Braughn and F. S. Ganter published a closet-drama called *Ravenswood* in New Orleans in 1873. Braughn, an attorney, organized the local Shakespeare Club, and served a term in the Louisiana Legislature.[36] The play shows some resemblances to older dramas of the storm-and-stress type, including a sketch of Lady Ashton in the manner

---

[32] *Theatre*, New Style, 16, Oct. 1, 1890.

[33] Brerton, *Lyceum and Henry Irving,* p. 279.

[34] T. Edgar Pemberton, *Ellen Terry and her Sisters* 2. 271.

[35] Smythe, *Life of William Terriss,* p. 101.

[36] Information concerning Braughn was furnished by the New Orleans Public Library.

of a Lady Macbeth. It draws the chief incidents from Scott, to be sure, yet the ending is more like that of the Elizabethan tragedy of blood. Accordingly, Douglas Ashton stabs Edgar, and Bucklaw fatally wounds Lucy. Caleb and the comic episodes at Wolf's Crag appear only by way of dramatic contrast to the serious portions of the play.

Stephen Phillips, the English poet, composed a prose drama in three acts and a tableau for his friends, the Martin Harveys, at Glasgow, where it enjoyed a successful season in March, 1908, and again in December at Birmingham. The action begins at Wolf's Crag, where Sir William and Lucy Ashton have taken refuge from the beating storm. At the end of the first act, Edgar appears brooding alone, by the dying embers of the grate in the hall at Ravenswood. Then follow the wooing and betrothal of the lovers, the absence of Edgar in France, with his belated return to Lammermoor, succeeded by the tragic events at the Hall of the Ashtons. Once more Edgar broods by the hearth at home. The final tableau shows three fateful hags in the moonlight, swimming in Kelpie's Flow, and leaving a silver wake behind them, to indicate the spot where the Master of Ravenswood has gone down in the quicksands.[37]

TRAVESTIES

For almost thirty years the rude hand of travesty spared the *Bride of Lammermoor*. Only when the first serious adaptations had outlived their usefulness, did the distortions begin to flood the playhouse. Among the first was *Lucy Did Sham Amour,* with words by Dr. Northall and music

---

[37] Phillips never published his romantic sketch. His old friend, Mr. Laurence Binyon of the British Museum, has kindly outlined the action as recalled by him. The *Glasgow Herald,* March 24, 1908, spoke of the piece as a 'sincere achievement,' but otherwise withheld any very definite praise.

by George Loder, for the Chatham Theatre of New York.
Ireland described this 'brilliant success' as a chief means of
diversion for several weeks of the summer season in 1848.
Both the operatic heroine in general, as heard in French
plays, and the various ladies who had acted as Lucy, were
touched off in humorous imitations. Some fun was drawn
from the oddities of the various librettos. Caroline Chapman for years was pleasantly recalled for her 'inimitable
imitations of the popular prima donna.'[38]

C. Helmerding made the words, and A. Conradi the
musical score, for a parody in German at the Wallner
Theatre of Berlin in 1859.[39]

Henry J. Byron, the ingenious provider of travesty plays,
cleverly hit off the numerous tribe of conventional operas.
One of his best is *Lucia di Lammermoor; or, the Laird, the
Lover, and the Lady,* which he announced as 'founded on
Donizetti's popular opera, and consequently very unlike the
romance.'[40] Many transformations greet us at every turn.
Alice Grey is changed from a sibyl to a rather common
lady's waiting maid, who 'speaks her mind pretty freely to
everybody.' Henry has become a villain basso-profundo,
but he succeeds only in making Edgar a little pale. Miss
Marie Wilton acted as Henry and staged the entire performance. Bucklaw outswells the typical stage dandy. Besides
Lucy, a Victorian 'simple dove-like creature,' ten additional
persons make up a medley of familiar caricatures. This
clever medley of effects by Byron amused many audiences,
beginning at the Prince of Wales Theatre, London, in the
autumn of 1865.

The bulk of the plot is overlooked, previous to the plight-
ing of vows by the lovers at Mermaiden's Well. The
opening scene introduces some byplay between Alice Grey
and Norman, who is characterized as 'head huntsman' to

[38] Ireland 2. 514.
[39] Information from the Library of Congress.
[40] So the title-page asserts.

Henry, for the reason that he is looking for Edgar's head, not that he is a forester, as the huntsmen of the novel are. When Edgar parts from his betrothed to go abroad, he exacts an elaborate promise from her not to flirt at parties. During the absence of the hero in France, Byron uses the incident of the forged letter as an excellent parody on the use of papers and letters as trite devices in melodramas. In having Bucklaw make love to Alice in mistake for Lucy, Byron gives us a delightful parody on stage-courtships, ending in the discomfiture of Bucklaw when Lucy herself appears on the stage.

Everything tends toward the return of Edgar from abroad, and the burlesque climax of the action follows closely the text of the original libretto. As Edgar comes into the Hall, something is said of the marriage contract, and the following dialogue results:

> *Edgar.* What do I hear?
> *Henry.* You've no right here, it's clear.
> So you may well remark, 'What do I here?'
> *Edgar.* Person! that lady is engaged to me.
> *Arthur.* For the next dance?
> *Edgar.* For life!
> *Arthur.* That cannot be;
> She's just accepted me.
> *Edgar.* Accepted you?
> Then what I heard was actually true.
> Tell me what I've done wrong.
> *Lucy.*   Oh, rubbish—stuff!
> What, you've done wrong?
> What you did write's enough.
> To send those letters—
> But the lot I've seen.
> *Henry.* And not to pay the postage:
> It was mean.
> *Edgar.* Mean? What d'ye mean? I'm in a fog.
> *Lucy.*   Continue in your fog; you won't be mist.
> *Edgar.* A heartless, venerable joke (*music tremuloso*).
> Oh, may you find that matrimony doesn't pay!
> May you find your fond adoring hub
> Pass his whole time at the convivial club,

> Until you hate him: then when you can't bear him
> May nothing from your presence ever tear him!
> May every play you go to turn out dull,
> May every evening party prove a mull.
> May he deny each debt by you incurred.
> May your dressmaker never keep her word.
> (*Lucy whimpers—agony on all sides*)

After another paragraph of malediction by Edgar, the entire group join in a concerted piece to the tune *Kafoozleum,* which is a hit on the sextette of the opera. The first lines of this begin thus:

> *Henry.* Pal-pitating is—palpitating is—pitating is.
> Pal-pitating is my breast with indignation.
> *Edgar.* There awaiting is—awaiting is—awaiting is,
> There awaiting is a carriage from the station.

These excerpts show the trend of Victorian travesty, but it would take several quotations to show all the verbal twists, elongated puns, allusions to events and persons of the time, which jostle one another on almost every page.

With a show of melodramatic energy, the bride at last bids Edgar begone. He remains to discuss with her the subject of their betrothal, the validity of which is attested by the broken coin. Arthur, in the meanwhile, is successively attacking all the dishes of the wedding-breakfast. Edgar argues that Scotch courts recognize as valid marriages those betrothals made by exchanging parts of broken coins. He continues:

> I've got a carriage.
> Bother this low preliminary marriage.
> No story now goes down, I vow this minute,
> If bigamy's an element not in it.
> In Scotch law you're my wife: I can't disown-ee.
> *Lucy:*
> The Scotch law is so vague on matrimony.
> If caught, my name in the newspaper columns—
> *Edgar:*
> Think only of the *heroine* in three *vollums.*

Shortly afterward a concerted piece is introduced by Alice and Edgar, which ends with this refrain:

> For a heroine she's a true
> Model, such as novel readers all take to.

Lucy herself joins in the last line. After considerable more fooling, the lovers drive off in the carriage. They are almost immediately pursued and arrested by soldiers, who bring them pompously back to Henry at the castle. The latter is waiting to forgive them in the most exaggerated style of theatrical melodramas.

Byron for many seasons was famous for the travestied outlines of various scenes in his light plays. As a sample of his deft workmanship, the synopsis for the final act of his *Lammermoor* is here cited:

> Scene four. Conservatory at the Castle. How, as in the Opera, Bucklaw and Lucy are made one, but by no means united, and how, as *not* in the opera, Lucy does not go out of her mind, but out of her brother's, accompanied by the object of her affections—but there is a breakdown, of the kind seldom seen in burlesque; and how Henry falls into a passion, Edgar falls into an error, Arthur into a trap, and Lucy into a puddle; and how appears a dead lock, when, compelled by the force of circumstances and the exigencies of Dramatic Law, Henry is obliged to give his consent, and after the hairbreadth 'scapes, moving accidents by flood and field, and innumerable ups and downs, all tending to illustrate the truth of the old motto that 'the course of true love never runs smooth,' Edgar and Lucy are permitted to pair off and
>
> ALL ENDS HAPPILY

SIGNIFICANCE OF THE LAMMERMOOR PLAYS

Little significance out of the ordinary attaches to the first Lammermoor plays. Thomas Dibdin failed for the first time to call forth any definite interest for his adaptation; but Calcraft, also for the first time, won a major hearing. In the middle period of the dramatic history of the tragic lovers, Cammarano and Donizetti's *Lucia* moulded the fashion for like operatic efforts for the next twenty or thirty years. The greatest compliment to the music of the gifted Italian composer is that it was used in almost all the varied operatic plays after 1835; the harshest of the criticisms of the libretto touch on the varied attempts in French and English to provide a better one than that of Cammarano. From Adelina Patti to Frances Alda and Marion Talley, some of the noble Donizetti scores have been sung by most of the great dramatic sopranos. The two sentimental romances, a little later, called forth the best talent of actors like Lemaître, Fechter, Ellen Terry, and Irving. In itself the late recrudescence of interest in the lovers of Lammermoor, long after the original zest had abated, is a tribute to the merit of the novel and the best adaptations of the poignant story. Even though the travesties by Byron have no literary merit, and so do not come within the range of serious consideration, in their class and magnitude they shine among the galaxy of stars of dramatic composition.

VI. IVANHOE

Scott's *Legend of Montrose* appeared as a novel, and as a drama, nearly six months before *Ivanhoe*. It will be reserved, however, for treatment among those narratives by Scott that inspired only minor melodramas and operas. Lockhart reports that *Ivanhoe* occasioned 'a more clamorous delight than any of the Scotch novels.' When it issued from the press a week before Christmas in 1819, the author had attained the peak of his ability as a narrator. His genius showed few signs of abatement. None of the prophecies had come to pass that the skill and vogue of the Great Unknown would quickly decline.[1]

Let the critics and historians of the novel decide for us whether *Ivanhoe* is indeed the greatest of the Waverley series. What we need recall just now is that this romance has consistently held the attention of readers of fiction during the last hundred years. Interest in some of the other narratives may have greatly declined, but *Ivanhoe* seems to hold its relative place year in and year out.

This work has aroused a greater number and a wider range of dramatic adaptations than any other Scott production. No fewer than thirty transcripts for the stage are now traceable, either in existent printed texts, or in criticisms among the dramatic annals of the nineteenth century. Fifteen printed plays at least are extant in the libraries; probably four or five texts have completely dropped out of sight, or are not now recognized in our large collections. With the exception of two or three decades, every period of ten years has brought out an important version of *Ivanhoe*. One good adaptation for schools appeared as late as 1917. Many recent amateur and juvenile plays are catalogued as copyrighted in the Library of Congress.

[1] Lockhart 2. 170, 172, 210.

Ivanhoe is remarkable in other points. In number of travesties, five in all; in shortened forms for the children's theatres, two of them; in variety of the operatic versions, though not in the worth of any single one, this novel is somewhat out of the ordinary. It took the playgoers of London by storm. Early in 1820, three separate versions were being acted at the same time, followed a bit later by two others. These, and one never acted, making six in all, came from the publishing house during the year—a record that stands alone in the history of the dramatizations of Scott.

Once more we learn that the novelist was inciting Terry to turn his hand anew to the writing of melodrama. Nearly a month before *Ivanhoe* came out on December 20, 1819, Scott advised Terry that the advance-sheets might be obtained, if his friend cared to avail himself of them. Yet Scott believed that the 'expense of scenery and decoration would be great, this being a tale of chivalry, and not of character.'[2] No definite evidence is available to show that Terry ever attempted to take advantage of the fame of this popular romance.

DIBDIN'S FIFTH DRAMATIZATION FROM SCOTT

For the fifth time before the spring of 1820, Thomas J. Dibdin had again outstripped every competitor among the playwrights. This list includes the *Montrose,* to be mentioned later, and his *Lady of the Lake,* not embraced in this discussion of the transcripts from Scott. His *Midlothian* and *Lammermoor* set the fashion among plays of the type, and now the *Ivanhoe,* first in the field, again caused others to try a throng of imitations, when it appeared at the Surrey on January 20, 1820.

Ivanhoe; or, The Jew's. Daughter, as Dibdin christened his play, retains all the complex background of mediæval life. We view the rude Saxon Hall of Cedric, the forest with

[2] Lockhart 2. 160.

Robin Hood and his men at their revels and glees, the dungeon and Isaac weighing out little by little his golden ransom, the picturesque arrangements for the burning of Rebecca, and the knightly lists. Dibdin tries to make all his characters real and vivid. By showing Brian more of a gentleman, and Reginald less of one, he straightens out some of the contradictions of the novel itself. Indeed, throughout he adds little touches here and there to motivate the entire drama. Since the plot resembles that of some of the others, it is not necessary here to give the details.

Imitations followed at once, and the precise relationship among them is not wholly apparent to the casual reader. Alfred Bunn, who compiled *Ivanhoe; or, The Jew of York*, professed to be entirely frank as to the source of his material. He borrowed it 'from the celebrated novel of that name, and from the contemporary plays on the subject produced at different theatres of the metropolis, with the addition of some speeches and situations and two songs.' In his preface to the edition issued in 1820 at Birmingham he said: 'It may be necessary to add that the play of *Ivanhoe* has been published under my name to prevent the chance of mistakes and to disarm criticism; and not to advance any pretensions to literary distinction, which I am totally unambitious of seeking, as I am totally incapable of supporting.'

Whether Bunn hints that Dibdin borrowed from him, one at present cannot fully determine. More likely, it seems to me, he alludes to another play that had the same title as Bunn's own. This may have been a drama that ran at the Coburg Theatre. All three of these dramas are similar. Those of Dibdin and Bunn are alike in general plan, outline, and in some of the wording, except that the order is changed now and then. For these reasons, one summary will suffice for both transcripts.

Wamba and Elgitha open the action with a bit of repartee. The clown has taken a dram or too more than he needs.

We soon get the information from the pair that Cedric is in a peevish mood, Ivanhoe has been banished for some little time, and affairs at Rotherwood Hall have been going worse and worse right along. Isaac and his daughter are forced by the lawless band of Brian de Bois Guilbert to seek refuge under the protection of Cedric. Already their leader has taken a fancy to Rebecca. Sherwood Forest is now revealed in all its gay and tuneful variety, while Robin Hood and his foresters join heartily in the old English ballads and glees. Another scene, by way of comic contrast, shows Isaac, now at home in York, greatly out of countenance because he fears he is going to lose, not only the rent-money, but even a perfectly good suit of armor, which he has rented to the Disinherited Knight for use in the tournament. Gurth soon appears, however, bringing the money for the suit. In another portion of the forest, Wamba is apologizing to the fair Elgitha for being tipsy when they last talked together. He now makes honorable amends by proposing. Elgitha accepts both the apology and the proposal, since 'matrimony is a foolish piece of business—and marrying a fool will but complete the matter.' Rowena and Cedric now appear, being joined shortly afterward by Isaac, who is once more fleeing from the knights in the train of the Templar. As the climax of the first act, the entire group is captured and carried off by a band of marauders.

The middle act carries the scene once more to Sherwood Forest, and then to Torquilstone Castle, where Rebecca is held prisoner through the designs of Brian de Bois Guilbert. Ivanhoe pays a visit to the cell of Friar Tuck, but disdains the simple fare of peas offered by his host. Considerable comic byplay is here introduced. Then follows a heavy scene, wherein Isaac is shown in a dungeon, refusing to give up his daughter, even though he may gain his own freedom at the expense of Rebecca. Wamba, in a friar's habit, enters the castle where Cedric and his party are held captive, allowing the old man to escape by borrowing Wamba's hat

and cloak.   Ulrica, broken by a long imprisonment at Torquilstone, comes to Rebecca, and intimates that one might
escape a living death by jumping from the parapet of the
castle.   For pure revenge she is willing to assist the dis-
traught Jewess.   Brian comes for the second time to perse-
cute Rebecca, who remains unswayed, even though he offers
her honorable marriage, which, the Jewess knows, the laws
of the Templars never would approve.   Rebecca outlines
the course of the battle to her father, who replaces Ivanhoe
of the novel, and other dramatizations, in this scene.   As a
grand culmination of the second act, the castle is enveloped
in flames, but Ulrica comes to the rescue of the Jewess.
Reginald is locked in his own high tower, from which there
is now no chance of escape, except by leaping from the
parapet.

    The final act contains but three short scenes.   Isaac has
escaped from the castle to the forest, where Robin Hood,
Ivanhoe, and some of the others await his coming.   The
jolly foresters set up a mock court, and exact from Isaac the
promise to pay six hundred crowns for the release of the
Prior, to say nothing of almost any amount for the release
of his daughter.   Rebecca is again captured on her way to
the forest, and falls once more into the seductive power of
Brian.   She is next brought before the Grand Master of
the Templars, who finally condemns her to be burned at the
stake as a sorceress.   After all the elaborate preparations for
the lists, Ivanhoe at last appears in the final moment of
grace, and announces himself as the champion of the Jewess,
who has just spurned a last appeal from Brian, and his offer
of marriage.   After a short period of combat, the drama
ends, as the novel does, with the defeat and death of Brian.
    Ivanhoe then addresses the chief Templar:

>   Proud priest, my king disdains any answer to thee.   His royal
> standard floats above thy temple mummery, nor all thy threats
> can pull that daring ensign from where a British hand with
> justice places it.   Beware!   thou'rt in the lion's grasp!
>   *King Richard.*   Templars, go where ye list, but rule not here.

> Come, Ivanhoe, thy destined bride, Rowena, and thy father's
> favour, await to crown thy gallant loyalty.
>   *Ivanhoe.* And dare such humble subjects as my dear Rebecca
> and myself intrude, with heart-felt gratitude to you and all, we'd
> say—our minds, our hearts, and means shall ever be devoted
> to our country and the good king we have so long revered.[8]

Bunn's version is indeed replete with life, color, and good
dramatic situations. Interest never flags for a moment.
Contrast is admirably secured through the alternation of
comic and tragic material. Madame Vestris in Elgitha, and
Mrs. Bunn in Rebecca, won many plaudits during the successful run at Birmingham.*

Four days after Dibdin's drama opened at the Surrey
Theatre, the rival Coburg playhouse, on January 24, 1820,
brought out an *Ivanhoe; or, The Jew of York,* which continued for two or three nights a week well into March. No
contemporary journal gave it any particular notice. During
the year, a play having the same title as the Birmingham
drama appeared in a London text. All the humorous portions are rigidly excised. Except for important additions
at the end, the remainder follows the novel, suggesting that
this might have been the play acted at the Coburg Theatre.

After defeating Brian in the lists, Ivanhoe and Richard
pay a visit in disguise to Rotherwood. The Lion-Heart
finally persuades Cedric to a reconciliation with his son, and
to countenance a marriage with Rowena, which for a time
the father stoutly opposes. The Jewess at the wedding
offers a costly necklace as her tribute to the bride. Rotherwood continues to be the happy residence of Ivanhoe,
Rowena, and their children, while Rebecca at times comes
over for brief visits from her home in York. Her heart only
once had been 'touched by love—that was for Ivanhoe.' She
therefore rejects all offers of marriage, lives contentedly at
York, and her fame spreads 'throughout England.'

[8] From p. 64 of the London edition of 1820. Some texts give this
last speech to Isaac.

This version deserves at least the credit of trying to bring about a more reasonable *dénouement* of the situation as found in Scott and practically all the other plays.

Romantic Drama by Beazley

Samuel Beazley compiled an ambitious melodrama, entitled *Ivanhoe; or, The Knight Templar,* for Covent Garden, where it ran for eighteen nights from March 2, 1820.[4]

An exceptional cast insured the success, since Macready as Front de Boeuf,[5] Liston as Wamba, Farren as Isaac, with Miss Foote as Rebecca, and Miss Stephens as Rowena, were among the best artists of their time.

A considerable flourish announced both the acting and the publication of the drama. The dedication reads: 'To the unknown author of *Ivanhoe* and the rest of those novels which have for the last seven years entertained the reading part of the population of England, and rescued our country. from the disgrace of those numerous Romances, which have brought discredit on the works of fiction in this country.'

Yet the dramatist did not honor the Great Unknown by adhering closely to the original narrative. Numerous little revisions occur here and there throughout the three acts. Though Sir Brian is one of the characters, much of his part is doubled with that of Front de Boeuf in this transcript. Ulrica becomes one of the major figures, to whom is given the final honor of speaking the epilogue, as a kind of tragic nemesis. This play ends with the burning of Torquilstone, not with the combat in the lists. Reginald Front de Boeuf

---

[4] The text was printed by W. Smith, London, 1820. Macready mentions Beazley as the author in his *Reminiscences,* edited by Pollock, p. 155. Additional comment will be found in the appendix to our present discussion.

[5] The *European Magazine* 77. 258 says that Macready 'threw a powerful interest around its repulsive ferocity,' speaking of the part of Front de Boeuf. Farren triumphed as Isaac.

persecutes Rebecca, much as Brian does in the novel, but he perishes among the flames of his own castle, where he has been locked by the betrayed Ulrica. In act two, however, at the time of the lists, brought earlier in the play, Reginald acknowledges his love for Rebecca in public.

The comic parts are somewhat exalted. Much is made of the humor growing out of the visit of Ivanhoe to the cell of the monk, and to Sherwood Forest, where he mingles rather freely with the greenwood revelers. Wamba, still tipsy, is more like a conventional stage-buffoon; and once, in trying to escape from the forest, he acts much as Shakespeare's young Gobbo. Tragic scenes alternate with the lighter ones: for instance, the scene of Wamba in liquor is followed by a very heavy one of Rebecca spurning Reginald at Torquilstone; Wamba escaping from Sherwood, after one similar scene, is followed by the picture of Isaac weighing out his golden ransom, with Sir Brian and his six giant slaves waiting to torture the old Jew, should he for a moment hesitate.

Four impressive climaxes occur at intervals. The dungeon-episode comes to a close with Isaac and Rebecca refusing all promised boons, and with Brian sulking ominously, because he has failed to bend them to his selfish purposes. Then, again, the tournament at Ashby shows a field of elaborate splendor, scarcely equalled in color and magnitude in any of the other Ivanhoe plays. Greatest of all are the intense scenes at Torquilstone, when the master of the castle seeks, through his arguments and personal magnetism, to break down the resolution of Rebecca, and once or twice she all but yields to his equivocal persuasions. The burning of the castle finally brings the series of powerful scenes to a highly theatrical close, with Ulrica emerging in savage triumph as a chief avenger, with Friar Tuck bearing out both Wamba and Isaac in turn, and with Ivanhoe at last carrying Rowena in his arms.

Front de Boeuf lingers through a collection of long

speeches, in which a seasoned actor like Macready could rise to heights of his art. Finally, the master of Torquilstone sinks back into the flaming mass of his own castle, and so eventually poetic justice is well appeased.

For transposition of the chief elements of the plot, so as to unify and intensify the whole, this drama could hardly be improved.*

Soane's Hebrew

Soane must have understood that his cue was to vary the action by making Ivanhoe acknowledge his love for Rebecca. Thus, at the outset, Ivanhoe has returned from banishment, in the disguise of a disinherited knight, only to hear himself roundly cursed at Rotherwood Hall. Not even Rebecca has recognized him. The knight makes friends with her, and eventually gets the Jewess to commission him to bear a scarf from her to the distant lover, should he happen to meet Ivanhoe in his travels. She had promised Cedric long ago not to countenance the suit of the banished son. When Cedric learns what has been going on under his own roof, he drives Ivanhoe forth once more, and incites Rebecca to renew her pledge.

From this point forward, the changes are fewer. Interest is focused on the dungeon-scene, the vivid interviews at the castle, and the romantic ending to suit the laws of melo-drama. The tensest moments of the play occur during the preparations for burning Rebecca at the stake for sorcery. Yet special emphasis is laid on the respite granted by the Chief Templar 'till yon black clouds shall dark the sky.' Just as the sun is commencing to be obscured, Ivanhoe rides into the lists as the champion for Rebecca. The details of the combat, together with the sudden death of Brian, follow the gist of the concluding part of the novel.

At the end, the printed text is somewhat ambiguous as to whether Ivanhoe and Rebecca were allowed to marry. Genest states that they are in love, but offers no further illumination.[6] We have the authority of the *European Magazine,* however, to the effect that old Isaac dropped dead of emotion, leaving Rebecca 'to the protection of her future husband, the Disinherited Knight, Ivanhoe.'[7]

The cast included such seasoned performers as Charles Kean for Isaac, Mrs. W. West for the Jewess, Penley for Ivanhoe, and Hamlin, ·a favorite actor from Glasgow, for Brian. Soane added a Miriam, a part of no importance.

A LITERARY DRAMA BY MONCRIEFF

W. T. Moncrieff's *Ivanhoe; or, the Jewess,* though one of the six dramas published in 1820, seems never to have been performed. The author was rather proud of his accomplishment in compiling a drama from the novel, with about fifty new lines of his own material merely to fill in the gaps. His curious preface expresses 'a strong suspicion that his play will have more literary merit than the others.' Moncrieff bemoaned the fact that another had preceded him by about three weeks. He therefore invited the unknown author of the Waverley novels to supply in advance the text of his next effort, so that Moncrieff might achieve priority. One might compare the original text of Scott with this drama to see how the fabric could be cut into acts and scenes, but such a scheme is outside the pale of our present treatment. Moncrieff himself asserted that many playwrights had 'obtained the reputation of excellent Dramatists, on no better ground than paste, shears, and a Scotch novel.' His own abortive drama certainly shows that it takes more than cutting the text of Scott into dramatic divisions to make a good acting play. No theatrical manager apparently dared undertake to produce this dramatic nondescript.

London had abundant chances to compare the merits of plays based on *Ivanhoe* in 1820. Dibdin's began a run at

[6] 8. 33. Soane's drama was among the six printed in 1820.
[7] For 1820, p. 256.

the Surrey Theatre on January 20; a second, four days afterward, at the Coburg Theatre; Beazley's on March 2 at Covent Garden; and Soane's at Drury Lane on the same night. Bunn's at Birmingham—and possibly also in London—and Moncrieff's, make up the variety for the season. All six went through the publishing house before the close of the same year.

REVISIONS FOR EDINBURGH

Both John W. Calcraft and William H. Murray, of the Royal Theatre in Edinburgh, tried their luck by modifying some of the numerous *Ivanhoes*. Neither printed a version, but Calcraft's was the prior attempt. According to James C. Dibdin, Murray made his play from 'detached scenes from the Covent Garden adaptation of the same name, from *Rebecca; or, The Jew's Daughter,* produced at the Surrey, and from the Calcraft *Ivanhoe.*'[8] Scotch audiences remained cold toward both pieces, though Murray's ran for a number of evenings.* The scenery and all the appointments were rather magnificent, though some of the paintings looked 'more like daubs.'[9]

OPERATIC PLAYS BEFORE 1850

Rebecca as a character gave rise to a number of operatic plays. Altogether *Ivanhoe* inspired more musical dramas than any other novel by Scott. No fewer than five distinct operas enjoyed some little favor before the middle of the century. These include a French *Ivanhoé* by Deschamps and de Wailly; Lacy's modification of this for the English stage; the *Templar und Die Jüdin* by Marschner and Wohlbrück; the *Templaro* by Marini and Nicolai; and an opera by Rossi for use at Milan.

During a brief sojourn in Paris, Scott wrote in his

[8] *Annals,* p. 307.
[9] *Dramatic Review* 6. 95.

journal for October 31, 1826: 'In the evening to the Odéon, where we saw *Ivanhoé*. It was superbly got up, the Norman soldiers wearing pointed helmets and what resembled much hauberks of mail, which looked very well. The number of attendants, and the skill with which they were moved and grouped on the stage, were well worthy of notice. It was an opera, and, of course, the story sadly mangled, and the dialogue, in part nonsense.'[10]

This production, put forth anonymously, has been identified by Barbier as the work of Emile Deschamps and Gabriele G. de Wailly. One of the French journals said: 'The play has no spring, no dramatic situation; but the scenes, though badly connected, are rather forceful,' and added that it was indebted to some of the English dramatic versions.[11]

The 'mangling' of the scenes between Brian and Rebecca is notable. The authors changed the characterization of Brian, making him far less repulsive, but they did not change the dialogue to correspond. At certain points it is truly absurd. We look in vain, also, for the familiar Gurth, Wamba, Ulrica, Rowena, Richard, and even Front de Boeuf. Instead, we are introduced to Ismaël, 'Mussulman steward of the king of France,' who does service for our old friend Isaac, Leíla, who is Rebecca rechristened and made into a mysterious lady. Leíla at last turns out to be the daughter of the old friend whom Cedric saw fall long ago in Palestine. At the conclusion, Cedric places the hand of Edith (that is, Leíla now identified) in that of Ivanhoe, giving him his blessing and announcing their troth.

M. Rophino Lacy made a bad translation and adaptation of this French opera for Covent Garden in March, 1839. His *Maid of Judah; or, The Knights Templars*,[12] lived by

[10] Lockhart 2. 546.
[11] *Moniteur Universel*, Sept. 17, 1826.
[12] Published in *Cumberland's British Theatre*, Vol. 25. Yet the New York Public Library has an independent text that shows some changes.

virtue of the original Rossini music. Both the setting and
the acting were beyond cavil. Many of the songs were
deservedly popular for a long time. They include the greenwood ballads, sentimental solos by Rebecca; a duet with
Ivanhoe, during which he promises to become her champion;
and a final grand chorus, celebrating the fall of Brian in the
lists.

When this *Maid of Judah* first appeared on the boards at
Covent Garden, Ivanhoe was played rather indifferently by
Wood, Brian in his usual excellent style by Warde, the
famous Irish actor, and Isaac quite suitably by Egerton.
Miss Paton 'evinced rare powers' as Rebecca, especially in
the scene where she demanded a champion of the Templars.[13]
In 1830, Warde and some other favorites produced Lacy's
play, after elaborate preparations, in Dublin. Yet the interest of this drama fell somewhat below that of some other
adaptations from French operas.

The *Templar und Die Jüdin* was first sung and printed in
1829 at Leipzig. Heinrich Marschner composed the score,
and also assisted his brother-in-law, W. A. Wohlbrück, with
the libretto, which some of the critics pronounced too heavy
for the music. It won a fair hearing at the Prince's Theatre
in London.[14]

Isaac, Cedric, and Wamba are reduced to lay figures, but
Robin Hood and his merry followers hold the centre of the
stage in several of the scenes. Much attention is given to
the old ballads, and to bits of German folklore. Richard
appears among the foresters as a mediæval knight, on
pleasant terms with all his subjects, though still a great
over-lord. Rebecca regains much of her original nobility of
action and temperament. At the close of the opera, she

---

[13] *Theatrical Journal*, 1829, p. 41. The *Drama Magazine* for Oct.
1, 1829, contains a portrait of Miss Paton as Rebecca.

[14] John P. Jackson, about 1833, published a translated and revised
text in English, which the title-page describes as 'a Grand Romantic
Opera.'

utters a strong appeal for sympathy, since she can claim no special boon, being of the despised race.

Several operatic dramas are mentioned by Towers and other authorities, but the *Templaro* by Gerolamo-Maria Marini, with music by Ottone Nicolai, is about the only one now remembered.* This piece centred the attention on the events at Torquilstone, omitting details of the forests and most of the story before the tournament at Ashby. Rebecca frankly appealed to Ivanhoe for his love at the close, but the English knight informed her that she and Isaac must return to their home in Syria. While Cedric and Ivanhoe turned to leave, the Jewess fell fainting into the arms of her father.

Dramas After 1850

Fox F. Cooper wrote the best play after 1850 for Astley's in London, where it was acted in 1870. King Richard proposed to award to Ivanhoe 'the maiden as his prize,' referring to Rebecca, but the ending is ambiguous as to whether they were allowed to marry. The final stage-direction ('they fall into each other's arms') might relate to Isaac and his daughter, or to Ivanhoe and Rebecca. This hesitation as to the ending shows the tendency, in the last plays, to break over the barriers set by Scott, who once justified his ending of *Ivanhoe* by saying that the times never would have sanctioned the marriage of a Christian and a Jew, and that poetic justice does not demand that the virtuous must always be rewarded for being good.

Andrew Halliday compiled a *Rebecca* for Drury Lane in 1871. Samuel Phelps in Isaac (the part he played forty years before in Bunn's transcript), and the talented Lilian Adelaide Neilson, carried off the honors of the play and of the entire season.* Everything was arranged to suit the romance and sentiment of the drama, as conceived by the beautiful actress.[15]

---

[15] Stirling, *Old Drury Lane* I. 290.

Among the later dramatic successes are a *Rebecca of York* at Liverpool in 1871; a piece by Cowrie for Dundee in 1874; one by Ernest Stevens for Glasgow in 1896; another for Manchester by William Palmer in 1906; and Arthur Shirley's at the Lyceum in 1913.[16]

As early as 1822, a condensed *Ivanhoe; or, The Jew of York* appeared in Hodgson's series of plays adapted to the use of children in home-theatres. Maud I. Findlay, almost a hundred years later, prepared a delightful children's drama by using most of the original words of Scott, with links contributed merely to bind the whole into a finished unit.[17] All the great scenes appear, though the interviews of Brian and Rebecca are judiciously curtailed. The tournament, the sylvan scenes, the refusal of Isaac to accept his freedom at Rebecca's expense, the comedy of Friar Tuck, the spurning of Brian by Rebecca in the tiltyard, are all specially elaborated. At the close of the play, Rebecca visits Ivanhoe and Rowena at Rotherwood, bearing gifts of costly ornaments, which Rowena declines. Rebecca then exclaims she will never more wear jewels.

Some of the Later Operas

A. Castegnier prepared the libretto and the score for a grand opera that was printed in London in 1882 under the title of *Rebecca*. Four years subsequently, renamed the *Normands,* it was revised, printed, and probably acted at Trouville. Both texts are identical, save for the omission of a character or two, with the consequent transferring of some of the speeches from one person to another. Only the serious portions are retained, but Richard appears among the foresters, who sing a few of the old ballads. Ivanhoe and Rowena pledge faith at the end, while Isaac and his daughter return to their home at York.

[16] Clarence, p. 220.
[17] Printed in 1917 by the Oxford Press.

When the new English Opera House was dedicated on January 31, 1891, Julian Sturgis arranged the words of the novel for a libretto, for which Sir Arthur Sullivan wrote very beautiful, but rather 'ponderous' music, more like the notes for a grand symphony. For twenty years, since the time he prepared lighter music for Plowman's travesty, *Isaac of York,* Sullivan had been interested in the subject, as one suitable for the highest type of operatic composition; and so he spent several weeks late in 1890 preparing his score for the Sturgis libretto.[18]   All the main essentials are preserved, including the conventional marriage at the end. Sullivan made new music for some of the ancient ballads, which were highly pleasing to the audiences that crowded the Lyceum for one hundred and six nights. Two entire casts were used during this lengthy run. Most emotional and dramatic of all the situations are the duets of Brian and Rebecca, which rise to great lyric heights. Two or three mirthful scenes, especially when King Richard appears in the Sherwood Forest among the merry men of Robin Hood, are not quite up to the standard of the serious portions.

THREE GOOD TRAVESTIES

Travesties at their best are ephemeral, with little chance to survive the popularity of the works they imitate.   Interspersed among the attempts after 1850 to continue the fame of varied Rebeccas and Ivanhoes, three fine burlesques were prepared by masters of the craft. They enjoyed considerable runs. Henry J. Byron, Robert B. and William B. Brough, and Thomas F. Plowman, drew forth considerable innocent fun by twisting the situations and characters quite enough to make them ridiculous.

Brough Brothers, at the Haymarket in 1850, broke the backs of the King's words in every possible fashion.   Their

---

[18] Fitzgerald, *Operas of Gilbert and Sullivan,* p. 125; Klein, *Thirty Years of Musical Life in London,* p. 335.

travesty on *Ivanhoe* abounds in elaborate and ingenious puns, many of them dragged in by the ears; in diction that runs into all sorts of blind alleys and lengthy lanes of meaning; in allusions to contemporary men and women that no doubt had sharp points, though they are dulled to our understanding; and in a plot that is twisted, broken, stopped, and started at will to suit every passing whimsy.

To imitate the custom of printing novels in a series of volumes, the Broughs divided their work into two parts, one having three chapters, the other having four. Rotherwood Hall is pictured in rather tawdry splendor (a hit on the magnificence of some of the canvas views in legitimate dramas). The chief hero, Isaac of course, is introduced in the business-house of Isaacs and Sons, dealers in cast-off clothing, rusty armor, antiques, and other curious things. The turret chambers and ramparts of Torquilstone are shown as the places 'where everybody fights everybody else and gets the best of it.' As a realistic skit in imitation of the vogue of final tableaux, this travesty arranges an elaborate grand exposition and extravaganza to show all the nations of the world in characteristic dress and action.

Besides Isaac, described already, other characters are thus named: Cedric, the original old English gentleman; the Palmer, otherwise Ivanhoe, a mediæval study; Prince John, a foolish young scion at play during the absence of the cat; Rebecca is the maid of Judah *par excellence;* and Rowena, to cap the climax, is described as the lady of a hollow heart, wearing the prettiest mask imaginable.

Henry J. Byron, in his *Ivanhoe in Accordance with the Spirit of the Times,* transposed most of the masculine and feminine parts. His skit was acted at the Strand, London, and at the Royal, Liverpool, on the evening of December 26, 1862, when Byron himself took the part of Isaac at the latter house.

Costuming, make-up, and acting apparently suited the descriptions of the persons as quoted from Scott. Isaac is 'a tall, thin old man, who, however, has lost, by the habits of stooping, much of his original height.' Rowena's 'complexion is exquisitely fair; her profuse hair, of a color betwixt brown and golden, was arranged in a fascinating and gracious manner, in numerous ringlets, to form which Art had probably aided nature.'

Byron used only enough of the novel to show that his play had some connection with the story. It specializes in intentional misrepresentation of a remark or description, through apparent misunderstanding. Everything is punny, if not funny to a later age, with a full quota of verbal twists.

Characteristic of similar travesties by Byron, his acts are described at some length. Thus the outline says: 'Scene the first. Dining room at Rotherwood. Paterfamilias of the period. How the wet Templar drops in, and how Wamba gets more dry than ever. How Rowena illustrates the truth of the saying that "absence makes the heart grow fonder," and how Cedric's countenance, like the sky, grows gloomy at the absence of her lover, and how the head's bawled at the absence of the heir. How Isaac walks in his sleep and catches cold because he does not know what room-it-is. The Palmer foils the Templar. Mutual hatred from that moment.'

Thomas F. Plowman, the English promoter of entertainments, put together two versions that bear somewhat on the story of Scott. Sir Arthur Sullivan contributed the music for the first of these, which was named *Isaac of York; or, Saxons and Normans at Home,* and which combined some of the serious with certain comic elements. In the first few months of 1871, this piece ran for over a hundred nights at the Globe in London, and later enjoyed a popular turn at the Gaiety, Drury Lane, and some of the provincial theatres. Fewer odd twists than those of the Byron and Brough travesties are noticed in the broken, rhymed metres of Plowman. Walter Hamm painted a number of good scenes for the background. Seven years later, Plowman made a dif-

ferent sketch for the benefit of the firemen of Oxford.
This was christened *Isaac Abroad; or, Ivanhoe Settled and
Rebecca Righted,* and the cast was made up of students of
the town.[19]

IVANHOE IN AMERICA

Numerous references to the production of several Ivanhoe
plays in New York are mentioned by Brown and Ireland.[20]
Some of the more important are the appearance of Maywood
and Mrs. Barnes at Anthony Street, New York, in 1820,
when their parts were 'exceedingly well played'; notable
revivals of Lacy's *Maid of Judah* at the Park in 1832 and
again in 1834, with Mr. and Mrs. Joseph Woods and their
English Opera Company; and also two years later, and
again in 1840, in Boston and other places. Mr. and Mrs.
John R. Duff won considerable fame at Baltimore in 1830;
E. L. Davenport at the Bowery, New York, in 1846, when
this version was produced with a large equestrian corps in
'one of the most brilliant spectacles yet seen.' Marschner's
German opera was sung at the Broadway in 1872.

Mrs. John Wood introduced a travesty in New York, with
which Dion Boucicault had some connection, not now fully
understood. Byron's sprightly burlesque attracted large
audiences at Kelly and Leon's in 1869, and elsewhere at
other times. John R. Blake and Benjamin Aymar arranged
a humorous version for the Columbia University Strollers,
using about a fourth of the original Byron travesty. This
was produced in 1893, and later in New York, Brooklyn,
and Philadelphia.[21] Finally, Universal elaborately screened
a version of *Ivanhoe,* with the background at Chetsworth
Castle, and King Baggot in the chief rôle.[22]

---

[19] The second edition was printed at Oxford in 1878.
[20] See Ireland 1. 364, 418; 2. 8, 455, 701; Brown 1. 121, and index
for others.
[21] Brown 3. 412, and a personal letter from Mr. Aymar.
[22] Information and scenario furnished by the Universal Company.

REVIEW OF IVANHOE ON THE STAGE

No single version of *Ivanhoe* enjoyed more than a temporary fame. Though audiences may have reasonably objected to the ending of the novel itself, they liked even less the transformations made by some of the later dramatists. According to usual habit, the foreign plays and operas changed the names, characterization, and many of the salient details of the plot. Competition among the theatres of London and Paris did not bring any one play into the foreground, unless it be for Beazley's, and one or two in the later decades. Yet the uncommon ferocity of the drama in which Macready distinguished himself did not prove acceptable to those audiences that loved sentimental melodrama. Though the great tragic actor must have been powerful in the closing scenes at Torquilstone, the terrible intensity of the action did not attract the playgoers, and so this drama ran for only fourteen nights.

Even the Murray piece in Edinburgh exceeded this number by more than half. Though Bunn made a real hit in Birmingham, the run was surprisingly short for such a fine production, as it was magnificently staged. No version, in fact, ever attained half the vogue of the Terry *Guy Mannering,* or the Pocock *Rob Roy,* or the Dibdin *Heart of Midlothian.*

Managers by this time were apparently insisting that the excerpt from Scott must have theatrical value, and not mere similarity or closeness to the original romance. Beazley's drama seems to indicate that they chose inferior texts, in preference to more literary versions that lacked melodramatic force or adaptability to the stage.

Through the capable acting of Phelps and Miss Neilson, Halliday's *Rebecca* ruled as a favorite for a brief time. It was more dramatic and emotional than the earlier forms. Altogether this melodrama netted the management upwards of eight thousand pounds, a sum considerably greater than

Scott received for the manuscript of his novel.[23]   Yet Plowman's travesty interested the public for a longer time, with a record of a hundred nights the first season, and numerous subsequent revivals.

Twenty of the plays and operas focus the attention on the tense scenes at Torquilstone Castle.   No better contrasting pair could be found than Brian and Rebecca.   Yet the playmakers hesitated a bit as to whether the original characterization of the Templar should be retained.   Tom Dibdin, Soane, and Beazley, together with the composers of all the foreign operas, toned down the villainy of Brian for very obvious reasons.   At the same time, however, they intensified the chief scenes, showing more humanly than Scott does the surging of emotions of both the Templar and the fair Jewess.   The operas by Deschamps and de Wailly, and by Marino, make Brian a most eloquent pleader for the regard of Rebecca, while she alternates between obduracy and despair, to which she all but gives way, or between weakness of resolve and the terrific power of mental and moral resistance.   Both Marschner and Sullivan bring out the striking conflict of two firm human wills, but agree with Scott in showing that Rebecca distrusts her wooer the more, as he protests that he is sincere and a man of honor.

Picturesque, comic, and tuneful elements cumulate in several of the plays.   Bunn cleverly alternates the comic and tragic material.   Beazley revived some of the older ballads, followed somewhat closely by such different artists as Sir Arthur Sullivan and Marschner.   Dibdin most closely transferred the scenic effects of forest, castle, and hall to his composition.   He revealed Torquilstone Castle and Rotherwood in various lights, and the tournament and scene of the lists in great pictorial splendor.   Much good scenery was wasted on some of the inferior plays, such as Lacy's, which made up in gorgeousness what it lacked in real dramatic effect.

[23] Stirling, *Old Drury Lane* I. 290.

Nothing could be nearer to Scott, and still further away, than the travesties. Byron and his fellows intended this to be so. They all chose to follow the story just enough to magnify all the little inconsistencies, until these overshadow the serious motives and nobler sentiments. They succeeded best, possibly, in the verbal and mental gyrations that abound on every page of the printed text. Some of the travesties proved attractive in spite of the changes, whereas Soane tried to gain applause by overcoming the inconsistencies of the plot, and got only a cold house for his pains. Wherein Soane failed, Halliday succeeded, because the latter knew how to exalt and idealize the romantic situations for the benefit of sentimental audiences.

How to deal with Rebecca at the end puzzled the dramatists more than almost anything else. Some, like Scott, failed to mete out the poetic justice to which average audiences thought her entitled. Others made bold to substitute Rebecca for Rowena as the bride of Ivanhoe, either in fact or by implication in the concluding scene. These likewise failed to convince the playgoers. Marschner sent Rebecca to her old home in Syria; others sent her back to her English home in York. One French opera transformed her into another, using the hackneyed device of disguised identity.

That many authors tried and failed to harmonize the elements of the novel itself indicates the genuine difficulty of making a good play out of a good novel.

VII. KENILWORTH

During the first weeks of 1821, *Kenilworth* leaped into favor which threatened at once to rival that of *Ivanhoe,* some eighteen months previously. In the interval, both the *Monastery* and *Abbot* had been published, and placed on the stage, but neither aroused any notable enthusiasm in the playhouse; hence they will be reserved for consideration among the minor pieces drawn from Scott.

Material in *Kenilworth* is rather less abundant, but certainly much more unified, than in the plots of certain Waverley novels. We miss the greenwood foresters, the light comedy group of Gurth and Wamba, and some of the vividness of events at Torquilstone, though we have, as a compensation, the pageantry at Kenilworth Castle, and the oddities of Wayland Smith and his understudy. Once again, the old question of a fortunate ending for a drama is raised by *Kenilworth.* Must Amy Robsart be spared for the edification of sentimental novel-readers and devotees of plays that leave the heroine unscathed at the end?

The dramatization of this novel began with a form that followed Scott even to the death of Amy. Next, Tom Dibdin departed rather far from the original tragic motive. His version aroused small interest at Covent Garden, though it continued later to appear for some fourteen nights at the Surrey. Once more the laureates of Edinburgh revised, clipped, and combined some of the older plays, improving the action, and introducing a new range of scenery. Samuel Heath made a conventional literary drama in five acts. For the second time, Andrew Halliday had the uncommon distinction of making both the best travesty and the best serious drama of the later years after 1850.

Six days before Dibdin brought out his own transcript, J. Robinson Planché staged his *Kenilworth Castle; or, The Days of Good Queen Bess,* at the Adelphi. It was never published. Planché spoke with pride of the mechanical arrangement, which was 'so cleverly managed' that Mrs. Waylett as Amy was supposed by the audience to fall through a trap-door in the stage, 'and the curtain descended to thunders of applause.'[1]

DIBDIN'S PLAY AND HIS CONTROVERSY WITH BUNN

Besides being outrun by Planché, Thomas J. Dibdin had two other reasons for feeling humiliated in regard to his *Kenilworth*. First, Elliston had asked him to write a drama, and then refused to produce it at Drury Lane.* Second, Dibdin lent his text to Bunn and Dimond for production at Bath; they, in turn, brought it back in revised form to the Elliston playhouse. In the resulting controversy, Dibdin had the able support of several critics who accused Bunn and Elliston of double dealing.

For the initial performances at the Surrey Theatre, Mrs. Dibdin played as Queen Elizabeth, Bengough as Leicester, and Miss Taylor as Amy.[2] Three weeks later, March 8, 1821, Dibdin transferred his piece to Covent Garden. Its run at the Surrey lasted fourteen nights, but the audience froze it after five at Covent Garden. From the opening night, though admitting some skill and likeness in following the original story, the *Times* began to damn Dibdin's play for 'merciless mutilation.' Genest, ten years afterward, explained the apparent failure by saying that the management forced Dibdin to huddle the action into a brief afterpiece.[3] By a 'fortunate catastrophe,' however, Varney himself fell though the trap-door he had arranged for Amy. The *Gentleman's Magazine* commended the mechanical contrivances, the scenery, and the costuming, but thought the subject had already been exhausted at the minor playhouses.[4]

[1] *Recollections and Reflections,* revised edition, p. 290.
[2] *European Magazine,* Feb., 1821; *Theatrical Observer,* Feb. 15, 1821; Dibdin, *Reminiscences* 2. 301.
[3] 9. 107, 172, 232.
[4] For March 12, 1821.

Dibdin issued the play in an authorized text when the acting ceased at Covent Garden.* The text itself shows certain faults plainly enough. Too little is made of the spirited parts of Wayland Smith and the mischievous Dickie Sludge. Amy is rather too sophisticated. Worst of all, however, the salient events, as Genest remarked, are indeed huddled into so little room that no chance is left for emphasis of the kind demanded by the lovers of melodrama in 1820. Several changes confuse the action at different points. Amy, for instance, is summoned to Kenilworth, whereas Scott has her escape from Cumnor Place, and appear at her husband's castle, without the leave she has begged in vain.

Yet the ending is well arranged. Goaded into rash action by the insinuations of Varney, Leicester has ordered his underling to 'get the blood' of his wife. Shortly afterward, however, the Earl issues a countermand, but his first request has already sped on its way toward Cumnor. The Earl and his companions attempt to overtake the original messenger. Meanwhile, at Cumnor Place, Janet Foster is shown explaining the mechanism that operates the trap-door situated in the upper hallway. When the Earl's group arrives, Varney rushes out of a room on the second floor, inadvertently steps on the trap, and falls to his death in full view of the audience. Then Amy appears at the door of her own apartment above, while the tableau represents the entire group arranged in various attitudes of surprise and horror.

Some of the veteran actors in the cast of Dibdin's play at Covent Garden were Farley in Foster, Vandenhoff in the Earl, Mrs. Vining in Amy, and Mrs. Faucit in the Queen.

No little controversy arose over a modified form of the Dibdin text, which Dimond or some other adapter prepared for the Bunn company to act at Bath. Dibdin had allowed them to use his play, with the stipulation that it should not be staged in London. Elaborate preparations were made in the Royal at Bath. These included the removal of two rows of seats from the pit, to allow the champion of the lists to ride through on his charger. The showy banquet at Cumnor Place imitated one held during the coronation festivities not long previously in London. Altogether the affair was arranged 'on a scale of expense hitherto unparalleled out of London.'[5] Genest called it 'the grandest spectacle ever exhibited at a provincial theatre,' adding the opinion that Bunn's *Kenilworth* and *Midlothian* were the greatest dramatizations of Scott.[6]

Among the twenty-one characters named in the *dramatis personæ* are Hamblin as the Earl of Leicester, Bennet as Varney, T. P. Cooke as Raleigh, Mrs. Bunn as Queen Elizabeth (in which part she subsequently acted scores of times), and Miss Jarman as Amy.[5] The play ran from December, 1821, till the middle of February, when Mrs. Bunn had to leave to fulfil an engagement in Dublin.[7]

Late in 1823, Tom Dibdin heard that Drury Lane was planning to produce the text that he had lent to Bunn for use at Bath. In the correspondence that ensued with Bunn, the latter was equivocal, and claimed that he was not infringing any of the original author's rights.* Though Dibdin at first threatened to bring suit, he at last contented himself by writing his complaint to the newspapers of London. A number of critics and friends rushed to his assistance.

'Peter List' commented thus: 'I know the manager of Drury Lane may say that this piece of goods is made out of cloth that is common property: but this won't do. Mr. Dibdin was the dramatic workman, and not a bit of his article has Mr. Elliston a right to use, without his permission.'[8]

'Verax' supported this declaration, admitting that he first suggested to Bunn that the original work of Dibdin might

[5] *Bath Chronicle*, Dec. 13, 1821; *Bath Herald*, Dec. 15, 1821.
[6] 9. 403.
[7] Levey and O'Rorke, *Annals of the Theatre Royal*, Dublin, p. 13.
[8] *Theatrical Observer*, Jan. 19, 21, 1824.

be used at Bath. 'Fair play, Mr. Editor, is a jewel, and if any man attached to the Drama deserves it more than another, it is Thomas Dibdin, whose indefatigable exertion during his ill-paid management as tenant of the Surrey Theatre, could only be equaled by the classical chasteness of the different pieces he produced on the stage.'[9]

Among the twenty-five persons in the cast, we notice such old favorites as Mrs. Bunn once more as Elizabeth, Wallack as Leicester, Terry as Foster, Archer as Varney, and Mrs. W. West as Amy.[10] With such a notable group, the drama should have succeeded, but Genest informs us that it terminated on the eighth night, after having been 'indifferently received.'[11]

Dibdin claimed the entire production, except for some awkward mutilations at the end, and the addition of a pageant, of which the *Theatrical Observer* said: 'But for the stupid pageant with which it concludes, it might have escaped disapprobation.'[10] After the death of Bunn his literary executor published the play. Comparison with the original by Dibdin shows few notable revisions, except that Dickie Sludge and Wayland Smith are omitted from the list of characters. Some inexcusable blunders appear in the printed text toward the end, which might be due to a badly written manuscript. Dibdin's version, as printed in 1821 in London, has a fuller account of the visit of Elizabeth at Kenilworth. The Dibdin text merely mentions the concluding pageant. Few other changes are made, except for some of the stage-directions, and now and then minor variations in wording.

REVISIONS FOR EDINBURGH

Beginning with an unidentified transcript for the Royal in December 1821, and a playbill which mentions the coming

---

[9] *Ibid.*

[10] *Theatrical Observer,* Jan. 6, 1824.

[11] 9. 232. See also Dibdin's *Reminiscences* 2. 85, 131.

of Tom Dibdin's *Kenilworth; or, The Merry Days of Old England,* Edinburgh saw a number of plays within the next five or six years. Calcraft eventually had a hand in revising one of them; J. L. Huie published a text in 1823; William Oxberry another not long afterward; and the Corbett Ryder players acted some sort of *Kenilworth* in 1826. One of these versions ran in 1822 for only eight nights, with most of the favorite actors of the Royal in the cast.[12]

Our remaining interest at present lies in reading the printed texts, two of which show considerable literary and dramatic merit. These are the Huie and the Oxberry plays, which are quite similar except for certain unimportant changes in wording, scenery, and arrangement of the action. Oxberry admits that his compilation includes material taken from a play already printed in Edinburgh, parts of others acted in London, aided by the pens of two leading dramatists, with an ending suggested by 'a great literary character of Edinburgh.' Here is collaboration for you! From what Lockhart says of Scott's interest in the production of plays in Edinburgh, one may reasonably conclude that the Great Unknown himself might have been the 'great literary character.'

Oxberry further complicated the subject, however, by printing the cast for Drury Lane in his edition. Genest said laconically, 'It was not the piece acted at Drury Lane.'[13] An independent comparison of the texts of the four printed plays, together with the remarks of Tom Dibdin and the *London Times,* confirms the statement that Oxberry and others introduced many minor changes.

Yet of all the texts, the Oxberry is the only one that outlines the concluding pageant at Kenilworth Castle in honor of Queen Elizabeth. It is thus described: 'An emblematic

---

[12] Dibdin, *Annals,* pp. 299, 339, 343. It seems impossible now to determine which is which among these works, but undoubtedly all of them were based on the Dibdin original as revised for Bunn.

[13] 9. 172.

representation of some of the festivities given by the Earl
of Leicester in honor of Queen Elizabeth's visit to Kenilworth Castle, in July, 1575, arranged from the authorities
of Robert Laneham, consisting of combats of horses, morrice
dancing, fight by men of Coventry, etc., concluding with a
grand scenic entertainment wherein Britannia appears,
exhibiting the homage of the four quarters of the Globe,
with the symbols of their different nations at the feet of
the Queen, etc.'

Since the two dramas printed in Edinburgh give the most
complete texts of the Kenilworth plays, it seems advisable
to outline the general plan, using the one printed by J. L.
Huie.

All the major events of the novel appear, with some
changes to modify the characterization and explain the
motives of the action. Amy Robsart is restored to her
rightful dignity, with all her old contempt for the confidant
of Leicester, but with somewhat increased fear of Tony
Foster. She shows a childlike love for display and tinsel.
The drama improves somewhat upon Scott in that Amy
shows regret for being unable to leave Cumnor Place to
visit her old father, who is ill. We are certain throughout
that she chooses to play the hazardous rôle of unacknowl-
edged wife of an earl, because of her love for power and
display. Yet Amy, in their interview at Cumnor, reasons
at length with the Earl that he must take her to court as
his acknowledged wife.

Varney throughout makes it clear that he wishes Amy for
himself. He is less repulsive by far than he appears in the
novel, but he uses his native cunning always to put the Earl
into a wrong position. Leicester himself loses opportunity
after opportunity to make himself right with the jealous
Queen, while, with each loss of resolution, he falls deeper
and deeper into the toils of his underling.

Wayland Smith, as of old, enters the action to warn both
Amy and Tressilian at critical moments. When he arrives
first at Cumnor Place in the disguise of a peddler of wares

for ladies, the scene recalls quite vividly the art of the Great Unknown himself. Smith again saves the Countess from the poison, which has been offered directly by Foster, not through Janet as an unsuspecting agent of her father. Dickie Sludge is made more of a real person, while he still retains much of his blundering mischievousness. That precious rogue, Dr. Alasco, is dispensed with as supernumerary to the drama. Tony Foster redeems himself somewhat, by refusing to go the whole length in helping to prepare the trap for Amy.

One happy touch in the drama, that does not appear in the novel, is the summons of Amy to Kenilworth by Elizabeth. Thus the Countess is spared the exercise of her own wilfulness in departing from Cumnor against the commands of her husband.

Everything after the middle of the play is simplified to bring out three powerful situations: the loss of the evidence that Smith might have used to expose the machinations of Varney; the finding of Amy with Tressilian in the tower-room at Kenilworth, and the consequent loss of faith in her by Tressilian himself; and the final interview, during which the Queen, roused to a frenzy of a thwarted and jealous woman, refuses to countenance any of the statements of the honest Tressilian.

The crux of the drama occurs when Tressilian cannot proceed in a direct accusation against Varney, because Wayland Smith has lost the important letters that wholly convict Varney of treacherous scheming. Leicester vacillates more and more, while his tormentor flits about, spreading new contagion through the entire Court. He turns all suspicion away from himself, by intimating in public that Amy is indeed the paramour of Tressilian. Then the Queen orders that Amy shall be removed under guard from Kenilworth to Cumnor Place. Varney goads the Earl into an impotent fury, and at last succeeds in getting the order that the Countess shall suffer the utmost penalty.

In a duel with the Earl, the disguised Tressilian is quickly disarmed and recognized. Shortly afterward, however, Wayland Smith appears with the damaging evidence that convicts Varney in the eyes of the Earl, and leads Leicester to try to make just amends by informing the Queen of his marriage to Amy Robsart.

Elizabeth takes the centre of the stage once more, but not as the imperial commander of the fortunes of her court. She has now become a typical and rather ordinary jealous woman, wanting an object for her scorn and punishment. Tressilian at first falls under her notice, and would have suffered from her unreasoning anger, except for his whole-hearted defense that he could not supply information against Varney—which Elizabeth accused him of withholding—because he did not have it until after the confession of Leicester. Then the infuriated woman turns upon Amy Robsart, commanding that she shall henceforth be known as plain Mistress Dudley, not as the Countess of Leicester.

At this moment, a grave old counselor of the court, claiming the right of advice that is due to his age and long years of service, reminds the haughty monarch that she does both herself and the realm untold wrong by putting her private feelings above the common weal. Thus recalled to her better self, Elizabeth countermands the orders made in haste, and decrees that Varney and Foster shall be arrested.

This was the scene that Mrs. Bunn played for many years with a skill that won universal admiration among patrons of the theatre.

From this point till near the end, the Huie play follows the main outlines of Scott and the older dramas. Varney, who has escaped from Kenilworth, bends all his energies toward seeing that the first command of Leicester is carried out. He overtakes Lambourne along the road, leaves him dead like a mere dog, and rushes on with the original order in his own possession. When this arch-villain arrives at Cumnor Place, Janet informs him that Amy is in her own apartment on the second floor. Foster is to arrange to spring the trap about midnight. At nearly the last moment, qualms of remorse and conscience, mingled with some superstition, overtake Tony, leaving him resolved not to bear any active part in the murder of the Countess.

Janet has possession of the key which unlocks the mechanism of the fatal trapdoor through which Amy is to fall. Foster asserts that Varney is below-stairs drinking, but Janet knows he is in a room off the upper hallway. She unlocks the trap, *while soft music is being played.* Now the sound of echoing hoofs comes nearer and nearer, until at last the Earl and his party of rescuers enter the lower hall. Varney rushes out of the room above to meet the Earl, steps on the trap, and suffers the fate his cruelty has designed for Amy Robsart. The tableau shows Amy emerging from her own room on the second floor, with the rest below in the hallway arranged in striking poses of surprise and horror.

Few of the Waverley dramas are more convincing than these Kenilworth transcripts, except with reference to the change at the end, making a fortunate *dénouement* out of one that is obviously tragic. Otherwise, the merits of these are evident and cumulative. The characterization is both vivid and happy, in that much of the trouble arises from the hesitation of the Earl, though the devilish cunning of Varney leads the action toward inevitable results. Leicester's underling is more human, less like Iago perhaps, than he appears in Scott, since the plays show that he really wants the Countess for himself. The Queen is clearly shown, with all her regal traits, but also as a jealous and pettish woman, vindictive toward a rival. Amy, on her side, is a naïve young girl, enamored of tinsel and display at court.

Two or three of the vocal numbers appear in questionable taste. Tressilian, for instance, has been hid upstairs at the inn by Cicely as a protection against the violence of some roisterers in the taproom below. Yet, while he is easily within hearing, he sings a song. The critics of the age, to be sure, mentioned some of these faults, though the play-goers may have cared little about the incongruities. When Janet unfastens the trapdoor, soft music is played. This, however, is only one of the host of instances showing the use of music to heighten the emotional effect.

ADDITIONAL DRAMAS BEFORE 1850

Five or six ephemeral attempts to change *Kenilworth* for use on the minor stage call for little comment, since most of them died of inanition after a few nights at most. *Tilbury Fort,* by Edward Stirling, followed a celebrated version by Ryder in 1829, being 'founded on *Kenilworth,* artfully rechristened' for production at Gravesend.[14]   M. Deschayes and Michael Costa arranged a ballet for the King's Theatre in 1831. Two years later, when it appeared at Covent Garden, the *Athenæum* called it 'magnificent beyond description,' because of the pageantry and beautiful contrasts. A *pas de deux* by Amy and the Earl made 'a living picture, full of tenderness and beauty.'

Samuel Heath compiled a curious literary drama in five acts, entitled *Earl of Leicester,* which was printed in London in 1843.   Elizabeth is much the most important character. Heath made some other drastic changes in the plot, all of which he justifies in the preface on the ground that Scott should not be followed too closely. The author believes in making plays correct in setting and staging, to suit the times in which the actions occur. To this end in his *Leicester,* he made considerable investigation into the historical backgrounds of the Elizabethan age.

Elizabeth finally exposes the Earl, in hearing of the entire court, while Amy and Richard remain at Cumnor Place. When Varney at last realizes that all is now lost, he invites Amy to drink of a poisoned cup that he has prepared. For a long time, the Countess hesitates; but finally, worn down

[14] Stirling, *Old Drury Lane* 1. 69.

by his importunities, and in sheer desperation because of his taunts that the Earl has forgotten her, Amy grasps the cup, drains it to the lees, and falls dead. When Leicester at last arrives at Cumnor, it is only the restraint of Tressilian that keeps him from killing Varney outright. The latter at the end stabs himself, declaring that nobody shall lay hands on him while he is alive.

Among several minor pieces that are mentioned by the authorities of the time is *Queen Elizabeth; or, The Princely Sports at Kenilworth,* which made a special feature of the equestrian scenes when it ran in Liverpool in 1838, as a benefit for the master of the horse of the Royal Theatre.

EARLY FOREIGN ADAPTATIONS

For fifty nights in the first months of 1822, great crowds thronged the Porte Saint Martin in Paris to witness a *Château de Kenilworth,* a 'melodrame en trois actes à grand spectacle tiré du roman de sir Walter Scott.' This was credited to J. B. E. Cantiran de Boirie, with some aid from a Frédéric, and H. Lemaire.[15] Save for some adjustments of the action at Cumnor, and a highly melodramatic ending, the chief parts follow Scott. Of course, we notice the usual changes to suit Gallic tastes. Once more Madame Dorval won a triumph as Queen Elizabeth. Previous to the ending of this piece, the chief points of interest are a plot by Lambourne and Varney to incite the Earl and Tressilian to engage in a duel, the subsequent reconciliation of these two knights when they learn the truth, the death of Amy as told in the novel, and the final promise of the Queen to punish all who conspired against the Earl and his Countess.

One quotation may be offered to show how the spirit and text of Scott are made more melodramatic. Amy is reconciling the two rivals for her favor.

---

[15] Frédéric is probably Frédéric Dupetit-Méré, the acknowledged author of other French melodramas.

> *Amélie.* Tressilian, you were not fated to be my husband.
> Become instead my protector and the friend of him, who, with
> yourself, desires Amélie's happiness.
> *Tressilian* (holding out his hand). Chevalier, I promise my
> eternal friendship.
> (*Amélie,* her dearest wish realized, sinks on one knee, while
> Leicester and Tressilian repeat their oath, raising their hands
> above their heads. Jenny shares in the happiness of her mistress.)
> *Amélie.* O God, may this vow find grace in Thy sight and
> bring Thy benediction upon us.[16]

Contemporary journals commended the pageantry at the
close; for it reminded the French of 'the conquests of Elizabeth and the happiness of her reign.'[17]   In 1823, the piece
again ran for some eighteen nights.

Shortly after the success of Cantiran de Boirie's *Kenilworth,* another piece was projected, but this did not reach
the playhouse till early in 1823.   Scribe and Joseph de
Mélesville collaborated in making the libretto for a light
opera for which D. F. E. Auber composed the music.   His-
torically, this drama marks the beginning of the fruitful
years of the association of Scribe and Auber, cut short only
by the death of the latter in 1861.[18]   During the first season,
it was produced twenty-five times, and by 1828, attained a
total of sixty.[19]

A few startling innovations are found in the printed texts.
Raleigh, for instance, doubles the parts of Varney and
Tressilian, yet old Hugh Robsart appears in the list of characters in something like the rôle of Tressilian in Scott's
novel.   Elizabeth at last declares her regard for Leicester,
forgives him for playing as a deceiver, and sends him into
a temporary banishment from court.   Two of the reviewers
complained of the slightness and unreality of the libretto.[20]

---

[16] Translation by Draper, p. 23.
[17] *Miroir des Spectacles,* March 24 and 29, 1822.
[18] *Ibid.,* Jan. 27, 1823; *Moniteur Universel,* Feb. 6, 1823.
[19] Contemporary notices and Draper, p. 25.
[20] The *Miroir* and the *Moniteur.*

By this time, then, the subject of the Earl, the Queen, and the girl had become a favorite in France. There and elsewhere, other modifications appeared from time to time. Alexandre Soumet made a five-act light drama for the Comédie Française, which ran from September 1, 1827, for nineteen performances. The author planned the piece to suit the acting of Mlle. Mars as Amy, who is shown as demented, with other variations from Scott.

Several years before Soumet completed his *Emilia,* Victor Hugo and he entered into an agreement to collaborate in a version of Scott's novel. This was to be called *Amy Robsart,* with three acts by Hugo, and the last two by Soumet. On comparing their first drafts, however, these gentlemen decided to forego the plan, because of differences in theory and method of composition. Later Paul Foucher, hearing of this abortive effort from Soumet himself, went to Hugo (who was his brother-in-law), and begged the unused manuscript. This was produced for only one night at the Opéra Comique, February 13, 1828. All the critics and Hugo himself regarded it as a failure.

Tressilian does not appear in the list of *dramatis personæ,* and the part of Wayland Smith is doubled with that of Flibbertigibbet or Dickie Sludge, who at the close helps to deal out some deserved punishments to Varney and his chief poisoner, Dr. Alasco. Part of the dialogue is copied from the novel, some is rather transformed, and quite a bit is wholly invented. Sir Hugh Robsart and Leicester, after becoming reconciled, plan to rescue Amy and take her to Flanders.[21]

Many other versions of *Kenilworth* are casually named in some of the histories of drama and opèra in France and

[21] See Draper's *Rise and Fall of French Romantic Drama* for a thorough account of the debt of Victor Hugo and the elder Dumas to various works of Scott. This book discusses the Hugo and Foucher *Amy Robsart* as a melodrama that prophesied the new romantic drama in France. See pp. 33-45.

England. In 1840, the Théâtre de Madame brought together a rehash of several older pieces, under the caption of *Comtesse de Leicester*.[22] Five seasons before, Fottola and Donizetti's *Castello di Kenilworth,* probably after running a time in Italy, appeared at Cruz in Spain as a three-act opera.[23]

J. R. Lenz composed a German tragedy for Mainz in 1826.[24] When the fortunes of Drury Lane were at a low ebb, Alfred Bunn tried to acclimate foreign opera, and to introduce a new *Kenilworth* by Francesco Shira, but a lack of patronage cut short the season.[24]

HALLIDAY IN VARYING MOODS

Andrew Halliday—whose last name was really Duff—made both a travesty and a serious drama out of *Kenilworth*. No author, save this versatile dramatist, could have succeeded with both types. Indeed, each is the best of its class after 1850, and, quite out of the common order, the parody appeared first. Halliday named it *Kenilworth; or, Ye Queene, Ye Earle, and Ye Maydenne,* or 'a novel of Scott's novel of that name; but such a long way after Scott as to let the author off scot free.' The printed text describes it as an operatic extravaganza.[25] Opening at the Strand at the end of December, 1858, this light piece continued for nearly one hundred nights. For a subsequent revival, the author retouched some of the scenes to bring them up to date.

The special features include variations of popular tunes, exchange of men's and women's parts, a sword fight between Varney and Amy, Elizabeth in her flightiest moods, and a burlesque transformation scene to make fun of the spectacular endings of the serious plays.

[22] Partridge, p. 225.
[23] Churchman and Peers, *Influence of Walter Scott in Spain,* p. 55.
[24] Grove 4. 265.
[25] Printed in Lacy, vol. 38; reprinted by French, New York.

Until the final scene, it is thought that Amy has fallen through the fatal trap. Mike so announces her death, but Wayland contradicts him, going out in apparent high dudgeon; after which the following dialogue concludes the play:

> *Mike.* Hold! (*staggering*).
> *Queen.* You hold enough, and make yourself too bold.
> *Mike.* Dead? I. Who? The Countess. Varney's ta'en her in,
>   She's fallen a victim to his cursed gin.
>   I? Delirium tremens? No, a worse mishap,
>   She's broken her neck by falling through the trap.
> (*Enter Wayland, with Amy on his back.*)
> *Wayland.* 'Tis false. She's saved—saved for the last grand scene—
>   Her feet went through but not her crinoline. (*He sets Amy down.*)

Elizabeth forgives the lovers, and announces that tears are appropriate at a wedding, whereupon all of the company follow her suggestion effusively.

Eleven years later, Halliday brought out his serious *Amy Robsart* at Drury Lane. Beyond all comparison, this work excelled the other melodramas after the time of the spectacle shown by the Bunn players at Bath. Every appointment was magnificent, but more notably so were the revels at Kenilworth for the entertainment of the Queen and her retinue.[26] The concluding scene was so cleverly managed that the actor who impersonated Varney, without substituting a dummy, seemed to fall twenty feet through the trap in the hallway at Cumnor Place, 'and the righteous gods shouted till they were hoarse.'[27]

The emotional acting of the gracious Lilian Adelaide Neilson charmed all hearts. No other actress of her generation, says the *Dictionary of National Biography,* could ever have excelled her Rebecca and Amy in the Halliday

---

[26] Stirling I. 289.
[27] James R. Anderson, *An Actor's Life,* p. 306.

romantic melodramas.[28]   Marston mentions her two main traits: a child-like devotion to the Earl, and an intense scorn of Richard Varney.[29]   She appeared in this part for her introduction to American audiences at Booth's, New York, in 1873 and again two years later.   The *Herald* critic, who disliked the drama, spoke warmly of her acting: 'There broods a sunset light of mournful beauty, and a subtle, strange melancholy sense of vague, impending danger and horror, which is, in high degree, imaginative and poetical.'[30]

Both Halliday transcripts appeared again in America. Brown mentions four revivals of the travesty in New York alone, including one by Lady Don, who had carried the same piece to Australia in 1862.[31]   Through her own 'personal charm,' the late Marie Wainwright revived and adapted the serious drama, but she failed to measure up to the standard set by the lamented Neilson, either in sincerity of mood or in vividness of imagination.[32]

Between 1871 and 1900, six or eight attempts were made to revamp the old story, but none of these met with more than temporary fame.[33]   These sporadic attempts reached the high-water mark in 1893, when the operatic *Amy Robsart* was sung at Covent Garden.   This was the work of Paul Milliet, translated from the French by Frederick Weatherley, and set to music by Isidore de Lara.   Sir Augustus Harris assisted in making the libretto, which the *Times* praised, but said the music 'hangs fire terribly.'[34]   Important changes showed that Amy made a fatal mistake in allowing the Earl to deny that she was his wife.   This weakness contributed,

---

[28] 40. 183.

[29] *Our Recent Actors*, p. 233.

[30] For May 13, 1873; see the *Tribune* also for April 27, 1875.

[31] 2. 279, 381, 527; 3. 113, 344, 532.

[32] *Tribune*, Sept. 8, 1891.

[33] See Clarence, pp. 22, 232, and the bibliographical list of plays at the end of this present discussion, for the titles of these versions.

[34] For July 10, 1893.

more than anything else, to the final tragedy, which was 'not shirked in any way' by the dramatists. Madame Calvé took the part of the heroine, making much of the duets with Leicester.

Curiously enough, the travesties multiplied, and all had some passing vogue. Among the best is the *Little Amy Robsart,* by Gordon and Mackay, for the Philharmonic in London, 1882. Many of the romantic situations were changed to suit the changing tastes of newer patrons. One great hit was a variation of the motive of the lost letter, which the villain abstracted from a modern letter-box. Some of the men's and women's parts were interchanged.[35] Finally, the Wig and Mask Club of the University of Pennsylvania staged a two-act burlesque, which followed only the broad outlines of *Kenilworth,* with such specialties. as songs and dances by a chorus, 'swaggering' by Mike Lambourne, and impersonations by Queen Elizabeth.[36]

FINAL IMPRESSIONS OF KENILWORTH PLAYS

Little need be said to generalize our ideas of the suitability of the adaptations from *Kenilworth.* Nearly all of the dramas failed at some point to interest the playgoers for more than a few months, or a season or two at best. Some of the good literary versions failed to gain a notable hearing. Dibdin for once missed the popular fancy, because he made his first drama too brief and too scrappy; but some of the others like Dimond, Calcraft, and Oxberry extended the original version till it made a very respectable showing. Heath wanted to arouse interest by his historical features, and by sending Amy to her death in a new manner. Auber in his French opera tried to win applause by introducing

[35] *Theatre,* New Series, 5. 169. See also Boyd, *Records of the Dundee Stage,* pp. 51, 68.
[36] *Daily Pennsylvanian,* April 16, 1893.

Raleigh as an important character, and by making the father of Amy Robsart another chief figure in the action. Soumet followed by omitting Raleigh altogether, but by making Amy more or less demented, for the benefit of an actress who could well present such a character. Halliday at last threw over the whole a beautiful coloring of romance and tragic emotion, winning favors which the others after 1850 failed to gain.

Once more the dramatists found themselves in a dilemma. One wing of the audience, which loved little change from the novel, found the characters in these plays too pale and listless. The other, which welcomed changes for theatrical reasons, found quite unsuitable most of those particular changes actually effected. It seemed necessary to offend either the one party or the other.

To make up for these inherent difficulties, most of the later adapters fell back to the old-time pageantry. They therefore consulted the antiquarian writers of the Elizabethan age for details of dress, customs, and historical verisimilitude. Here again, however, the gallery gods were not appeased. At last, travesty alternated with serious drama, a somewhat unusual condition, since the burlesque versions commonly followed after the reign of the serious ones had terminated. Yet the motives of the lost letter, the conventional villain, the forsaken and wronged damsel, and the haughty queen, all gave rise to the best art of a man like Halliday. On the whole, finally, the frequent revivals of the Kenilworth theme after 1850 show alike the interest in the subject itself and the failure of all but a play or two.

The rôle of Amy Robsart brought Mrs. Waylett again into notice as a capable actress, though she was more successful in parts like those of David Gellatley and other youths. Her cousin, Mrs. William West, added Amy to her Meg Merrilies, and later rounded out her reputation in Waverley dramas by enacting Berengaria in a Talisman play. Though she liked her own Bianca in Milman's *Fazio* best of all her impersonations, Mrs. Alfred Bunn attained greatest fame for her Queen Elizabeth in a modification of Dibdin's play, and for the same character in a celebrated translation of Schiller's *Maria Stuart*. No one of these left nearly as finished an impression as that made by the gifted Lilian Adelaide Neilson, whose career was soon cut short by an early death.

VIII. REMAINING NOVELS BEFORE 1823

Fifteen novels in the Waverley series appeared between 1814 and 1823. Already six of the major ones have been discussed with reference to the stage-productions; the rest have been deferred for consideration in the chapter to follow. This second minor group, made up of the novels not previously discussed, includes *Waverley,* written in 1814 and not dramatized till 1822; the *Black Dwarf, Antiquary,* and *Old Mortality,* all published in 1816, and dramatized after eight months, two years, and five years, respectively; the *Legend of Montrose,* 1819; *Abbot* and *Monastery* a year later; *Pirate* and *Fortunes of Nigel* finally in 1822— after the time of *Kenilworth,* the last of the major novels to appear on the public stage These later novels all came to dramatic honors within eight or nine months after publication. Shortly after *Kenilworth,* however, the vogue of Scott began to decline on the stage. Several very fine dramas appeared afterward, but the old zest of the public seems to have abated.

THE BLACK DWARF

It would be indeed hard to explain just why the very mediocre tale of the misanthrope of the moor came to the playhouse before that of the sturdy Covenanters or the humorsome Jonathan Oldbuck. Probably it appealed more to lovers of melodrama than did certain stories. Once again Terry had proposed to make a play out of the life of Elshender, the moorland recluse, but Scott had written that he doubted whether the public would approve. This was before *Rob Roy* achieved such a prodigious success: only *Mannering* had reached the playhouse. Instead of the *Black Dwarf,* Scott recommended two plots to his dramatic friend, one of which the author himself used finally for his

Doom of Devorgoil.[1]   Some unknown dramatist, evidently not Terry, brought out a new melodramatic romance, how-ever, with score largely by C. E. Horn.   It ran for a number of nights, beginning on July 26, 1817, at the new English Opera in London.   Some of the chief actors were Bartley, H. Johnstone, and Miss Kelly.   Much was made of the painted drops, including an old Saxon Hall, Mucklestone Moor, Hengfoot Farm, a Gothic chamber, and a brilliant Gothic chapel for the final scene.[2]   Since Horn was in America in 1843, this version was probably the one that was presented at the Chatham Theatre, New York.[3]

THE ANTIQUARY

Speaking of his *Antiquary,* which the author inclined to make his favorite, Scott admitted to Morrit and Terry that the plot is not dramatic.   'It wants the romance of *Waverley,*' he wrote, 'and the adventure of *Guy Mannering;* and yet there is some salvation about it; for, if a man will paint from nature, he will be likely to amuse those who daily are looking at it.'[4]   Though this novel sold at the rate of a thousand a day for a time, the dramatists left it severely alone for two years.   Isaac Pocock made a piece for Covent Garden in 1818, but it fell flat on the first night, while *Guy Mannering* continued to draw respectable crowds.

By 1820, when Pocock no longer served at Covent Garden as dramatic laureate, Terry was called upon to compile anew an *Antiquary,* but he used the original Pocock as a ground-work.   How much is to be credited to each collaborator one cannot now tell, for the draft by Pocock in his collected works, and the Terry printed drama, seem to be identical.[5]

[1] Lockhart 2. 36.
[2] Lyceum playbill.   Praised highly by *European Mag.,* 1817, p. 154.
[3] *Ireland* 2. 397; the *Herald* of the same date.
[4] Lockhart 4. 15.
[5] Pocock's executor printed the play; the Terry text was published in London in 1820.

Terry's preface, however, explained that Pocock had excised the two most dramatic incidents, the storm and the duel. Terry, in his preface, disclaimed any literary credit for this drama, 'where Plot, Incidents, Characters, and even the very Dialogue, are already supplied by the Novelist.' He also added: 'The task of compressing Tales of three volumes into Plays of three acts is only of mere technical and mechanical drudgery, which no one would willingly undertake who could do better things: and he who performs it must be content to resign the title of Author, for the humbler and juster appellation of Compiler.'

That Scott himself gave Terry more of this than the mere novel affords, neither Lockhart nor Terry admits. Taking Terry's own concluding statement literally, one might believe that Terry regretted that Scott had not again helped him, as he undoubtedly did in *Guy Mannering*. For the preface expressed the wish that 'the mysterious and powerful pen' of the unknown author of the Waverley series 'had sometimes turned its wonderful force directly to the Drama.'[6]

Pocock's *Antiquary,* as thus revised by the friend of Sir Walter Scott, is lavish in spectacle and stingy in characterization. Little is made of that curious old beggar, Edie Ochiltree, or even of the oddities of the Antiquary himself. Such material indeed, even though interesting enough in print, is not easily made theatrical on the stage. So Terry furnished the spectacle that Pocock overlooked, including a magnificent water-scene that would do credit to modern stage realism. Isabella and Sir Arthur, caught in a tremendous storm, are forced to cross a wide gulf while the waters below are swirling furiously. Old Edie arrives just in time to carry Isabella over the tumbling cataract. Lovel himself climbs down the face of the cliff, but the rising flood now

[6] Cumberland's *British Drama* reprinted this play once more in 1832, with notes by George Daniel, including an elaborate eulogy and original poem in honor of Walter Scott.

forces the lovers to retreat, and Isabella is drawn up again over the precipice by means of ropes. The *European Magazine* speaks with enthusiasm of the mechanical ingenuity of this rescue, and of the 'prodigal scenery.'[7]

On the whole, the drama follows Scott well enough, except that the characterization lacks a certain charm and vividness. *Blackwood* said that most of the persons are 'like unfinished etchings from the novel,'[8] and a modern reader certainly gets this same impression. Genest thought Terry made a blunder in not writing the play for himself in Glenallen, rather than so much for Liston in Oldbuck.[9] The latter was indeed censured in London for making the Antiquary too much of a buffoon, but Farren succeeded admirably in the part for several subsequent revivals.

Altogether the run was high above the average—twenty-eight nights in London and twenty-two in Edinburgh. Murray, who touched up the text, and added somewhat from the novel, failed to gain the favor of the critics. One of them said caustically that he made Oldbuck 'more like a rude, ignorant, choleric English squire than a learned Scotch antiquarian.'[10] Calcraft in Lovel, Terry in Lord Glenallen once more, and Mrs. Renaud in Elspeth, made the occasion 'eminently successful.' Yet again the chief honors went to Mackay as Edie, the old 'blue gown,' in which part he 'fully sustained the reputation he had gained in *Guy Mannering* and the *Heart of Midlothian.*'[11]

Old Mortality

Three and a half years after *Old Mortality* came from the press, Covent Garden at last sponsored a transcript by

---

[7] 77. 166.
[8] 6. 625.
[9] 9. 52.
[10] *Caledonian Mercury,* Dec. 28, 1820.
[11] *European Magazine* 77. 166; *London Magazine* 1. 303.

Charles Farley, one of the actors there, which ran for some ten or twelve nights. All the reviews are unfavorable, except for the brief mention that Macready in the chief rôle 'much distinguished himself.'[12]   *Blackwood* remarked bitterly: 'The after piece, called *The Battle of Bothwell Bridge,* professes to be founded on *Old Mortality;* but it appropriates little of that work but two or three of the battles and some of its dullness.'[13]

The printed text shows some fitful energy in the battles but relatively little real dramatic action.   As literature, the Farley drama is commendable, but as characterization it is sometimes weak and ineffective.   Henry Morton, for example, writes to Claverhouse that he has joined the rebel Scotchmen to show these Covenanters how obstinate a course they are pursuing.   This is rather absurd, and a long way from Scott.   Burleigh ascends a tree, and is picked off by a rebel sharpshooter.   This, again, is rather out of keeping with the original narrative.

Spectacle and historical accuracy in costuming partly make up for some of the lapses.   One highly effective scene, though difficult to enact, shows the visit of Henry Morton to the secluded lair of the morose Claverhouse beside a lonely chasm.   After a rather churlish interview, Morton starts to go, but his host suddenly throws down the log over which lies his sole avenue of retreat.   Henry jumps for his life, while some of a party coming to rescue him are precipitated into the raging flood below.   This spectacle might be mentioned along with that of Terry's *Antiquary,*[14] in which a great flood was imitated on the stage.

One of the directions reads thus: 'Enter Lady Margaret Bellenden, drest in a scarlet riding habit, and high-crowned hat and feathers, as worn in the time of Charles II—very formal and dignified, with a gold-headed cane.   They are

[12] *Annual Register,* Vol. 62, part 1, p. 638.
[13] 6. 310.
[14] Printed in London for Lowndes in 1820.

preceded by domestics in armor, and by Mrs. Jennie Dennison.'

Nor was Calcraft any more convincing in his original form of the tale of the Covenanters. For once the dramatic laureate at the Royal in Edinburgh failed to gain an audience. On the contrary, one criticism at least was scathing, for the piece was called 'a gross libel upon all that Scotchmen most reverence.' The dramatist was roundly scored for announcing in advance in the printed copies that his play was then 'being acted at the Theatre Royal with the greatest applause.'[15] In fact, quite the opposite proved true.

Evidently the Scotch felt that Calcraft's work was unpatriotic. Later in Perth, however, and always in Dublin (especially after Calcraft entered upon the management of the Royal there), the *Old Mortality* proved rather a favorite. It was enacted in New York in 1827, and was published in *Waverley Dramas* in 1872.[16]

Thomas J. Dibdin's *Old Mortality; or, Burley and Morton* failed to impress the public, though a humorous preface in dialogue between the author and Jedediah Cleishbotham—Scott's imaginary scribe—caused no end of merriment, as a skit on the methods of the Great Unknown himself.[17] Pocock's *Cavaliers and Roundheads* drew on some of the foreign operas.[18] This, like three or four late versions, aroused no special interest.

Likewise the foreign operas and melodramas are more numerous and confusing than important. They include J. A. P. F. Ancelot and J. X. Boniface's *Têtes Rondes et Cavalieri,* from which Pocock drew somewhat; Count C. Pepoli's *I Puritani di Scozia,* for which Bellini wrote noble

---

[15] *Dramatic Review* 8. 31; 9. 73.
[16] Lawson, p. 271; Brown 1. 88.
[17] Playbill for June 20, 1820.
[18] *Gentleman's Magazine* 4. 644.

music. *Los Puritanos de Escocia* was produced at Cruz, Spain.[19]

A TYPICAL FRENCH MODIFICATION

One French modification has been left for treatment as typical of the revisions usually made by the Gallic authors. This is the vaudeville called *Exilé,* composed by d'Artois, Anne, and de Tully, and represented at the Vaudeville, Paris, in the summer of 1825.

All the familiar outlines of the novel have disappeared, except for the romance of Lord Evandale, Edith Bellenden, and Henry Morton. Thus the gods of unity are well appeased.

Edith and·Henry, lovers of long standing, are now separated by the exile of the hero in Holland. Not hearing from her affianced in many months, Edith becomes engaged to Evandale, whose ward she has been in charge of a chaperon at his castle. At last Henry returns disguised, for the penalty is death if he is seen in Scotland during the term of his banishment. While Edith is making ready to sign a marriage-contract, Henry secretes himself in a cabinet. As in the story of the bride of Lammermoor, the lovers have broken a ring between them in token of their troth. When Henry manages to drop part of the ring on the table, Edith starts up with a cry, refuses to sign the contract, while Henry escapes during the confusion.

Early in the second act, Henry comes out into the open. While he has been away, a dishonest justice of the peace has secured control of the estate that was left to Edith in a will. The rascally lawyer has Lord Evandale arrested, and then threatens Henry himself. When Edith endeavors to get Evandale to protect Henry, the latter complicates their affairs by accusing Edith of trying to break her promise to him.

[19] Churchman and Peers, *Influence of Sir Walter Scott in Spain,* p. 66.

Events in the third act move to a swift culmination.   Henry is revealed as Lord Melville, the Lieutenant of the country, now restored to all his old rights and dignities.   When a constable leads Lord Evandale in for final sentence, Henry tears to bits the original order of arrest, reminds Evandale of his former kindness to the lovers, and offers to resign any prior claims to the affections of Miss Bellenden.   Not willing to be outdone in magnanimity, the noble Lord insists that he himself has no real claims to the hand of Edith. The common laws of love and romance are now invoked, and the lovers are allowed to announce their formal betrothal. In the meanwhile, as one might already guess, Henry has thwarted the designing justice, who was trying to acquire the estate that belongs to Edith.

Shortly afterward, Lord Evandale is killed in a skirmish between his own men and the forces of the rascally lawyer. Thus tragedy and comedy are mingled, so as to remove all obstacles to the happiness and fortunes of the lovers.

The *Pandore* spoke with enthusiasm of this operatic play, commending the new music by Adam, the romantic turns in the situation, and the vivid play of emotions.[20]   The production ran for more than thirty nights between July and October, 1825.

THE LEGEND OF MONTROSE

Opinions doubtless differ as to the merits of Scott's *Legend of Montrose* as a romance.   The structure shows numerous weaknesses, and the whole composition reveals many examples of little mistakes, due to Scott's rapid methods of writing; yet the situations are wonderfully impressive, and entirely suitable to the needs of the stage. Except for the fact that so many Scott plays had appeared already, this novel would have interested the average audience to a remarkable degree.   Dalgetty is indeed one of

---

[20] For July 10, 1825.

Scott's most original creations.   So is the moody Allan in his struggle against his 'weird.'

Less than a month after the ink had dried on the last printed sheets of *Montrose,* Thomas J. Dibdin had his transcript acted at the Surrey Theatre on July 5, 1819.   Though the portrait of Dugald Dalgetty created much amusement, little interest followed the piece as a whole.

Glasgow received loyally the dramas of Scotch life and character.   Two excerpts from this novel originated in that city, one in 1820 and the second in 1847.   Both plays, which are anonymous, have undoubted literary charm of a kind lacking in most melodramas.

The 1820 version changes the narrative at some points, but presents most of the scenes in their true picturesqueness. Even the faithful steed, Gustavus Adolphus, might be named among the *dramatis personæ;* for we hear much of him from his valiant master, Dalgetty, and see him in action in a battle or two.   Many scenes stick in the memory.   One recalls them with no little enthusiasm, some of the best being the solemn conclave of the Scotch chiefs, broken somewhat by the hesitancy of Dugald as to whether he shall join their cause; the pathetic melancholy of Allan, which the harping of Annot Lyle, above all else, can dissipate; the visit of Dugald to the lair of the Duke of Argyle, with all the incidents of his imprisonment, his meeting with old Ranald of the Mist, and their escape from the dungeon.   At the close, the betrothal of Annot to the Earl of Menteith, with the departure of Allan for the solitude of the Highlands, stands out as one of the best scenes in all the dramatizations of Waverley romances.   Though by no means as theatrical as some of the earlier dramas, this Montrose play deserves a place among the best of the literary transcripts for faithfulness to the original, and for that peculiar 'Scotch feeling,' which the residents of Glasgow could well appreciate.

Little else could be added to intensify the outlines or color of the background.   Notice, for instance, the pictures of wild scenery in the Highlands, with many lakes in their secluded nests; the marshaling of the clans, with their picturesque tartans and multicolored, emblematic banners; and the stirring scenes of the final conflicts, out of which Dugald emerges without his steed, but not without glory.

Montrose; or, The Gathering of the Clans, a five-act revision of the earlier play, arranged by a 'Gentleman of Glasgow,' achieved a triumph that was long recalled.[21]

By 1847, however, the quixotic Dugald had lost some of his gallantry, and considerable of his impetuosity. Gustavus Adolphus still appears as the centre of the knight's affection, until he dies bravely in battle, and then Dugald is presented with a new steed, called Loyalty's Reward by the friendly chiefs. The comic interest is heightened by several references to Marischal College, Aberdeen, where Dugald received his higher education. The Rittmaster himself, however, is made too absurd and pedantic in this second play—almost a caricature of his real self, and as such he is far less likable than in the novel or the earlier drama.

Toward the close, one stumbles upon this interesting bit of conversation between the chiefs:

> *Montrose.* Were there an academy for the education of horses annexed to Marischal College, Aberdeen, Sir Dugald Dalgetty alone should fill the chair.
>
> *Menteith.* Because, being an ass, there would be an obvious relation between the professor and his students.

A great deal is made in both dramas of the celebrated story of the incautious Scots laird who boasted in England that he had six golden candlesticks as good as any he had seen south of the Tweed; and, when he was drawn into a wager on the subject and had to make good his boasts, the canny Highlander made them appear in the form of six giant countrymen, each with a torch in hand.

---

[21] Both printed texts afford no hints, further than this, as to the names of the authors.

Dugald is indeed a good comic contrast to the serious leaders, with all his dickering over fifty cents a day that one side may offer more than the other to a knight who has fought beside King Gustavus Adolphus. The second *Montrose* reveals in picturesque sternness the children of the mist, with their love of old Ranald, their leader.

For simple pathos, the concluding scene could hardly be amended. Allan MacAuley is shown, contrasting with the robust Dugald, as a man fighting against the weird of gloom when 'his dark hour' comes upon him. The fair Annot Lyle loves him as a sister, not as a sweetheart, and charms him with her harping whenever he is caught in the shadow of melancholy. When Annot stands by the side of the Earl of Menteith at the altar, Allan steals upon them unobserved. Menteith is saved from the dagger of Allan, because he wears a metal cuirass; and Allan, now fully dominated by his weird, a creature of ruinous hopes and once noble resolves, slinks off alone to die among the scenes of gloom in his favorite mountains.

Both these Glasgow dramas, though in need of curtailment, are interesting and dramatic, if not indeed actually theatrical. The scenery of the 1847 version is highly picturesque. Some of the pictures are those of the children of the mist in their wild home, rooms in Darlinvaroch Castle, the plaided Highlanders marching with banners unfurled and pipes playing, the grounds of Inverara Castle and dungeon, and various wild bits of country traversed by Dugald and Ranald after their escape from the dungeon of Argyle.

Isaac Pocock wrote the text, and Henry R. Bishop, with some assistance, the musical score, for a *Montrose,* which ran for twenty-two nights at Covent Garden in February, 1822, and for eleven more in Edinburgh during March. In the final conflict, sixteen horses were used on the stage. Pocock[22] included a fair proportion of the salient incidents,

---

[22] The Pocock text was printed in London in 1822.

some of which appear in dwarfish form, though old Erorcht, the wife of Duncan Campbell and mother of six stalwart sons that have been hanged in the public square, appears as an amazon of the Helen Macgregor clan.   Both the author and the painter of the scenery went to great lengths to make the background original and picturesque, with Highland vistas, plenty of rocks and water, the clans marching once more in the moonlight, and the six Campbell men hanging on the gallows at Inverara.

Bath used one of the versions in the spring of 1822, at which time John Genest, a resident of that town, remarked tersely that it 'was wrong to bestow much scenery on so poor a play.'[23] Hodgson's *Juvenile Drama* reduced the Pocock text from 70 to 24 pages, showing admirable skill in shortening the significant portions.

Montrose appeared in Edinburgh with Mackay as Dugald, when he once again won great public recognition, including some kind words from Walter Scott himself.   Somehow the Pocock text offended the Scotch, however, in regard to the quarrels among the nobles and the character and language of Dalgetty.   A modified form removed the objections, and allowed Mrs. Renaud greater freedom in the part of Erorcht.[24]   One judicious change saves Allan MacAuley from trying to take the life of the Earl of Menteith.   Instead, on seeing Annot Lyle, Allan hesitates, changes his purpose, and at last exclaims, 'My arm falls when an angel intervenes.'

THE ABBOT

Scott's *Monastery* preceded his *Abbot* by six months, but the latter, in turn, had the priority on the stage by five full years.   Both treat of similar persons and themes, and hence they will be considered together.

Tottenham Street Theatre, London, brought out an ambitious literary drama, named *The Abbot; or, Mary of*

[23] 9. 173.
[24] *Dramatic Review* 5. 64.   Murray or Calcraft made the changes.

Scotland, in September, 1820. The published copies credit this to Henry Roxby Beverly, and describe it as 'a serious, melodramatic, historical burletta,' since it appeared in one of the unlicensed houses. The preface asserts that the drama 'was nightly repeated to crowded audiences with unbounded applause,' but this may have been an advertising 'puff-preliminary,' before the public actually expressed any approval. At any rate, further commendation is lacking in the usual sources of dramatic criticism.

The dramatist followed Scott rather faithfully, except for the wise omission of many details of the opening chapters and some of the strife and unpleasant scenes at Loch Leven, including the attempt to poison Mary of Scotland. In the drama the Abbot remains much of a lay figure, while the chief persons move in their real elements: the mysterious Magdalene Graeme and her spirited son, Roland; the arch and elusive Catherine Seyton; the humorous Sandy and Mattie, once more done perfectly; the romantic and self-effacing George Douglas; and, in all her true colorings, the forsaken and tragic Queen.

Everything rises to a climax when Mary escapes at midnight from her virtual imprisonment on the island of Loch Leven. We hear Roland fumbling for the keys he has intentionally lost, while Mary is rowed further and further out into the lake toward the opposite, friendly shore. Likewise from time to time we hear the spreading of the alarm, with attempts to launch the boats in pursuit of the fugitives, and finally the glad news that the Queen has set foot on the farther shore beyond all immediate danger. Mary is last seen ready to depart for a safe refuge in France, with some of her faithful liegemen around her, while the curtain descends to 'appropriate music.'

ANONYMOUS NEW YORK DRAMA

Neither the contemporary press nor the recent historians of the drama in New York mention the name of the gentleman who was credited as the author of a *Mary of Scotland; or, The Heir of Avenel,* which ran from May 17 to July 6, 1821, before the Anthony Street Theatre was demolished to make way for a church.[25]

Nor does the printed text give us any definite clue, though an interesting preface mentions the play as an experiment to determine, first, whether the 'diffused action' of the novel could be compressed into a good acting drama, and, secondly, whether the public inclined to favor 'indigenous efforts.' Though a bit long, this piece is a noble instance of dramatic condensation, without following Scott too slavishly. Some of the initial events give way to heighten the action at Loch Leven. The acts abound in contrasts, a fine sense of both humor and tragedy, a number of picturesque speeches, and good scenery, for which special drops were painted—a rather uncommon procedure for New York in those days. The mysterious flittings of the White Lady of Avenel rise to a climax when she announces to Sir Halbert:

> Knight, no more the holly wear,
> Avenel claims its rightful heir.

William H. Murray made a *Mary Queen of Scots* by taking some of the material that others rejected, such as the events leading to the attempt to poison Mary at Loch Leven. The climax is the flight across the lake. The single scene of act two shows the death of the romantic Douglas.

Besides six or eight other English plays having to do with the life of the Scotch Queen, several translations of Schiller's *Maria Stuart* were freely used in England and America. Critics often neglected to inform their readers as to which particular drama was being enacted. It seems clear, however, that Madame Vestris revived the Murray melodrama when she assumed the management of the Olympic Theatre in 1831. Maria Foote proved an acceptable Mary. Charlotte Cushman acted as Lady Loch Leven at the Chatham

---

[25] So the *Evening Post,* Brown, Dunlap, Ireland, and Weglin.

Theatre, New York, on the last night of January, 1857, in a version announced as 'played for the second time in America.' For a generation, almost every Scotch comedian acted Sandy Macfarlane, the quaint humorist in Murray's *Mary of Scotland*. Mlle. Rachel in 1841 made a profound impression as Mary when she visited England.[26]

A French Melodrama

Alert as usual to the romantic elements of the story of the tragic Queen, R. C. G. Pixérécourt, a prolific French writer of different types of drama, brought out his historical *Château de Loch-Leven* in December of 1822, at the Gaieté. The text shows the typical command of the entire situation, a unity of the events, excision of all irrelevancies, and a clever adaptation to the tastes of French playgoers.

Mary here refuses to sign the articles of abdication offered her by the English nobles, even though she is urged to assent by her loyal admirer, George Douglas. He intends to have Mary wear a new suit, designed originally for Roland Graeme, as a part of the plan of getting her away secretly from the island of Loch Leven. When the page fancies that Catherine Seyton is going away in the company of a man, he becomes intensely jealous, and unwittingly betrays the plan. Douglas confesses his part in the plot to have Mary leave with Catherine, and then throws himself into the neighboring lake.

Old Randall, during the revels at Kinross Fair, warns Catherine Seyton that Roland must not find her there in disguise. During a dance with her, however, Roland becomes suspicious, and hints to the fair one that he might be willing to assist Queen Mary. The Queen next escapes being poisoned by some liquid that Randall has obtained from Dr. Luc-Lundin, ostensibly to rid the island of snakes. Though Roland himself detects the plot, it is Catherine (and not he as in the novel) who forces Randall to taste some

---

[26] *Dict. Nat. Biog.* 27. 43; Martin, *Essays on the Drama* 2. 35.

of the food that has been prepared for Mary. Instead of changing dishes as in Scott, Catherine has the poisoned one removed altogether; but Randall goes out boasting that he has at last rid them of all fear of the troublesome Queen of Scots. Meanwhile, the faithful George Douglas, a warm admirer of Mary, has returned with a list of all those who will aid in the escape, with an indication of what disguise each will wear.

During the confusion of calling a doctor, Catherine and Mary conceal themselves in the garden, where they await Douglas and his party till about midnight. When the faithful boatmen at last appear, the arranged signals are set, one of them being placed unconsciously by Lady Loch Leven herself. We hear Roland fumbling with the gates, and professing to look for the keys that he has thrown into the lake. As Mary is being rowed toward the opposite shore, Douglas is pierced by an arrow intended for the Queen's boat. His last loyal act is to inform his mother, the Lady Loch Leven, that the hated Mary of Scotland is now for ever out of reach of those who would do her injury. A rocket now trails along the sky, indicating that the boat has reached the protection of friends on the opposite shore.

For the sake of unity, several of the minor persons are doubled in this French melodrama—Dryfesdale and Randall, Lindesay and Ruthven, for instance. Henry Seyton, brother of Catherine, does not appear. In spite of the condensation of the story, this piece follows Scott almost verbatim for whole pages at a time. As a variation from the common run of historical plays based on the fate of Mary of Scotland, the French greatly admired *Château de Loch-Leven*. It ran for upwards of thirty nights in 1822 and 1823.[27]

The Monastery in French Opera

Once more Scribe and a gifted collaborator happily interpreted the wishes of the French patrons of opera. This

---

[27] *Miroir des Spectacles,* Paris, 1822-3.

time he received the help of Boieldieu, master of light effects
in music. Thus their *Dame Blanche* opened at the Opéra
Comique in December, 1825, and three months afterward
began a triumphal tour of the provinces with a first performance at Rouen. No operatic drama ever captivated
more audiences, for a longer time, in France. For this
reason, we are interested in the outline of the plot, and in
the subsequent stage-history of this remarkable arrangement.

Scribe's libretto is based on *Guy Mannering,* the *Monastery,* and a trace from the *Abbot.* The chief persons are
George Brown, who turns out to be the lost Julian of Avenel;
Gaveston, steward of the Avenel estate; Dickson, a simple
farmer of the Dandy Dinmont type, but not half so valiant
as the 'honest' rustic in *Guy Mannering;* Anna, adopted
child of the late lady of Avenel, who takes a rôle similar
to that of Lucy Bertram; and the mysterious White Lady of
Avenel, a tragic nemesis of the Meg Merrilies type, though
more elusive and supernatural.

Brown, an English officer on leave from his regiment,
has lived for a time with Dickson, tenant on the large estate
of the absent laird of Avenel. For many years, tradition
has circulated the report that a White Lady flits about at
times in the neighborhood of the Monastery. In the castle
itself is a statue that goes by her name. While the laird
of Avenel is forced to live in exile, on account of his
sympathy for the Stuarts, the estates and the ward have
fallen under the control of Gaveston, who cunningly plans
to dispose of the property and marry the ward.

Being aware of most of his plans, Anna assumes the
disguise which the White Lady is said to wear. Through
superstition and fear, Dickson hesitates to give her aid.
At last she enlists the help of Brown, who is given a palpable
hint that soon he may become acquainted with a lady who
once saved him from death while he was dangerously ill.
At the auction of the castle, Gaveston proposes to bid it in.
Still in disguise as the mysterious lady, Anna reveals a

treasure in the statue in the hall of the castle. Gaveston
tears off her veil, only to discover that she is the rightful
heir to all the Avenel estates. Not long after she and Brown
have been married, it transpires that he is the Julian of
Avenel who disappeared many years before when a mere
child.[28]

One French theatrical journal, the *Pandore,* frequently
praised the opera, and predicted great fame for it during
the initial run.* Ponchard, Roger, and Achard in turn took
the important part of Brown, with Mrs. Rigaut as the first
Anna, Henri as Gaveston, and Peréol as Dickson. Critics
agreed that the music excelled the libretto. 'The harmony is
rich and grand, the songs graceful and elegant. Some
passages denote the desire of complying with the taste of
that part of the public which loves hardly anything in Italian
music except the superabundance of ornament.'[29]

Sir George Grove exclaims with enthusiasm, '*La Dame
Blanche* is the finest work of Boieldieu, and Boieldieu is the
greatest master of the French school of comic opera.'[30] Year
after year this piece brought forth continued enthusiasm,
until in 1864 the announcements in the newspapers mentioned that it was being offered for the thousandth time, and
Draper informs us that it ran three hundred and forty times
more by 1875.[31] This seems to be the record for the Scott
transcripts in France, unless it be for the *Lucia di
Lammermoor.*

English translations of the *Dame Blanche* never proved
so popular as some others from the French. Probably the
variations from the style and plot displeased some English
audiences, though the music captivated many. T. S. Cooke,
in the autumn of 1826, made selections from the French

---

[28] Upton's *Standard Operas,* p. 49, outlines the story.
[29] *Pandore,* Dec. 11, 1825; see also *Constitutionnel,* Dec. 12, 1825,
and *Moniteur Universel,* Dec. 10, 1825.
[30] *Dict. of Music and Musicians* I. 352 (N. Y., 1904).
[31] Draper, p. 27; contemporary journals of 1864.

work for Drury Lane, adding new songs and other 'inter-
polations' of his own.   Within the next few months, a complete translation was brought upon the stage at the other
patent theatre.   Though the first accounts mentioned that
it had been announced for repetition 'without a dissenting
voice,' the length of run extended to only nine nights, even
with the celebrated Miss Paton in the chief rôle.   J. Howard
Payne won a 'triumphant success' at the Park Theatre in
New York for his rendering of the Scribe libretto in 1832.
During the same season, the original was sung in New York
by a French operatic company.   Similar troupes from abroad
appeared in Dublin in 1850 and 1875, and again in New
York in 1867 and 1870.[32]

The Pirate

With the exception of the *Monastery,* which was delayed
in reaching the theatre, all the novels thus far considered in
the present chapter were published and dramatized before
Kenilworth.   In both the novel and the play, the *Pirate*
appeared just after the narrative of the times of Elizabeth,
and her visit to central England.   Scott, with his matchless
wizardry, shifted at once, after he wrote *Kenilworth,* to the
scenes of the northwestern islands of Scotland and the
children of the storm.   Tom Dibdin, however, followed the
romantic imagination of the Great Unknown wherever it
went or whatever it pictured in the Waverley novels.
Dibdin at once perceived the wealth of dramatic material
in this tale of the people of Zetland.   Within two weeks, his
transcript went into rehearsal at the Surrey, where it opened
during the first week of January, 1822.[33]

Nothing essential is lost in his version.   Something is
indeed gained by a few transpositions and modifications for

[32] *Gentleman's Magazine* 1. 66;   Clarence,. pp. 269, 482;   Ireland
2. 52;   Brown 2. 55, 457;   Levey and O'Rorke, *Annals of the Dublin
Stage,* pp. 41, 60.
[33] Printed in London and Baltimore in 1822.

the sake of unity and suspense. Thus the second wreck is introduced in the fourth of the six scenes that make up the second act. In the novel, the identity of Cleveland is not revealed until somewhat after the duel in the moon-light between him and his half-brother Mordaunt under the windows at the home of Magnus Troil at Hofra; in the drama it is made known almost at once after the duel. On the contrary, some minor details introduced early in the novel are kept until toward the end of the drama.

Enough of the rugged scenery has been transferred to the play by Dibdin. There one finds the snug house of Magnus Troil at Hofra, scene of many convivial nights; the barren waste of moor, with the house of Mertoun resting gloomily, like its owner, not far from the ocean; the land-scapes in sunshine, rain, and moonlight, shifting back and forth like drops in the theatre. Some of the painted views showed all of these, but the most picturesque scene is that of the curved bay at sunrise, with a handsome privateer, and a sort of pleasure-vessel, both riding easily at anchor. An arched rock appears in the foreground, with a picture of the sea showing through it in the far distance. Finally, one of the painted canvases revealed the fight between the revenue cutter and the pirate craft, in full view of the dwellers on the island.

Norna herself is a natural companion of the wilful storm, as it sweeps across the deserted moorland. She arrives just in time to save Mordaunt from the steel of Cleveland, when they fight a duel under the windows of the fair Brenda and Minda at Magnus Troil's. Her wildness has more of the elemental than the madness of Meg Merrilies, with some-thing more also of romantic tension. It is entirely possible, however, that, ere this play reached the stage, a considerable part of the theatre-public had tired of the long line of the type represented, only with individual variations, by Meg, Helen Macgregor, Madge Wildfire, Magdalene Graeme, old Elspeth, and finally here by Norna of Fitful Head.

Mordaunt himself is a man of moods, only somewhat different from his father, who sits brooding for years at home, while his son goes and comes almost at will. Both novel and play are full of dramatic ironies. Norna moves in the midst of them, while she watches over the son of the man who once loved her, protecting him from the wrath of Cleveland, who—but Norna does not know it—is both her son and Mertoun's. Mertoun himself once called Norna a quack and a witch, not knowing that she is the Ulla Troil who bore him Cleveland years ago.

These ironic situations are well emphasized by Dibdin. Besides, he draws many clear portraits. Taking a few from his gallery, we behold the gay and treacherous Cleveland, as much of the pirate as his father, Mertoun, once was before him; the tricky peddler, Brice Snailsfoot, pitting his soul against the driving of shrewd and dishonest bargains, a lover of petty gossip, and bearer of trouble throughout the island; the contented Magnus Troil, Udaller of Zetland, master in his own house, hospitable to the last extremity, proud of his fair daughters, and a kindly foster-parent to the lonely Mordaunt.

As one peruses the text of the Dibdin romantic comedy, one marvels not at all that the *Theatre Magazine* predicted that this would rival Dibdin's renowned *Heart of Midlothian*.[34] If the cast for the Surrey had been of higher calibre, the run might have been long, instead of merely respectable. After an early drama had finished its course, the Caledonian Theatre in Edinburgh turned to Dibdin's *Pirate,* with a happy result in 1825.[35]

Three rivals followed in rapid succession. Within a week after Dibdin introduced his transcript, the Olympic Theatre brought out a similar draft written by J. Robinson Planché, while Drury Lane pushed forward a third on the next

[34] 2. 206.
[35] Dibdin, p. 243.

evening. Thus, by January 15, 1822, all three pieces were running simultaneously in London. Some undesignated composer provided good music for the Olympic drama, of which the songs far outranked the lyrics at Drury Lane. The scenery of Planché's drama imitated that of Dibdin's. At least it included some of the same pictures, such as the rustic home of Troil, the shore and the wrecks, the stormy moorland, and a rugged view, bordered by 'a green loch, as described in the novel.'[36]

For some reason not fully cleared up by the contemporary allusions, the Drury Lane piece met with stubborn resistance on the opening night. Though it was subsequently revised somewhat, it ran for a total of only nine times, even with such favorites in the cast as Cooper, S. Penley, Munden, Mrs. W. West, and Madame Vestris.[37] For this and the Bath performances, Mrs. West impersonated Norna, a character well suited to her style of acting.[38]

Proudly heralded as licensed for the Royal in Edinburgh, a new *Pirate; or, The Reimkennar of Zetland* started on a brief course, March 29, 1822. New scenery was painted for the occasion, and the critics commended the 'good taste of the Manager' in getting for the public a wholly original drama; yet the patrons remained cold toward it, as the *Dramatic Review* at last perforce had to admit.[39]

THE FORTUNES OF NIGEL

One morning in October, 1821, Sir Walter Scott, Daniel Terry, and John G. Lockhart paced the banks of the Tweed, while the author read the first instalment of the *Fortunes of Nigel,* fresh from the hand of the master. All agreed

---

[36] As the undated London text announces.
[37] *Gentleman's Magazine,* part 1, p. 80. This operatic form was never published.
[38] Genest 9. 145.
[39] 8. 107; Dibdin, p. 308.

that here was 'every prospect of a fine field for the art of Terry-fication.'[40]   Once again Terry failed to profit; for Edward Ball, within three weeks after the novel came out, was the first to rush his play into rehearsal for the Surrey Theatre.   Audiences continued to be pleased for a time, with Bengough in the humorsome and droll King James; Burroughs, a spirited and independent Nigel; Buckingham, a stingy and miserable Trapbois; and Gomery, indeed a generous Heriot, jeweler and money-lender to the impecunious king.[41]

Each of the three acts rises to a high pitch of excitement. The play opens with the wounding of Richard Monoplies in front of the shop of Tunstall.   The main details of the novel are followed, with special emphasis on the scenes of the negotiations of Nigel with the King, ending at last when the monarch pledges the royal jewels as a guarantee that he will eventually pay his honest debts.   Closing the first act, we see the spirited encounter of Nigel with Lord Delgarno near the forbidden precincts of the public walk, followed by the flight of Nigel to 'Alsatia,' the refuge of insolvent debtors, over which old Trapbois presides.

Here Lord Nigel is seen trying to get the old miser to give him a generous loan.   In the meantime, the friends of the young lord are continuing an energetic search.   Margaret Ramsay, who admires Nigel, tries vainly to make some of her wealthy friends understand that the lord is in need of funds, since King James refuses to pay Nigel's loan to him.   Excellent comedy is provided in one scene, where Jen Vincent and Mrs. Suddlechop, during the absence of the master of the house, are fooling, and taking a nip or two for company.   Trapbois at last succeeds in obtaining from

---

[40] Lockhart 2. 260.

[41] *Theatre Magazine*, 3. 84.   This drama bears no relationship to Ball's operatic *Crown Jewels*, which is based on D. F. E. Auber's celebrated *Diamants de la Couronne*.

Nigel the paper of James which pledges the crown-jewels. Next the old Hebrew is seen counting up his own store of gold, when suddenly he falls into the hands of some extortioners who have crept silently into his private sanctum. Nigel is attracted by the commotion, and fires a shot which fatally wounds one of the intruders; but Trapbois is also killed in the fracas.

The final act shows how Nigel cleverly escapes from his dangerous refuge in Alsatia. Margaret Ramsay, disguised as a young man, obtains an interview with the King, during which she exacts a definite promise from him that Nigel shall not be prosecuted for fighting with Lord Dalgarno in the grounds which the King has forbidden to gentlemen who have debts of honor to settle. Yet Nigel is soon afterward arrested, but is promptly ransomed from the Tower by Dick Monoplies, who secures a final promise from the elusive James that Nigel shall no longer be molested. Then the King himself visits Nigel to inform him of his release, and to assure him that his second arrest was only a little joke. In the meantime, Lord Dalgarno has been caught trying to elope with Mrs. Christie, though he is not picked off by a chance shot, as described in the novel. To bring down the house, the generous Dick Monoplies appears, somewhat inebriated, but inordinately proud that he has won for his bride the misshapen, but highly gifted, Martha Trapbois.

In this drama Ball did a creditable piece of adaptation. The portrait of King James vividly shows his dialect and mannerisms, superstition, and at times rather undignified fears. Years afterward Ball mentioned this play as the real foundation of his dramatic successes.[42]

Six months later, Covent Garden introduced a second drama, known as *Nigel; or, The Crown Jewels,* which was staged by Charles Kemble, who requested Isaac Pocock to

---

[42] *Thirty-five Years of a Dramatic Author's Life,* pp. 94, 103. See Ireland I. 490.

imitate Ball's play, after Kemble had admired it at the Surrey. Very unfortunately indeed, Pocock cast his drama into five acts of blank verse. He likewise changed some of the details of the plot, without gaining any pronounced advantage.

Some of the more noticeable revisions of the story may be mentioned. Instead of being shot, Dalgarno is made ridiculous and contemptible. Trapbois meets death by strangling, when Dalgarno and his accomplice steal into his rooms in Alsatia. Comedy is made out of the awkwardness of Nigel, and his dislike for being identified in public places. James carries the royal jewels in his hat. When Nigel, who has them as a pledge, leaves them on a table below-stairs, his landlady admires each gem in turn, offering a humorous monologue. Two parts introduce a rather antiquated style of playcraft: one laid in the tap of the inn, with roistering and songs; the other in the Tower, with much scurrying about when Margaret Ramsay is discovered there in the dress of a page. The texts allude to a mask that followed the main play.[43]

Pocock's effort ran for only one night, though the staging and cast were fairly good. Three contemporary magazines disliked it, and Genest called it 'a poor piece,' inspired solely by 'the rage for dramatizing the novels attributed to Sir Walter Scott.'[44] Drury Lane apparently intended to bring out Terry's version, but Pocock outwitted them, and his failure put an end for the time being to all similar efforts.

William H. Murray revised the Ball text for Edinburgh, calling his adaptation *George Heriot; or, The Fortunes of Nigel*. This amended form ran for eighteen nights, with several revivals during the same season and in other years. He excised one scene of the tower as being 'tedious,' modified many of the lines to suit conditions of acting in Scotland, abandoned the original music, made considerable of

[43] Printed, 1823, in London.
[44] 9. 199.

the doings in Alsatia, and introduced the Duke of Buckingham and his cronies in some lively action.[45]

J. C. Dibdin recalled this melodrama as 'another of those
trump cards,' quite worthy for the same hand that included
Guy Mannering and *Rob Roy.* Mason as Trapbois won a
triumph, while Denham, with his Scotch burr and knowledge
of the character of King James, received the warm commendation of Walter Scott himself.[46]

Forty-five years after these first Nigel dramas held the
boards, Andrew Halliday composed three plays in honor
of the centenary of the birth of Scott. These were the
King o' Scots, Amy Robsart, and *Rebecca,* with music for
all three by the talented Irish composer, W. C. Levey. In
the first of these, Samuel Phelps doubled the parts of James
and Trapbois, while Lilian Adelaide Neilson supported him
as Margaret Ramsay at Drury Lane late in September, 1868.
Dutton Cook described the crowds on the stage as 'animated,'
the scenes in Alsatia and the hunt in Greenwich Park with
real hounds as 'triumphs' of realism, and the style of Phelps
well suited to the language and spirit of the original
narrative.[47]

Blackwood said of Phelps: 'His command of the Scotch
dialect is wonderful in an Englishman; his walk, his look,
his attitude, are as palpable indications of character as the
language he employs. . . . As an exhibition of how a great
performer can vivify a whole play, in spite of all drawbacks,
we pronounce the acting of Mr. Phelps, in some respects,
without parallel on the modern stage.'[48] Chatterton said
years afterward that he as manager turned to Halliday to
save the house from disaster, when 'Shakespeare spelled
ruin and Byron bankruptcy.'[49] This drama also won great

[45] Printed in Edinburgh, 1823, and in *Waverley Dramas,* 1872.
[46] *Annals,* p. 305.
[47] *Nights at the Play* 1. 81.
[48] Quoted in *The Stage and its Stars* 1. 105.
[49] Stirling, *Old Drury Lane* 1. 282; Odell, *Shakespeare from
Betterton to Irving* 2. 258.

applause at Liverpool, Sadler's Wells, Astley's, the Princess, Dundee, and other playhouses.[50]

WAVERLEY

After eight seasons of delay, this first romance by Scott went through 'a sort of Terry-fication,' for the entertainment of the King at Liverpool in 1822, when all the dignitaries of the town, assisted by numerous Highlanders in their plaids, reminded the people of several scenes in *Waverley*. Corbett Ryder followed the suggestion a year afterward, with his *Waverley; or, The Forty-Five,* at the Caledonian in Edinburgh, which the *Theatrical Observer* scored for huddling the scenes together, and for missing 'many beautiful incidents' of the novel.[51]

Edward Ball, in his operatic play, succeeded at both the Adelphi and Coburg Theatres, London, in 1824. Much was made of the pranks of Davie Gellatley, in which part Mrs. Waylett, 'that lovely syren,' sang exquisitely.[52] By excising the first ten or dozen chapters, except for the quarrel at the inn and a few other lively scenes, Ball gave more attention to the hero and his friends, Fergus and Flora M'Ivor.

The closing scenes were notably melodramatic. Both Waverley and Flora appear in turn at the cell of the condemned outlaw. One fine picture shows Fergus standing, with cap in hand, waving adieu to his young friend. Flora now rushes in, supported on either side by the Baron and Rose Bradwardine. She has secreted a dagger in her clothing. Yet the Roman Catholic priest, who has come to offer Fergus the consolation of the Church, fixes her attention, as she thinks of her vow to make way with herself. As the father raises his crozier, Flora 'fixes her eyes torpidly upon it. The dagger falls, and raising her eyes to heaven,

---

[50] Clarence, p. 234; *Dundee Stage,* p. 69.

[51] Lawson, p. 273; Peter Baxter, author of *Drama in Perth.*

[52] Ball, p. 149.

she is sinking into the arms of the other characters, so as to form a fine affecting picture, as the curtain slowly descends to the accompanying music.'[53]

Calcraft tried to improve upon the Ball text. He succeeded only in making it more tedious by extending the speeches, and by reducing all the gay humor and mischief of Davie, with his songs and oddities. About the sole offsets are two or three spectacles, including a scene of 'a grand chorus with Military instruments.' Mackay acted as the Baron, Calcraft himself as Fergus, Murray as the Laird, and Mrs. H. Siddons as Flora. When Calcraft took a benefit on the second evening, the critics were so severe that all subsequent presentations cut down many of the long dialogues.

Evidently Calcraft did not act as Fergus on the night of his benefit. A contemporary critic accused him of 'very conveniently' catching cold, and withdrawing at the last moment from the cast. 'This novelty brought an overflowing house to Mr. Calcraft,' the critic reported, 'and, as according to the Scotch proverb "a fore sorrow is a light sorrow," we trust he bears with Christian patience the unfavorable reception which his drama met with.'[54]

That the piece greatly needed pruning is shown by the remark of a reviewer in Dublin that the performance in Ireland, though 'tolerably well received,' took four hours and nine minutes on the stage.[55]

Numerous attempts to revive or revamp old dramas show that *Waverley* did not call forth much enthusiasm. Jones and Mackay brought out a new version at Perth in 1825, but this proved almost a failure. Some of the forms were tried in New York again in 1829, in Edinburgh at the Adelphi in 1852, and again at the Royal in 1871, without

[53] From London edition, 1824, and *Waverley Dramas,* 1872. Calcraft's play was issued in Edinburgh in 1824.

[54] *Theatrical Observer* 9. 31.

[55] Levey and O'Rorke, *Theatre Royal,* Dublin, p. 152.

creating much of a stir.[56]   Fritz von Holstein, a young officer of the German army, made an opera from the novel in 1852.   This piece came under the favorable notice of the great dramatist, Hauptmann, who finally persuaded the author to abandon his military life in favor of literature and music.[57]

[56] Lawson, p. 273; Ireland 1. 612; *Dict. Nat. Biog.* 41. 37; Clarence, p. 477.
[57] Grove 2. 423.

IX. NOVELS DRAMATIZED AFTER 1825

Twelve of the remaining novels were published after 1823, and most of them appeared in dramatic form within a season. Unless they are not now traceable, having been obscured, or combined with other material, the *Betrothed,* the *Surgeon's Daughter, Castle Dangerous,* and *Count Robert of Paris,* never reached the playhouse.

Even in 1823, Scott was still prompting his friend Terry. 'I think I have something now likely to be dramatical,' wrote the author to the dramatist, on forwarding a copy of his new *Peveril of the Peak.* Yet the facile Ball once again rushed his transcript into action at the Surrey within three or four weeks. Under the name of *Peveril; or, The Days of King Charles the Second,* it ran for over a month during the winter season. One critic mentioned it as 'an excellent adaptation, . . . only varying the catastrophe as regards Fenella, for the purpose of adding to the theatrical effect.'[1]

Scott frankly confessed that he failed somewhat to make this young girl wholly real. Fenella is difficult to describe in a novel, and doubly so in a drama. Yet Ball succeeds in making us understand her position from the start. She is feigning to be a deaf mute, is in love with Julian Peveril, but wants to be generous and self-effacing. Throughout, she is buffeted between conflicting interests, mainly between selfishness and altruistic love. During the first of the drama, she is under the baleful influence of Christian, whom she supposes to be her father. When she discovers that he is only her uncle, she throws off his tutelage, and espouses the cause of her friends. She therefore is willing to protect the King and the Countess of Derby from the plots of Christian and Hudson, the dwarf. Though Scott hints at times that this is the situation, and though at last he makes

---

[1] *Theatrical Magazine,* Feb. 24, 1823.

it evident enough, Ball at once sets us right on some obscure details. Thus, it is not surprising that Fenella willingly stands between the Countess of Derby and the dagger of Christian, after she has revealed the plot of the dwarf.

Genest remarks that the Ball version was 'rather hissed' at Bath.[2] Certain changes were made for Edinburgh, where it first appeared at the minor house, and then at the Royal. The *Caledonian Mercury* censured the whole piece for departing too far from Scott, for making Hudson 'even more absurd than in the novel,' and for reducing Alice and Julian to 'sighing lovers, who have little else to do than vent their passion in an occasional song.'[3]

Yet the story, as printed in the Scotch capital, improved over the Ball text.[4] Julian is made clearer than in both the novel and the other play. He hesitates to stir up any more controversies between Protestants and Catholics, but he will never betray the packet that the Countess of Derby has asked him to carry to her friends in London. This explanation accounts for the strange actions of Julian. From the outset, it is also made plain that Major Bridgenorth considers difference in faith an insuperable barrier to the marriage of Julian and his daughter.

Fenella, too, is brought into clearer focus. One stroke of dramatic genius makes Fenella promise to release Julian if he will renounce his love for Alice Bridgenorth. Again, at the supreme moment of suspense and danger, Buckingham maliciously whispers in Fenella's ear that Christian is only her uncle, not her father. Immediately, she considers all obligations broken, and so she willingly allows the malignant Hudson to stab her, that she may save her King, and atone for the wrong to Julian and Alice.

Both printed texts end with some directions that were

[2] 9. 218.
[3] For April 12, 1823, after the first production in Scotland.
[4] The Edinburgh text is dated 1823; the London is undated.

intended to appeal to the highest motives of melodrama. Of the final tableau we read: 'Music—Fenella, lifting her eyes in silent prayer, joins the hands of Julian and Alice, who kneel; she then sinks back on the Countess of Derby's right arm; the Countess stretches her left hand toward Heaven, forming a fine picture of awe and devotion. A striking group is formed, and the curtain slowly falls.'

Isaac Pocock's operatic *Peveril,* magnificently mounted and 'tolerably well received,' engaged the audience at Covent Garden for nine nights in the autumn of 1826. Charles E. Horn, credited with the score for a version of Scott's *Black Dwarf,* composed the music.[5]

Of the fifteen lyrics by Pocock, as printed in his *Collected Plays* in London in 1826, there are five glees and choruses, seven solos divided between Alice and Julian, two duets, and one quartet. The opening chorus welcomes the knight of Peveril Castle:

> Look out, look out, 'tis the good old knight,
> He's kind in thy Hall and he's brave in the fight.

Three other numbers by the chorus are 'Boots and Saddle,' a convivial song having no connection with the novel; a grand finale to act second, celebrating the close of the period of danger; and a final 'Long live the King.'

To illustrate the type of sentimental song of musical plays in the age of the Pocock opera, one might quote from the opening solo by Alice, in act one:

> When sorrow speeds the venomed dart,
> And rends the love-lorn maiden's heart,
> Soft music with her silver sound
> Can lull the pain and heal the wound.

---

[5] The musical score and copy of the lyrics, in manuscript form, are a part of the Brown Collection, Boston Public Library. Horn conducted the Handel and Haydn Society, Boston, from 1846 to his death three years later.

One of the songs by Alice Bridgenorth illustrates the lively, humorous type of lyric:

> Oh, I never will marry a Puritan lad,
> So dull and so formal, so solemn and sad.

This is her playful reply to the protest of affection sung by Julian:

> My fairest, my dearest, sweet maid, believe!

No conspicuous other attempts to use *Peveril* on the stage came until the autumn of 1877, when W. G. Wills rather boldly adapted the romance for Drury Lane, under the title of *England in the Days of Charles II*. Only a shadow of the plot, and some of the names of the characters, remained from the novel. Indeed, a contemporary remarked that a knowledge of the story in Scott would only make 'confusion worse confounded' in the drama.[6]

QUENTIN DURWARD

For a novel that was 'frost bit,' as Scott remarked in the spring of 1823 when the public received coldly his *Quentin Durward,* this production attained great honor among the dramatists. They at once seized upon its many vivid incidents as the veritable stuff from which great plays are made. Had some of the versions appeared when the public remained keen for Scott plays, they would have enjoyed a lengthy run. Though not specially popular at home, the novel itself aroused an enthusiasm in France that compared with the interest in *Ivanhoe* in England, and *Rob Roy* in Scotland.

Almost before the ink of the first edition was well dried, the Coburg Theatre brought out a transcript that followed the main thread of the narrative. One contemporary announcement ascribed this drama to 'a Mr. Haines,' an

---

[6] For Sept. 27, 1877. See also Stirling, *Old Drury Lane* I. 315; *Dict. Nat. Biog.* 62. 49. Wills' play was not printed.

actor in the cast making his initial appearance on the boards.[7] It seems to be the work of John Thomas Haines, afterward a prolific purveyor of dramatic wares; but the description by the critics fits fairly well a printed drama, issued in London in 1823, and credited to R. Haworth. The only notable change from Scott is mentioned as a 'trifling deviation' at the end, making Quentin a victor in the lists without specific aid from his Scotch uncle.

Critics disagreed somewhat as to the quality of the acting. One writer said the piece 'was well played.'[7] Another commended the author for his fidelity to the original plot, language, and characterization, but roundly condemned the players. 'Surely, if the author [Scott himself] could see his best parts cut and mangled by the above gentlemen in the most heartless manner,' said the caustic reviewer, 'he would throw down his winged pen and never write for ever.'[8]

Corbett Ryder secured a native version from 'a Gentleman of Edinburgh,' which won 'the greatest applause' at the Caledonian in June, 1823. The *Dramatic Review* felicitated Ryder for having the enterprize to bring out a play written at home, while Murray of the Royal 'we presume, will continue to nauseate the public with the offals of the London theatres, or some of Mr. Calcraft's choice productions.'[8a]

No fault could be found with the choice of the events from the novel. Quentin is given a trifle more of the action than in the novel. The bloody events incident to the murder of the Bishop of Liège are wisely omitted. Toward the end of the story, the scenes become more forceful, leading up to the final tournament, in its picturesque detail and colorful settings. Some excuse may be allowed to the Scotch author on the ground of patriotism in making the Duke of

[7] *Mirror of the Stage*, June 23, 1823.
[8] *Theatre Magazine* 2. 304.
[8a] 2. 151, 161.

Burgundy offer this flattering judgment: 'But why should I grudge this youth his preferment; since, after all, it is sense, firmness, and gallantry (which the Scots possess in ample degree) that have put him in possession of *wealth, rank* and *beauty?*' 'Picture is formed—Curtain drops to music.'

Next in order of time is Edward Ball's 'grand' opera, with music by Henry Laurent, Jr., which did not score a hit at Covent Garden in 1848. Though the *Theatrical Times* complained that much of the story had been curtailed, and some of the characters wholly omitted, the printed text shows commendable emphasis on the chief scenes.[9] Necessarily in the operatic form only the main core of incidents could be retained.

As an example of the mid-Victorian final chorus, the ending is fairly typical:

> Like crystal streams, which bubbling start
> From flowery banks to greet yon sky,
> Joy's fountain gushes through this heart,
> In one bright thrill of ecstasy!
> Love and bliss,
> Can know but this,
> This dear delight! Oh, ecstasy!
> Chorus:
> Victoria!
> Victoria!

Several good French operatic dramas drew largely from *Quentin Durward*. Casimir Delavigne based his *Louis XI* on the novel and on the memoirs of Commines. Jean-Marie Mély-Janin's 'slavish imitation,' as *Figaro* called it, ran for more than fifty times from February, 1827, to the time of the death of the dramatist in December. Contemporary journals complained that this piece violated some of the rules of classic art, but the author himself, reviewing his own play in the *Quotidienne,* asserted that it had unity of

---

[9] First acted Dec. 6, 1848. *Theatrical Times,* Dec. 7, 16, 1848.

action, and some scenes not taken directly from Scott.* *Figaro,* in a piquant and humorous rejoinder, again insisted that Mély-Janin had made a play that violates the spirit of French prose drama. Michelot as Louis, and Firmin as Durward, gained no little fame in this production.[10]

Expensively mounted, and well acted by Jourdin as the Scotch lad, and Coudre as Louis XI, a version appeared at the Opéra Comique, late in March, 1858. This serious poetic drama in three acts, resembling the average French opera, was the work of Cormon and Michel Carré, with music by Gavaërt. The authors skilfully performed their task of 'cutting out of W. Scott's novel the dialogue of a three-act drama. . . . interesting, clear, and complete. . . . We know of no grand opera in five acts that is conceived with wider proportions and lasts longer.'[11]

This French operatic play, which may have been published, seems to have suggested the *Louis the Eleventh* by J. A. Coupland. If the English form shows the excellence of the original, Mély-Janin's play must have been high above the average of its class. Dunois, for one example, improves over his counterpart in the novel, in that he is shown vacillating between the daughter of Louis, to whom he is formally betrothed, and his real regard for Isabelle of Croye, who at times acts as if she despises him. Coupland well shows that Louis, for this reason, designs to have the Countess fall into the ruthless hands of the Wild Boar of the Ardennes, as William de la Marck is named. Another wise revision shows that the Bishop of Liège dies in a perfectly fair fight, and not by assassination. Scott richly embroidered the scenes of the conflict of wills between Louis and the Duke of Burgundy, when the latter accuses the wily French king of playing fast and loose with him. Coupland

---

[10] For Feb. 16, 17, 19, 20, 1827; *Quotidienne* and *Constitutionnel* for Feb. 19; Partridge, p. 225.

[11] *Moniteur Universel,* March 28, 1858.

makes this situation the climax of his drama, and not the scenes of blood toward the close.[12]

Apart from the use of suggestions from Louis for his *Richelieu,* a number of late attempts have been made to revive the fame of this subject in dramatic form.[13]

ST. RONAN'S WELL

'We had a new piece t'other night from *St. Ronan,*' wrote Sir Walter Scott to Terry in the summer of 1824, 'which, though I should have supposed very ill adapted to the stage, succeeded wonderfully—chiefly by Murray's acting the Old Nabob, which he did very well. Mackay also made an excellent Meg Dods, and kept his gestures more within the verge of female decorum than I thought possible.'[14]

Scott is speaking of the piece announced at the Royal as the work of R. Planché, who might be J. Robinson Planché, a well known and prolific author of different types of drama. For a benefit-performance, a bit afterward, Scott himself added a characteristic humorous epilogue for Mackay to recite as a curtain-call, in the character and style of Meg Dods. This proved tremendously popular.

St. Ronan's soon lost caste, however, in the playhouse. Along with other dramas for the Scott centenary in 1871, M'Neill revised some old play, or made a similar one for the Edinburgh Princess, where it won good applause for nearly a month.[15] Besides a Ronan piece by David D. Fisher for Belfast in 1876, only the sentimental romance by Richard Davey and W. Herries Pollock commanded any

[12] Coupland's play was issued in London in 1889. Not having any text of the older drama at hand, one cannot tell how closely this is followed by Coupland.

[13] See list of plays at the end of this discussion for other titles. See also Paul Wilstach's article in the *Bookman,* April, 1902.

[14] Lockhart 2. 341.

[15] Since M'Neill married a daughter of Corbett Ryder, this may have been a manuscript that came from the old days.

notice on the stage.[16] Instead of dying a demented and wronged woman, as in the novel, Clara Mowbray lived on, 'leaving the spectators to imagine that the heroine will end her days as the wife of Francis Tyrel.'[17]

Only because James Ballantyne absolutely insisted, Scott had canceled some twenty-four pages of the original draft of his novel, for the sole purpose of toning down the idea that 'a high-born damsel of the nineteenth century could suffer any personal contamination.' The author always maintained that this change spoiled the *dénouement* of his story, and once he said to Ballentine, 'You never would have quarreled with it, James, had the thing happened to a girl in gingham. The silk petticoat can make little difference, either in fact or in fiction.'[18]

REDGAUNTLET

Besides 'a milk-and-water adaptation' brought out at the Surrey, in the midsummer of 1824,[19] and a final version by M'Neill in 1871, only one other Redgauntlet play won favorable consideration. Murray produced a fair transcript, 'very probably from his pen,' in Edinburgh. Mackay was so realistic in Peter Peebles that many said this part by him excelled all his others in the Waverley list. Emphasis was laid on the songs of the lovers, but the speeches of the tedious old litigant were much curtailed.[20]

Two drafts from *Redgauntlet* appeared briefly on the stages of Paris, and one was accepted by the Théâtre des Nouveautés, but seems never to have been used in the original form. This last is called the *Quittance du Diable; or, The Devil's Receipt* in English, and is in the form of a

---

[16] Clarence, p. 395.

[17] *London Times,* June 13, 1893.

[18] Lockhart 2. 340.

[19] *Theatre Magazine* 6. 249.

[20] *Caledonian Mercury,* May 29, 1825; *Dict. Nat. Biog.* 39. 415. See also Dibdin, p. 484, and Boyd, p. 68.

short three-act tableau drama written by Alfred de Musset about 1830.[21] The substance is taken from that picturesque tale told by old blind Wandering Willie Stevenson in the eleventh letter of the novel. Only the young laird, son of the original Redgauntlet of Scott, and Stenie Steenson, are taken from the story, while a young lady and her governess, Johny, and some minor characters, were added by de Musset. Old Sir Robert enters the account only as a skeleton in the family tomb, to which Stenie and his guide, John, the rambler, proceed, and bring off the receipt in triumph, in spite of the ghostly crew made up of the companions of the old laird in a sort of hell above ground.

Stenie is provided with a sweetheart, the young lady mentioned, who has to be separated from her governess before the real love-making may proceed. Johny is accused of poaching by the young laird, and in revenge he conducts Stenie to the tomb to obtain his due in form of the receipt for rent paid to the elder Redgauntlet. Thus, we observe, that only half comes from the story told in the novel by Scott. Indeed, the piece is deflowered of its picturesque and vital elements, save for the scene at the tomb.

Another piece drew good houses for thirty nights at the Opéra Comique in 1834. This musical transcript, named the *Revenant,* seems to have little or no connection with the de Musset version. It follows all the main details of the novel, including the payment of the rent to the old Redgauntlet by Stenie, the death of the violent old laird before he could make out the receipt, and the journey of the tenant to the lower regions to secure his quittance. The piece touches the other possibly at one point, in that there is a 'commercial traveler of the devil,' who leads Stenie to Hell for the receipt.[22]

[21] Draper informs us that the *Revue Bleue,* 2 and 9 May, 1914, prints the complete text.

[22] *Figaro,* Jan. 3, 1834; *National,* Jan. 4, 1834. No mention is made of the author, but Gornis prepared the music.

Paul Henri Foucher and Jules Edouard Alboise de Pujol based an opera on the tradition of a wonderful sign that appeared on the forehead of any Redgauntlet who might become angry.*   An abandoned child also provides a chief motive, but the rest of the novel appears only in barest outlines.   It was acted at the Ambigu-Comique on February 18, 1843, after which time no further notice has been found in the journals or dramatic criticism of the period.[23]

THE TALISMAN

Several dramatists found the romantic elements of the *Talisman* highly suitable for melodrama.   Once again Samuel Beazley, a maker of composite dramas, obtained the lead with his *Knights of the Cross; or, The Hermit's Prophecy*.   With music by Bishop, and the difficult rôle of Berengaria taken by Mrs. W. West, this affair won a good hearing at Drury Lane in February, 1825, after which the text was printed.

To the reader, the action seems hard to follow, even though some of the salient events are well set forth.   Some of the main threads of the story are the visit of Sir Kenneth of Scotland to the hermit, all the events growing out of the removal of the English banner by the Austrians, and the arrest of Kenneth, his rescue of Richard, and the final engagement to Edith Plantagenet.

Neither the first playbill for the opening night, June 22, 1825, nor the *Caledonian Mercury* mentions the name of the author of a Talisman play at the Royal, Edinburgh.   This 'new historical drama' proved a genuine hit, running for sixteen nights, with Murray as the Knight of the Leopard, and Mrs. H. Siddons as Edith.   It might have been merely a revision of Beazley's piece, which found favor in New York in the spring and again in the winter season, 1828.[24]

[23] *Revue et Gazette des Théâtres*, Feb. 23, 1843.
[24] Brown 1. 34, 37 ; Ireland, pp. 549, 595.

Later efforts include a printed text by Catharine Swanwick, a version for schools by Maud Findlay in 1917, in which all the major incidents are delightfully presented, and a film that was released by the Associated Authors in 1923. All the usual events are presented in the scenario, with no sparing of the picturesque backgrounds. Some additional thrills are provided by a surprise of the main party of the Crusaders by the forces of Saladin, but the attackers are beaten off by a small company of English and Scots knights. Kenneth also rescues Edith from the unholy power of Conrad, and Richard in person fights Saladin in a spirited combat, out of which comes a treaty of peace and fellowship.[25]

Andrew Halliday sought to bring forward all the picturesque colorings incident to the romantic adventures of the royal lovers. His *Richard Coeur de Lion,* at Drury Lane in 1874, despite his close adherence to the original story, brought upon his head the condemnation of the reviewers in the *Athenæum,* who called it a 'pageant or circus entertainment.' As a final touch of contempt, the critics flung this dictum to the management of the playhouse: 'The days of burlesque must shortly come to an end, since human ingenuity can scarcely outgo, or human voices outrave, the extravagances of that which is put forward as a serious entertainment.'[26]

Edward Stirling, who managed the theatre at the time, mentions two of the 'spectacular' elements: a troup of acrobats, and a Moorish fête, introduced to please King Richard at his request. He also adds that the 'lack of female interest unfortunately rendered the piece a comparative failure.'[27]

With reference to travesties, the critics may have had in mind Brough Brothers' *Talisman; or, King Richard Coeur de Lion,* which interesting bit of drollery had a good run at

[25] Information from scenario published in advertising circular.
[26] For October 3, 1874.
[27] *Old Drury Lane* I. 297.

Drury Lane in 1853.[28]   Twenty years later, J. F. McArdle also made a hit in Liverpool, when he produced his *Plantagenet Preserved in a Salad-in Pickle*.   This, or else a third burlesque, appeared at the Philharmonic, London, in March, 1875.[29]

Few of the operatic transcripts received any special attention, save for a posthumous work by Michael W. Balfe, and Foucher's *Richard en Palestine* in Paris.[30]   The celebrated Irish composer spent some time during the closing year of his life in trying to get his opera produced by an English manager, though he refused an opportunity offered by the reigning Napoleon to produce it in Paris.*   Four years after the death of Balfe, the original libretto by Arthur Morrison was translated by Signor G. Zaffira into Italian, and the music was revised and augmented by Sir George Macfarren. As *Talismano,* the revised opera gained moderate attention at Her Majesty's Opera House, London, in June, 1874, the chief parts being taken by Miss Christine Nilsson, Signor Rota, and Signor Campanini.

Mattison omitted the scene of the curing of Richard, making no mention of any talisman, and also the arrest of Kenneth for allowing the Austrians to steal the English banner.   Otherwise most of the chief incidents of the novel are preserved.   Accordingly, the affairs of the two lovers assume a major place, rising to the grand duet of the Knight of the Leopard and Edith at the tent of Queen Berengaria, who has invited Kenneth, and who thus causes him to neglect the English banner.

The *Athenæum* censured the libretto for being over-picturesque, and the music for 'transformations' in the manner of the grand operas of Meyerbeer and Wagner.[31]

[28] *Drama Register,* 1853, p. 113.
[29] Clarence, p. 435, and information from the Liverpool Public Library.
[30] *Siècle,* Oct. 14, 1844; Partridge, p. 288.
[31] For June 13 and 20, 1874.

When the opera proved more successful in 1878, the critics of the *Theatre* argued that the original lack of interest derived from Zaffira's translation in a form not suited to the music of Balfe.[32]   In Dublin, the former home of Balfe, all his operas called forth great enthusiasm. When the *Talismano* appeared, however, the clergy denounced the scene that showed a chapel and altar on the stage, with nuns and acolytes in procession. 'This piqued the curiosity of the general public, and proved a capital advertisement.'[33]   In 1891 a worthy revival of the opera occurred in Liverpool. It was used several times in New York, especially at the Academy of Music in 1875 and 1878, and at the Irving Place Theatre in 1894.[34]

WOODSTOCK

'Don't fancy that I am going to stay at home to brood idly on what can't be helped. I was at work on *Woodstock* when you came in, and I shall take up the pen the moment I get back from court.' These brave words of Scott to a friend on January 17, 1826, allude to the announcement only that morning of the failure of the firms in which the author had allied himself in publishing the novels. Just before *Woodstock* came from the press in May, Lady Scott died, after a somewhat prolonged illness. These, and other troubles during this spring, might have crushed a man of lesser resolution.[35]

From the time of the financial catastrophe, Scott produced five long and three short stories, besides numerous prose criticisms and historical works. By this date the vogue of the novels on the stage had greatly declined, though now and then a genuine success had its day before the public.

---

[32] For August, 1878.
[33] *Athenæum,* Oct. 3, 1874.
[34] Brown 2. 78, 87, 235; Clarence, p. 435.
[35] Lockhart 2. 481.

Isaac Pocock compiled the first dramatization of *Woodstock*. Yet, in spite of competent acting by favorites like Charles Kemble, Cooper, Warde, and Farren, this ran for but six nights at Covent Garden in 1826.[36] There were good portraits of Henry Lee, the old Cavalier, of Cromwell, the stern, superstitious, and at times not unkindly general, of the gallant Everard, and of the mysterious Louis Kerneguy, as King Charles II in disguise called himself. Altogether, this is indeed a drama of characterization more than of action. Some excellent dramatic action occurs, however, in the scene where Cromwell is deeply touched on seeing his own picture on the *back* of a portrait of the King, and also in the scene where Everard fancies that the visitor is too friendly with his own beloved Alice Lee.

One modification by some of the Edinburgh dramatists ran for only seven nights.[37] In 1892 George R. Sims and Robert Buchanan prepared a version for the Adelphi. Between these two plays, the interval is bridged by several French melodramas. *Charles II,* by Alexandre Duval, maintained its lead for a score of nights in 1823. Except in putting Charles at the head of his partisans, this drama followed Scott in most details; for it was recognized by the public as one more clever specimen of the type that Duval had been writing, and the playgoers applauding, for more than twenty years.[38] *Charles Stuart* by de Croisy and Beraud fared less well, because Charles became ridiculous, and Sir Henry Lee appeared 'as one of the many unhappy fathers we see in every melodrama.'[39] Albert Lee and Everard have become one person, who does much to assist Charles to escape. Some mountaineers are also introduced, of a kind that one fails to notice around Woodstock in Scott's

---

[36] Genest 9. 350.
[37] Dibdin, p. 318.
[38] *Figaro,* March 12, 1828.
[39] *Pandore,* Sept. 9, 1826.

picture of the estate.   Though numerous speeches are carried bodily from the novel to the play, the revisions just noted, and the general spirit, make it more French than English.

Page de Woodstock, a third French sentimental play, excels the other two in fidelity and Scottish spirit.   Some scenes are shifted, a few of the names are changed, and many details are omitted to secure a greater unity of the whole.   The King and Everard all but come to actual blows over Alice; but Albert and Charles finally depart, before the troops arrive, leaving Alice and the plot to manage themselves.   According to Draper, this piece, which ran at the Vaudeville in March, 1828, is credited to Xavier de Maistre, Duvart, and Dupeuty.[40]

I Puritani by Count Pepoli, and Bellini and Romand's *Dernier Marquis,* are somewhat reminiscent of certain parts of *Woodstock.*[41]

The Fair Maid of Perth

Scott grew to consider most of his people in the novels from the standpoint of good dramatic timber.   Once he wrote in his journal: 'Suppose a man's nerves, supported by feelings of honor, or, say, by the spur of jealousy, sustaining him against constitutional timidity to a certain point, then suddenly giving way, I think something might be produced. . . . I am hard up as far as imagination is concerned, yet the world calls for novelty.   Well, I'll try my brave coward, or cowardly brave man.   *Valeat quantum.'*

Out of this grew Conachar in the *Fair Maid of Perth,* which novel the playwrights recognized as uncommonly dramatic.   Henry M. Milner and Thomas Hailes Lacy were the first to reach the stage with their play at the Coburg in June, 1822.   All the main incidents are wisely transferred to the boards.   Special notice is taken of the

[40] P. 28.
[41] Hubbard, *Cyclopedia of Music* 4. 153.

picturesque 'bier right,' to determine who murdered Oliver Proudfute. Many nooks and corners of Perth are represented in the scenery. The Highland lakes, with the gathering of the clans, the choice of a new chieftain, and the banquet of the warriors, appear in natural colorings.

As a minor action in the drama, the Prince follows Catherine Glover, the Fair Maid of Perth, and her father to the Highlands, where he is imprisoned and finally put to death by Bonthron, though Catherine lets herself down by a rope into his dungeon, in the vain hope that she may assist the Prince to escape.

The last act shows the vivid details of the battle of the Inch. By this time, Conachar has proved himself a craven, and Smith has taken his place as leader of one of the clans. Two powerful scenes conclude the action. In one the old king pitiably bewails the death of his recreant son. In the other we view the romantic grounds of St. Hunan, with the Falls of Campsie Linn as the background of the last struggles of Conachar, the 'brave coward,' who once held so important a place in the home and affections of Simon Glover and the fair maid of Perth.

If this production had reached the stage during the early vogue of the Waverley dramas, it would have created something of a sensation. It is one of the best of the later plays, reminding a reader of the old spectacles like *Kenilworth* and *Ivanhoe,* when great audiences flocked to the playhouse to see everything new that came from the works of the Wizard of the North. Some of the special scenery, showing views in Perth and the Highlands, excelled anything of like nature after 1825 in the production of Scott dramas.[42]

During 1828 also, the company of Charles Bass brought out their *Fair Maid of Perth* at Perth, Dundee, and in 1829 at Edinburgh.[43] This version, which some attributed to

[42] Printed in Lacy's *Acting Drama,* vol. 71, undated.
[43] Dibdin, p. 345; Lawson, *Scots Stage,* p. 276.

Bass himself, 'was welcomed by an overflowing house' when first produced for some nine nights—a good run for a town like Perth. D. V. Bell, also in 1828, compiled an original play, which ran during the year at two houses in New York City, and in the following year was revived. It never was printed.[44]

St. Georges and Adenis furnished the libretto, and Georges Bizet the music, for an operatic *Jolie Fille de Perth* for the Théâtre Lyrique in Paris, late in December of 1867. Théophile Gautier commended the libretto for cleverness, but said that only Glover, Catherine, Smith, and one or two others appear, and they indeed in much modification from Scott. 'The local color of Scotland that gives such charm to the novel is poorly represented in the plaids and the quadrilles of the actors.'[45]

The Two Drovers

H. Goff compiled a two-act piece in six scenes from Scott's tale that was entitled *Two Drovers*. The dramatization named *Second Sight; or, Prediction,* appeared first at the Surrey in 1828, later at the Queen's, and finally at Perth in September during Hunt Race Week. Both the tradition of the Highlands and the warnings of a sibyl are given considerable prominence in the story and in the transcript.

Two friendly drovers are leading their flocks toward the grazing fields of Cumberland. Robin Oig (Little Robin) remains behind a moment to snatch a last kiss from the lips of his sweetheart. Old Elspeth, a Highland woman given to clairvoyance, solemnly warns him that there is blood on his dagger. She walks three times around him, stops suddenly, and cries, 'The music stops.' At last she persuades Robin to leave his dagger with another shepherd.

On arriving a bit late at the grazing-fields, impulsively he

[44] Ireland i. 613.
[45] Grove i. 334; and Gautier in *Moniteur Universel,* Jan. 6, 1868.

quarrels with his friend over precedence in taking the most desired place for the sheep. Later in the day, some men at the inn during the noon-hour taunt Robin to the point where he feels he must fight the other shepherd, or be proclaimed a craven. He is thrown in a wrestling-bout by the rival shepherd. Somewhat bruised in the tussle and greatly mortified, Robin rushes out, soon meets the shepherd who has his dagger, gets him to give it back, and then quickly returns to pick a quarrel with Harry Wakefield, the other man, who now makes all friendly advances in good faith. Robin, however, refuses to forget, and opportunely stabs his former friend to death, just as old Elspeth and the sweetheart rush in to prevent him from taking such a rash step. In utter contrition for his failure to heed the prophetic warnings, Robin Oig now buries his blade in his own breast. Then follows the concluding 'picture of consternation and horror.'[46]

The Royal in Edinburgh produced a similar play in 1828, which J. C. Dibdin thinks differed materially from the London piece by Goff. No further evidence is available, except that it was revived four years later, and then finally in 1841, when the artist M'Ian created a deal of favorable comment in his portraiture of Robin.[47]

ANNE OF GEIERSTEIN

No particular notice seems to have been taken of the romantic story of the fair Anne of the mountains, except for a single play in New York in 1834. The Bowery Theatre made elaborate preparations, which called for the closing of the playhouse for a week, the painting of a number of new scenes, and some enlarged space for the stage. 'Every effort has been made,' said the announcements in the *Post*, 'to produce this effective drama in a style

[46] Printed in 1828.
[47] Dibdin, p. 324.

superior to anything hitherto witnessed.' During the scene of the battle of Liège, sixteen horses appeared on the stage. Other vivid scenes showed the rescue of Arthur by Anne from the tree which overhung the chasm, the rising of the mist, 'as described in the novel,' and finally all the splendors of the court of the Duke of Burgundy.[48]

THE HIGHLAND WIDOW

Dougal the Piper; or, The Highland Widow, drawn from one of the short narratives of Scott, ran for nine nights in Edinburgh in 1836, with a successful revival in 1852.[49]

[48] March 2, 1834.
[49] Dibdin, pp. 369, 431

X. A BROAD VIEW OF THE WAVERLEY
DRAMAS

Offhand, one might think that a master of playcraft could transfer at will any good novel into a fine acting drama. As illustrations, one might offer a respectable list of transcripts from fiction since the age of Shakespeare. Yet the failures are probably more numerous and more conspicuous. Recent authorities therefore inform us that it is indeed considerably harder to make a suitable play out of a popular novel than it is to make a wholly original one. Brander Matthews and Bliss Perry agree that this is true.[1] The former points out that ten or a dozen plays were made out of the favorite story called *East Lynne*. The best of the entire lot was a French melodrama written by persons who never had read either an English or a French version of the original, but who obtained the plot at second hand from an actress that retailed it to them in the essential features.

Such dramas succeed, not for following the narrative of this book or that, but because they show that the methods of the stage are not the methods of the printed text. Many novels are not at all dramatic. Thus *Huckleberry Finn,* and even the *Pickwick Papers,* according to Mr. Matthews, are doomed to fail on the stage, since they 'do not contain the stuff out of which a vital play can be made.' Several of the Waverley novels fall undoubtedly into this classification; but the rest have enough incidents that are truly dramatic and theatrical to make excellent stuff for plays.

Scott himself realized that some of his characters are not suitable to the stage without some changing, for he distinctly mentioned Robert Pattison, the old Covenanter, the Antiquary, Fenella, and Clara Mowbray. He feared even for his friend, Nicol Jarvie. Among the rest, one thinks

---

[1] Matthews, *A Book about the Theatre,* p. 100; Perry, *A Study in Prose Fiction,* p. 71.

of Henry Morton, Peter Peebles, Claverhouse, the Earl of Montrose, Cromwell, Charles II, Guy Mannering, Lord Nigel, and Diana Vernon as among the considerable number that had to be touched up more or less for the stage; else, if left too nearly like the originals in the Waverley romances, they failed to please the audiences.

Over against such a list, however, may be placed a longer and more representative group of persons that gave life and blood to melodrama. One may cite some of the best known characters, like Dominie Sampson, Bailie Jarvie, Dugald Dalgetty, Edie Ochiltree, Jeanie Deans, the laird of Dumbiedikes, Caleb Balderstone, Wamba, James I, Meg Dods, Peregrine Touchwood, Louis XI, Meg Merrilies, Rob Roy, Norna of Fitful Head, Magnus Troil, Edgar of Ravenswood, Roland Graeme, Rebecca of York, Mary Queen of Scots, and Richard of the Lion Heart.

Growing out of differences in potential availability, two opposite theories of dramatic composition were applied to the Waverley plays. The average playgoer wanted no emasculation of the originals, and many of the critics were inclined to take precisely the same stand. Later dramatists, and some who held no brief for either the novels or the author, deliberately made revisions to observe dramatic laws, by adding, changing, extending, and unifying both the characters and the plots. For these efforts, they were often roundly damned by the critics, and at times were rewarded by half-empty theatres. In a few extreme instances, these conditions had to be modified. For instance, in England a few endings had to be changed to appease the gods of sentimental comedy; in Scotland, some national traits and beliefs had to be favored in certain plays; in France, the laws of unity held in check the diffusion of material, since they wielded a despotic power over both playwright and dramatic critic.

Suppose we bring now, from scattered parts of the preceding chapters, only a few citations that show how these conditions were exemplified.   First, we call forth the testimony of John Genest.   He once remarked that the large revisions of one play 'disappointed and therefore disgusted' the audience.[2]   He scored Pocock for 'one gross and unpardonable blunder—he has reduced the interesting and spirited part of Diana Vernon to a mere singing girl.'   Dutton Cook called Soane's *Rob Roy* a 'bungling adaptation,' and one other critic pronounced it 'a hoax on the public—a springe to catch woodcocks.'   Oxberry mentioned Jerrold's *Guy Mannering* as 'a bad imitation or rather continuation of the novel.'   *Blackwood* said that characters in one *Antiquary* were 'unfinished etchings from the novel.'   According to one journal, the Edinburgh *Old Mortality* 'appropriates little of that work but two or three of its battles and some of its dulness.'   Dibdin's *Kenilworth* was censured for 'huddling' the incidents into two acts, and his *Bride of Lammermoor,* though good in all other parts, for adding a spectre-lady that 'contributes nothing to the plot, but very much to the annoyance of the nerves of the audience.'   On the other hand, his *Midlothian* was voted by Oxberry, who ought to have known, 'a piece which may fairly be stated to be the best adaptation ever made from a novel.'   Terry, however, made so many revisions in his story of Jeanie Deans that the Birmingham reviewers said tartly: 'Were it possible to suppose Walter Scott deserving of punishment, what could we wish him worse than to see his matchless novels as they are at present dramatized?'

These are only a few instances that show how the dramatists varied from the beaten paths only at their own peril.   After 1850, though the conditions changed somewhat, some of the critics still continued to speak unfavorably of all except the most necessary changes from Scott.   Even as late as 1897, the reviewers spoke unkindly of Robert

[2] Having already been made in footnotes, definite citations to text and page will not be repeated here.

Chambers for modifying too much the story of Scott's *Guy Mannering.*

Minor Adjustments in Waverley Plots

It would be a misconception, however, to believe that none of the narratives changed in minor details in their journey from the publisher to the playhouse. Though the critics sometimes passed them with great reluctance, not a few found favor with audiences. These chiefly have to do with changes in characterization, and notably in some of the tragic endings.

Terry felt justified in making Julia the sister of Colonel Mannering, not the daughter, and Scott evidently approved. Pocock changed the ending of *Rob Roy,* to tone down the fierceness of the hero, and to make the close more picturesque. Artistically, Scott may have been right in the original conception of the ending of *St. Ronan's Well,* but the dramatists, as well as the original publishers, knew that the melodramatic audience would not approve the ruination of Clara Mowbray. Several little changes had to be made in the *Pirate,* to justify the position and prophecies of Norna of Fitful Head. Likewise, *Nigel* had to be made more human and interesting to the average audience; *Peveril* had to be cleared up with reference to Fenella; and even *Lammermoor* needed some changes for the sake of toning down the death of the lovers. Both *Old Mortality* and the *Antiquary* called for certain revision, but no playwright seems to have taken the right cues; for no drama is wholly convincing as to the action of Henry Morton and Claverhouse, or as to the old collector and his friends.

These are some of the more striking changes, but numerous little modifications might also be cited to show that, whether the audiences and critics always recognized the conditions or not, the dramatists themselves knew perfectly well that many such were imperative.

With the multiplication of versions, as in the cases of the *Ivanhoe* and *Bride of Lammermoor,* new devices had to be tried to maintain the public regard. All the dramas, however, emphasize the fervid interviews between the Templar and Rebecca at Torquilstone. Beazley and two of the French dramatists reach the summits of the sensational. Two other versions make Isaac and his daughter the central figures. Three plays emphasize the ballads of Robin Hood and his jolly foresters. One German piece mingles folklore from the Rhine with ballads of the greenwood crew, and Sir Arthur Sullivan composed new music for several of the old glees.

Four of the dramas arrange the ending quite differently from that of the novel. One operatic French piece changes Rebecca into an elusive Léila, who at last turns out to be the long-lost daughter of Cedric's old friend in Palestine. So it comes about naturally that she and Ivanhoe shall wed; Rowena is, of course, dispensed with altogether. Marschner's German opera follows the conventional ending, but brings out more dramatically the loneliness of Rebecca, thus separated by custom and fate from Ivanhoe. One Italian version allows Rebecca to appeal for the affection of the knight, but Ivanhoe gently reminds the Jewess that she and old Isaac must indeed return to their own home in Syria.

In one or two of the Jew of York transcripts, Rowena and Ivanhoe are pictured with their children in the old manorhouse at Rotherwood, where Rebecca and her father sometimes come to visit them; but the fair Jewess has never been touched by love of any knight save Ivanhoe. Thus once more an ending is revised for the edification of sentimental playgoers, who probably did not agree with Scott that the Jewess never could have married Ivanhoe in their time, and that poetic justice does not always demand that virtue must receive definite rewards.

Some have said that *Lammermoor* is the most dramatic of all the Waverley romances. Little changes had to be made here and there to adapt some of the later versions to new conditions of the playhouse, or to create a new interest in an old story, already seen on the stage. Edgar, then, is drowned in Kelpie's Flow; or the lovers are both drowned while trying to escape from Lammermoor to Ravenscrag; or Edgar falls by the dagger of a domestic. In one of the modified forms, Lucy herself is stabbed by Bucklaw, and Edgar by Ashton. Likewise, in some of the operatic plays, the heroine does not die insane, but lives to elope with Edgar, only to be swallowed up with him in the quicksands.

Several authors emphasize the sharing of the token by the lovers. One or two provide a ring, which is divided between them. In one scene, Edgar, returning as Lucy waits at the altar, tears the ring from her hand so violently that an Ashton follows him from the Hall, and issues a challenge, which is promptly accepted. On the contrary, Soane has Lucy remove the ring, and hand it to Edgar as a sign that their troth is ended. This reviser also excises the scene of the wounding of the bridegroom by the infuriated Lucy. Some dramas resemble Simpson's in hardly more than mentioning the madness of the bride, but one French drama makes Lucy rave at length upon the stage.

Some make Lady Ashton the moving evil genius of the action; others hardly mention her at all; a few omit the elder Ashtons entirely. Braughan, in his closet drama, transforms Lady Ashton into a modernized Lady Macbeth, who boasts that she commands the destinies of the family. At least two dramas mention that Henry Ashton needs money so much that he feels obliged to force his sister to marry the rich, but foppish, Bucklaw. Irving's *Ravenswood* had a final tableau showing old Caleb watching the sea near Ravenscrag, where the lovers have gone down in the quicksands.

Three conditions of the drama, at this point, are fairly obvious. First, the average audience, for the first years of the plays at least, wanted to see the story transferred from Scott without vital change. Tragic endings are exceptional, in that the playgoers often wanted them made into something more sentimental and far more melodramatic. Again, numerous passages in the Waverley novels were not easily transferred to the stage. Many of these simply had to be motivated or adapted, but the critics approved some changes reluctantly, and indignantly rejected others. Finally, with the increase of versions of the same novel, something new had to be introduced to justify another drama. Different devices were used, many of which left the critics frowning and the public cold.

REVISIONS FOR SCOTLAND

Native dramatists were not prolific in Scotland. Yet several of the managers and playwrights, like Ryder, Bass, Calcraft, and Murray, sometimes struck twelve when they adapted English plays to northern tastes and stage-conditions. Besides acting about a score of Waverley characters, Murray had a versatile Shakespeare repertoire that included Autolycus, Cassio, Edmund, Sebastian, and Launcelot Gobbo.[3] He found time to adapt numerous London successes, and to make original transcripts of Scott's *Abbot, Heart of Midlothian, Redgauntlet,* and *Pirate* probably. His Gilderoy melodrama, one of three on this subject, stood next to *Rob Roy* at times as the best glorification of the Highland freebooter. With the aid of such trained performers as Mrs. Henry Siddons, Calcraft, Mackay, and Miss Stephens, Manager Murray raised the fortunes of the Royal to the pinnacle of success, thanks to *Rob Roy* and similar plays borrowed from the works of the Great Unknown, who was a warm friend and supporter of Murray and his ventures.

Calcraft, the real dramatic laureate of the Royal Theatre,

---

[3] J. R. Anderson, *An Actor's Life,* p. 23.

proved versatile in the art of 'compilation.' He realized just what London favorites could be garnished for a Scots audience. He knew just how to amend the original dialect to make it real Scotch, and how to assort the Highland lochs, passes, and mountain views to fascinate most of the lovers of Walter Scott. Calcraft and his fellows found how to adapt the favorite airs and lyrics for celebrated singers to use as interludes and sentimental appeals.

Now and then the playwrights of London grumbled over the free use of their wares north of the Tweed. The lack of adequate laws protecting the rights of dramatists, and the customs of the time, permitted theatres of one country to borrow, without money or permission, much of the work of foreign talent. During the time of the great vogue of the Waverley plays, these conditions prevailed. It was not till 1832 that J. R. Planché brought matters to a head when Murray borrowed his *Charles XI* for use in Edinburgh. The author complained so loudly that the subject was aired in Parliament, with the result that a select committee, after several months of hesitation, proposed an act in 1833 which from that day protected dramatic writers on both sides of the Tweed.[4]

In the meantime, the public generously welcomed all original efforts in dramatic composition. Besides the Murray and Calcraft plays, with other sporadic works in the North a gentleman of Edinburgh compiled an effective *Quentin Durward;* Huie published a *Kenilworth,* which might have received some touches from his hand; the Ryder company brought out two original *Rob Roys,* one of which at least was entirely new; Perth sponsored a romantic piece that celebrated the charm of the fair Catherine Glover; and a few stray drafts from the novels certified to the craftsmanship of other native authors. Still, the custom of borrowing and revamping was so prevalent that critics hailed an original

[4] *Dict. Nat. Biog.* 29. 415.

work with extraordinary praise. The reviewers could hardly say enough, for example, when Ryder secured the *Quentin Durward* from 'a gentleman of Edinburgh.' They threw this nasty gibe toward the Royal: 'Murray, we presume, will continue to nauseate the public with the offals of the London theatres, or with some of Mr. Calcraft's choice productions.'[5]

THE VOGUE OF SCOTT IN FRANCE

Fourteen novels by Scott inspired thirty operas and melo-dramas in France, and at least a dozen in other European lands. Six modifications of the *Bride of Lammermoor* in French, two or more in Italian, and another in Spanish, attest the fame of this tragic story. Of *Kenilworth* there were six adaptations in French and one in German, and of *Ivanhoe,* three and two, respectively. For almost thirty years after 1820, the vogue of Scott in France fell just below that of Shakespeare, with Byron and Fenimore Cooper coming next, and the older dramatists of the eighteenth century, a poor fourth, Goldsmith and Sheridan being about the only ones then famous.*

As early as 1823, the *Corsaire* exclaimed: 'Grand nouvelle pour les amateurs de romans! Le célèbre Walter est, dit-on, arrivé à Paris, avec une cargaison d'ouvrages inédites. Messieurs les fabricants de mélodrames, taillez vos plumes.'[6] Four years later, a new critic reported that Scott might justly claim a pension from the French play-houses, since the authors of some of the most popular dramas had long borrowed from his novels.[7] Speaking in 1829 of *Henri III et sa Cour* by the elder Dumas, Charles Mangin thus relieved his mind: 'God be praised! There's

---

[5] *Dict. Nat. Biog.* 45. 395.

[6] For Sept. 26. For this and several other quotations of the same import, see Eric Partridge's *French Romantics' Knowledge of English Literature*, beginning at page 198.

[7] *Courrier des Théâtres,* Jan. 11, 1823.

a drama that is imitated from neither Walter Scott nor Cooper.'[8] A contemporary bemoaned the borrowing of themes from other nations by French dramatists, 'who do not seem to lack invention in the matter of details.' This critic mentioned Scott, above all others, as the chief provider of material for librettos.[9]

Scores of stray English versions—modified, unified, and transferred into foreign settings—enjoyed at least a passing vogue in the French centres of drama. Armand de Pontmartin recalled that three from the Waverley list were running once in Paris on the same evening, followed by a fourth the next afternoon.[10] In 1830 the critics began to assert that Scott had been drained dry by the French borrowers,[11] and yet the transfusion continued for upwards of a decade more. Dumas loved Scott so much that he leaned heavily upon his English friend in some dramatic experiments. Later in life he freely admitted that he drew from *Kenilworth* for some traits of his Christine; from *Quentin Durward* for a gypsy scene, from the *Talisman* for some items for his *Charles VII;* and from *Peveril of the Peak* for his *Laird de Dumbicky,* besides the abdication scene for his *Henri III*[12] from the *Abbot.*

Similar conditions existed in Italy. Paul Hazzard quotes from the contemporary *Spettatore Lombardo* to show the great popularity of Scott, and his influence on Italian drama and opera. M. Hazzard adds: 'Des noms nouveaux

---

[8] *Globe* for Feb. 14. Curiously enough, however, Dumas himself admitted, according to Partridge, p. 243, that the abdication-scene in his *Henry III* came largely from Scott's *Abbot,* in the scene where Murray and the other regents seek to get Mary to sign her abdication.

[9] *Revue Française,* July, 1829.

[10] In *Mes Memoires,* Seconde Jeunesse 3, as quoted by Partridge, p. 225.

[11] *National,* Sept. 23, 1830.

[12] Partridge, p. 242.

s'imposent, comme celui de Walter Scott, dont l'œuvre est lue, goûtee, admirée, imitée, pillée, dans le peninsule autant qu'en aucun lieu du monde.'[13]

When one turns to the journals of England in this same period, he notices many statements that look nearly like literal translations from the corresponding French periodicals. The playwrights of both nations were running, neck and neck, in a race to see which group could borrow more from the literature of the other land. Thus the *Theatrical Magazine* informs the reader that London playhouses, out of a total list of only fifty-one titles, in two years after January 1, 1828, borrowed thirty-eight pieces from the French.[14] The nondescript shows have not been included. When a bill for abolishing the patent rights of certain theatres was being argued in 1833, Lord Bathurst testified that 'if the choice lay between a bad translation of a French piece and the same in the original, I should prefer the latter.'[15] Such was the rage for making poor translations of foreign dramas.*

Companies of players went back and forth across the Channel. French troupes often appeared in London, and now and then one attempted an English drama in English, though the staple was opera in French or in Italian. Players from Scotland and England, within twenty years after 1822, made elaborate tours of the French centres of drama, taking with them such seasoned actors as Mrs. W. West, Penley, Wallack, and T. P. Cooke.[16]

These borrowings show clearly the main differences between English and French methods of dramatic composition. Early adapters from Scott in England and Scotland

---

[13] In a paper published in the *Revue de Littérature Comparée,* April-June, 1926.

[14] For April 1, 1830.

[15] Dutton Cook, *On the Stage 2. 208.*

[16] Partridge, p. 193.

were expected to follow the original plots rather literally, save for a small range of allowed variations. French librettists, on the contrary, were expected to unify the stories according to the laws of Gallic drama. Now and then, critics were not too harsh on their French contemporary dramatists who followed Scott, instead of the classic laws of Gallic playwriting. Yet these were somewhat exceptional.

Let us cite a typical specimen from the criticism of each nation to show these differences in point of view. Insisting that audiences went to the playhouse to see how the drama compared with the original romance of Scott, one English critic remarked: 'But those who truly admire and appreciate these splendid works feel that it is a species of profanation to touch and tamper with them at all—much more so to cut and carve them about, and transpose the language and sentiments, so as to adapt them to the taste of modern audiences, and the talents of favourite actresses. But how is it possible, and if it were, how is it desirable to think of Meg Merrilies under the disguise of Mrs. Egerton?'[17]

Compare with this the views of a French critic, which are representative of many others in the same period. He pointed out that 'the delightful, fresh, and living works of the Scotch novelist' could not be literally transferred to the boards. Some who tried direct borrowing had failed altogether to make attractive melodramas or operas. 'The playwrights cannot make up their minds,' he concluded, 'to sacrifice a given situation or to omit such and such a character. . . . He alone will successfully transfer Scott to the stage who manages to extract an interesting, simple, and single action, free from all accessories; something that will, in short, form a play and not a novel divided into acts: something that will reflect Scott without being a slavish copy.'[18]

Undoubtedly, the best French compilations followed the

[17] *Blackwood* 6. 624, censuring Soane's *Hebrew* for unlikeness to Scott.

[18] *Journal des Comédiens*, March 10, 1831.

laws of technique as understood and practised by standard writers of nineteenth-century melodramas. Unity and climax were always kept to the front. Necessarily the love-making was typical of French manners and customs. Many changes in social rank seemed advisable to French lovers of conventional plays of the time. Social ideas, too, needed some adjustment. As instances of the failure to realize these requirements, the Odéon *Ivanhoé,* and Scribe and Auber's version of *Kenilworth,* have already been cited.

Certain revisions made in France are interesting to the student of comparative literature. The rank and manners of the people in *Guy Mannering,* to begin with, are greatly modified. The Colonel has become a lord, Glossin a sheriff, and Hatteraick a military lieutenant. Intrigue is suggested by the addition of a second lover, who is displeasing to Julia Mannering's father, as Guy is called. In the *Bride of Lammermoor,* Sir William has become Lord Ashton, Governor of Lammermoor Castle, while those two sprightly rogues, Craigengelt and Bucklaw, are known as Lords Seymour and Melval, much transformed in manners as well as in titles. Great changes are made in some of the Ivanhoe plays by making the conflict between French and Normans a chief interest. Thus, Lucas, the Chief Templar, is now head of all the Norman forces opposing the French; Isaac is wonderfully transformed into the Mussulman steward of the King of France; and Rebecca proves eventually to be only the ward of the Jew, and in reality the daughter of an old friend of the Saxon Cedric. Though this last change is absurd from the point of view of Scott, it makes a highly melodramatic ending of the conventional sort that would charm the average audience. On the whole, the French playwrights made many such revisions for the sake of dramatic effect, and of the sort that English critics would have disowned.

Numerous details drop out of the story; other are combined; not a few appear for the first time. Characters are fewer, style is exalted, consistency is chosen as absolutely required, and unity appears in every move of the dramatic development. As far as the laws of composition are concerned, the average French transcript improved greatly over Scott.

Where the English bungled the history and characterization of the Covenanters as found in *Old Mortality,* the French ignored all this, and threw the emphasis on the love-triangle of Henry, Lord Evenden, and Edith Bellenden. Likewise, in dramas made from the *Abbot* and *Woodstock,* the French revised the plots according to their own ideas of English history. No English maker of dramas felt authorized to combine incidents from a number of novels, as some of the foreign authors did in forms like the *Dame Blanche,* which is a modification and extension of certain parts of *Guy Mannering,* the *Monastery,* and the *Abbot.*

Thus we notice that the French borrowed almost at will from the Waverley novels, but they differed from the English playwrights in that they better suited the scenes to the tastes, customs, and prejudices of average theatre-patrons.

Variety of Dramatizations from Scott

One could never hope to discover all the native and foreign dramas, melodramas, musical pieces, operas, and variety-entertainments that borrowed surreptitiously from Sir Walter Scott. Nor is it always possible to distinguish one version from another among the works that contemporaries either praised or blamed. There was much borrowing, overlapping, revamping.

No fewer than two hundred and fifty titles of these performances of varied sorts are noticed in the records of drama in the nineteenth century. Nearly a hundred found their way into the printing-house, of which a few are not now extant. Yet, altogether, at least seventy-six printed texts have been examined during the course of the writing of this dissertation.[19]   Ten or a dozen of these have been studied by proxy in unique copies found in libraries like those of the British Museum or of Paris.

This impressive total includes twenty-five operatic pieces, not counting a dozen or more stray titles mentioned casually by Grove, Towers, and Partridge.   Forty transcripts other than English and Scotch range in kind from grand opera to light vaudeville.   Outside of those versions made for London, no fewer than fifty were prepared for Perth, Glasgow, Edinburgh, and New York.   Of this impressive total, the great bulk of celebrated works were actual melodramas, or imitations with incidental songs.   Yet five or six of the serious operas outlived their own age, of which *Lucia di Lammermoor* is the best known in the twentieth century. At the opposite extreme, a score of travesties ran their course after 1840, with two or three of them before the public for a decade, when the audiences no longer loved Scott well enough to abhor all liberties taken with his text or his serious intentions.

It has not been found possible to include a study of the plays related to the metrical romances of Scott.   Some of the chief examples, however, may be mentioned by name. Generally speaking, the poems fell into the class of spectacle and incipient melodrama, when they reached the playhouse.

The *Lady of the Lake* and *Marmion* led the list in the number of poetic adaptations—the one with eleven different transcripts, all but two being published; the other with four, two being published.   After the Waverley novels appeared on the stage, the poetic dramas lost caste, though three or four were often revived for a few years.   Important dramatic *Marmions* by Stephen and Henry Kemble and by Edward Fitzball won considerable attention.   The Kemble tragedy is one of the legion of closet-dramas that lack the spark of

---

[19] Yale University seems to have the largest single collection of plays taken from the Waverley novels.

genius, but the verse is fairly good, and two or three scenes have a nervous energy not at all bad, thanks probably to Scott. Fitzball's piece, made some years afterward, is merely one more of his musical and spectacular efforts. James N. Barker, an American manager and dramatist, compiled a *Marmion* that 'ran through the American theatres.' To make the original performance attractive, the bill announced Thomas Morton, a famous English playwright, as the author, since his *Lady of the Lake* already had appeared successfully in New York.[20] Thomas J. Dibdin, always a prolific maker of dramas, copied all the spectacular parts from Scott. Edmund J. Eyre drafted an early *Lady of the Lake* also, and Andrew Halliday another many years afterward that enjoyed liberal runs. Good burlesques by Mortimer Thomson and Robert Reece provoked much merriment in several playhouses. Quite unlike the novels by Scott, the poems attracted few foreign dramatists, the *Robert Bruce* by Beauvallet being the only important poetic drama in France.[21]

Production of the Waverley Dramas

During the heyday of melodrama, twenty buildings at least were dedicated to the dramatic muse in London alone. Not all of these, of course, were open at the same time. Once four different *Ivanhoes* were running in the same month. Covent Garden led with fourteen Waverley plays, Drury Lane followed with ten, and the Surrey, in the management of Thomas J. Dibdin, produced quite as many. The range extended from the dignified patents, which finally descended to all sorts of entertainments, to the houses that played the lightest travesties.[22]

[20] Dunlap, *Hist. of the American Theatre*, p. 379.

[21] Partridge, p. 228.

[22] See Dutton Cook, *On the Stage* 2. 159; Percy Fitzgerald, *History of the English Stage* 2, chap. 3.

Compared with similar efforts, the adaptations from Scott maintained long runs, and some of them established records for melodramas, approaching the vogue of 'legitimate' plays. The great majority failed to survive the first season or two, but at least a dozen continued to interest audiences for a decade or more. *Rob Roy* leads with a total of two thousand nights at least in Scotland, and several hundred more in other lands. Its main competitors were *East Lynne,* some of Shakespeare, and a play or two by Goldsmith or by Sheridan. In Paris the *Dame Blanche,* by the middle seventies, reached the one hundred and fortieth performance, after which it continued at intervals for a decade or two longer. For length of run during a season, Dibdin's *Heart of Midlothian,* with a total of one hundred and seventy nights, seems to hold the record for melodramas from Scott. *Lucia di Lammermoor,* among the operas, has steadily maintained a favored place, with hundreds of revivals of the sextette and the chief solos by eminent artists the world over. Other plays that ran for upwards of a hundred times were *Guy Mannering,* in which Charlotte Cushman appeared for so many at least; the *Ravenswood* in which Irving and Terry starred; the *Ivanhoe* by Sullivan and Sturgis. Even a few of the travesties, like the *Kenilworth* by Halliday, and the *Ivanhoe* by Plowman, continued to be demanded for a long time after they attained the hundredth performance.

Conditions in Paris resembled those in London, so far as length of run is concerned. In addition to *Dame Blanche,* with a record of more than thirteen hundred nights, others like the *Prison d'Edimbourg* were inordinately popular. The *Lucia* and *Talismano* led among the operas with totals that extended into the hundreds for the former alone. Other notable records are these: a French *Abbot* for upwards of thirty nights; one of the numerous Lammermoor plays, this one exalting Caleb Balderstone, for fifty-two nights, and another by Ducange from the same source, for at least fifty; one operatic *Kenilworth,* for forty-nine; a vaudeville based on the story of Henry Morton, for thirty-one; and a Charles II play, for not fewer than twenty.

Such popular compositions held their own along with the classical plays and operas. Many of them equaled the fame of the most attractive melodramas not based on foreign novels.

SOME ELEMENTS OF MELODRAMA

Originally melodrama meant any form similar to the French *mélodrame.* Shortly after 1810 in Great Britain, however, the meaning was greatly extended to include any play having unusual effects of various kinds. Some of these were new, but most were simply old spectacular elements now exaggerated. Sadler's Wells and other houses, for a number of years, had specialized in nautical and spectacular shows. In a few of the large playhouses, the platforms became too ample for ordinary drama, the audience-pits too far from front to back, and the requirements for the mounting often too exacting. The taste of the patrons had largely changed in favor of more striking action, incidental songs, and highly pictorial and emotional endings.

Variety in names meant little or nothing; for the unlicensed playhouses had to resort to subterfuge and misbranding to avoid an open breach with the patent theatres like Covent Garden and Drury Lane. By the time that the Waverley dramas reached the stage, patrons understood well enough what was meant when the managers announced one such play as 'a serious melodramatic, historical, burletta'; Bunn's *Ivanhoe* as 'a new grand chivalric play'; and the stage-form of the *Fair Maid of Perth* as 'a grand historical, national drama.' Between the second and third of these and the first lay no differences, except that the first was produced in an unlicensed house, while the others came out in a patent theatre.

Some of the exaggerated effects will now be considered under six appropriate headings. There is, necessarily, some overlapping, and some few forms may not classify under the names chosen. Yet the main divisions might well be described as the following:

1, The use of song and recitative; 2, picturesque scenery and theatrical stage-effects; 3, contrasts of tragic and comic scenes and other effects; 4, sentimental endings; 5, odd characters, star-parts, and types of emotions; 6, exaggeration, struggle, surprise.

These will next be considered separately.

SONGS IN THE WAVERLEY DRAMAS

Incidental songs appear in nearly all the melodramas drawn from the works of Scott. Sometimes they were designed merely to protect a minor playhouse from running afoul of the licensed theatres. Two or three times the scraping of a few fiddles, or the singing of a few familiar songs, made all the difference between a burletta and a regular play. Some pieces designated as operas differed little from ordinary melodramas, except for the addition of a few extra songs. Many favorite ballads were interpolated into some plays, or the songs of Burns were suited somewhat to the occasion.

Yet in many instances, however, the musical parts had little relation to the text of the play. In the first *Guy Mannering,* and some earlier dramas besides this, few of the songs bore any direct relation to the plot. The opening chorus of loiterers in the tap of the inn at Kippletringan celebrates the approach of winter, but the season is not late autumn, as one might infer. This song was introduced because it was popular with the audience. Similar lyrics are sung by the crowds in two or three of the *Kenilworths.* In Pocock's *Rob Roy,* Francis sings *Auld Lang Syne,* which is quite out of keeping with the occasion of the quarrel between him and one of the English officers. In Terry's *Guy Mannering,* a convivial song is introduced just after Hatteraick is captured, and the crowd adjourns to take a 'dram' at the inn; but both the song and the scene are so obviously out of place and character that they were usually marked for omission in the printed texts. In one Kenilworth drama, Tressilian sings a ballad while secreted upstairs at Gosling's inn to avoid a brush with some roisterers below. How they could possibly fail to overhear him is not revealed by the dramatist.

These are a few of the typical instances from the considerable list that might be mentioned. Topical songs often brought down the house. Some of the most famous were Mackay's rendering of the 'Good Fat Hen,' in the character and awkwardness of Dominie Sampson; the 'Tramp Chorus' by the women of Aberfoyle; and a quartet made up of Francis, Owen, Jarvie, and Miss Mattie in the tolbooth of Glasgow.

Not a few of the sentimental songs, however, were appropriate and in good taste. An effective example is Lucy Bertram's solo of parting from the old scenes at Ellangowan. This well expressed her actual emotions on leaving the old home she had loved since childhood. Scott's *Lullaby of an Indian Chief,* in this same drama, gave Charlotte Cushman a great opportunity to show her powers as an emotional actress. Nothing could have been so suitable here as this lyric, with which Meg Merrilies awakens the slumbering memories of Henry Bertram. Terry in his *Heart of Midlothian* adapted a poem from Burns, 'I'm wearing awa', Jean' for Effie Deans to sing when her sister came to her in the jail. Jean herself used another plaintive ballad, called 'The Lily of St. Leonard's,' the words and music of which were hawked about the streets of many cities in Great Britain for a number of years. Edinburgh and Dublin playwrights were always interpolating new or popular songs to catch the ear of their patrons.

Turning to the operas themselves, one recalls instantly a long list of favorite lyrics and famous singers. Besides the many solos, such duets might be mentioned as those of Edgar and Lucy, the Templar and Rebecca in a number of operas; Kenneth of Scotland and Edith Plantagenet in one of the interesting Talisman plays; Amy and her Earl in several Kenilworths. Moreover, some of the great musical artists of the nineteenth century provided the scores, such as Henry R. Bishop, director of music at Covent Garden for years, Donizetti, Rossini, Carafa, Bizet, Boieldieu, Balfe, Marschner, and Sir Arthur Sullivan.

Scenery and Mechanical Effects

Attempting to approximate the descriptions in the novels, the painter of scenes went to great lengths of originality, daring, and expense. In Edinburgh especially, the patrons wanted to get some authentic glimpses of the Highlands, and of the haunts of their favorite characters in the romances of Scott. Now and then spectacle and gorgeous scenery compensated for the lack of dramatic matter in the plays. Yet the best managers risked little on the dramas that did not follow Scott in the main outlines of plot and scene.

From the large list of interesting devices to vivify the plays and operas, only a few typical effects can be cited now. One of the 'Gentlemen' who reviewed the drama in Dublin reported that the burning of the Portanferry buildings in a Mannering play was 'the finest and most sublime scenery and scenic machinery that we ever witnessed.' At Bath, Genest described the concluding pageant of the Bunn *Ivanhoe* as the most elaborate of its kind ever shown out of London. Even in New York City, where the same drops oftenest served for a variety of scenes, sixteen horses appeared on a stage which had been specially enlarged to receive them for one of the plays based on the *Abbot*. In one of the Montrose dramas in London, besides a number of other steeds, the famous charger of Dugald Dalgetty held the centre of the stage. Some of the pageants at Kenilworth concluded with historical displays of morris-dances, games of skill in horsemanship, and other ancient sports.

Pocock led the fashion in natural scenery which raged unchecked for two or three decades. He always provided for a generous assortment of Highland crags, narrow mountainous defiles, romantic views of lochs, and numerous clans, arrayed in their typical tartans, marching to battle in the moonlight. This description would fit almost any of the Scotch plays. A familiar direction in one *Montrose,* for example, reads: 'Wild and romantic scene: night, rocks, mountain pass, uncertain moonlight.' Evening scenes appear in several dramas based on *Ivanhoe, Midlothian, Pirate, Montrose,* and *Abbot.* Pitt's *Whistler* had a convenient display of cliffs from which the wild unnamed youth—who turns out to be the lost son of George and Effie Robertson—jumped to his death among the jagged rocks below.

Real cataracts of water were rather numerous. Shepherd's *Heart of Midlothian* had a rustic bridge, with a torrent flowing underneath; so did *Old Mortality,* when some friends, coming to rescue Henry Morton from the spite of Burleigh, were precipitated into the raging flood. Several Lammermoor dramas had quicksands into which Edgar and Lucy seemed to sink; in one of them, Craigengelt and Bucklaw pursued Edgar into a cataract of real water. The *Antiquary* and some others had imitations that varied only with the ingenuity of the different mechanisms employed on the stage.

Scott provided an abundance of scenery for the stage in *Ivanhoe.* All the versions take full advantage of the descriptions of Rotherwood Hall, the varied scenes, with Robin Hood and his merry men in the centre of the stage, the picturesque setting of the lists, the grim dungeon in which Isaac weighs out his ransom in pure gold, and the landscape that made a background for Torquilstone Castle. Lacy added a storm at Rotherwood, Torquilstone aflame, and more of the sylvan scenes. Dibdin showed Sherwood flooded with moonlight for the rustic games. Doubtless the most vivid of all the many scenes was that of Macready acting the death-throes of Front de Boeuf, locked in the tower of his own flaming castle at Torquilstone.

The interior scenes were varied in all their appointments. These included the audience-hall at Holyrood Palace, which appeared in several of the descriptions; the altar made ready for the installation of nuns in an Abbot drama; and the solemn procession of nuns and acolytes in at least one Talisman adaptation.

Indeed the range of interiors is almost limitless. We see the throne-room of King John in very elaborate setting; some banquets in *Kenilworth, Quentin Durward,* and several others; a coronation now and then; cells of nuns and friars like those of St. Cuthbert's, St. Mary's, and Copmanhurst, and even the refuge for debtors, called Alsatia, where old Trapbois keeps miserly court. Gothic chambers, libraries, and cloisters are mentioned in ten or a dozen plays. Halls, Gothic rooms, apartments and towers of Torquilstone, the Tolbooth and near-by church, Wolf's Crag, appear according to the skill of the scenic artists who painted for the playhouse. At the opposite extreme are taprooms in eight or ten plays at least. We are introduced to the cells of the Tolbooth in Edinburgh and Glasgow, the common jail at Portanferry, the dungeon where Dugald runs across old Ranald of the Mist, another in which the Prince of Scotland is put to death at the hands of Bonthron, and still another in which Isaac, watched by the stalwart slaves of Brian de Bois Guilbert, weighs out his ransom in finest gold.

Sometimes the wish to be original led to daring scenic effects. Not content like the rest with simple moonlight, Soane added the aurora borealis in one of his pictured backgrounds. Pocock, in *Montrose,* arranged the bodies of five men on the gallows in the public street of Inverara, and one Midlothian melodrama showed a gallows arranged on the stage for the execution of Effie Deans.

Both the *Fair Maid of Perth* and the *Legend of Montrose* have extraordinary scenic effects. Besides the peculiar 'bier-right' in the convent to determine who murdered Oliver Proudfute, we have in the former the interesting pictures of the Wynd of Perth, a bird's-eye glimpse of the city from the battle-field of the North Inch, picturesque gatherings of the clans on an elaborate scale, the ceremonies incident to the choosing of a new leader to replace the recreant Conachar, a characteristic Highland ballet, 'and a terrific battle of twelve' champions in the lists.

Besides the movement of the clans, the serious conclave of the chiefs of Scotland, the filthy dungeon where old Ranald and Dugald are confined, the different Montrose dramas have no end of pageantry. One remarkably vivid scene discloses six giant Highlanders, each with flaming torch in hand, in lieu of the silver candlesticks which an incautious Scotch laird, away from home, boasted that his house possessed. Having been inveigled into a wager on the subject, he determined not to be outdone in strategy, even though he was by his English friends in the possession of silver ornaments; and so he dressed up the tallest men he could find, to stand in his dining-room to represent the six silver candlesticks. Sir Walter Scott himself had somewhat elaborated this incident from an actual experience that had been reported to him, and the dramas went him one better in the picturesque details of the scene.

Comic Relief in Melodrama

Following the lead of the older dramatists whose works Scott read and admired, the author of *Waverley* alternated many comic and serious scenes in his various romances. He once wrote to Terry that a certain novel could not interest the public in dramatic form because it had no *vis comica*.

Numerous little touches in his own criticisms of other works, besides the evidence of the novels themselves, show that Scott held that comic and serious parts should often be alternated. Dominie Sampson and Nicol Jarvie are, of course, two of the best illustrations found in the novels. The poor, befuddled Dominie contrasts with the stern and impassioned Meg Merrilies. Even when Meg is trying to arouse him to the need for instant action, the Dominie delays with his scraps of bad Latin, this scene of rare comedy being followed almost at once by the tragic death of Meg. The Bailie likewise breaks into the midst of several tense scenes with his unconscious foolery, like that of his being caught in the thorn-tree, and his running at the English officers with the 'het poker.'

Recalling some other good illustrations, one might cite the comic passages between Sandy and Mattie in the Abbot plays, followed at once by the scene in which Mary is forced to sign her abdication. The whimsical explanation of Caleb Balderstone, rehearsing an ample—but quite imaginary—bill of fare, is followed by the scene in which Lucy and her father are driven by a storm to take refuge at Wolf's Crag. Again, Caleb's fitful expedition in search of provisions, with his snatching of the dinner which a good woman of the village is roasting on a spit, soon gives way to the tragic appeal of Lucy to her brother to be spared from marrying the foppish Bucklaw.

Further evidence of the alternation of serious and comedy material is readily found in a number of dramas. Jen Vincent is seen taking a dram with Mrs. Suddlechop, in the absence of the lord of the house, and next appears the trepidation of Nigel, when old Trapbois invites him to settle for his lodgings in Alsatia. The hesitation of Dumbiedikes, which some dramatists turned into farce, gives way to the very serious consideration of Jeanie's trip to London to obtain the pardon for her sister. Finally, one clearly recalls the flittings and the jokes of Wamba and Gurth, together with the following merriment of Friar Tuck and his foresters, after which comes the scene of the condemnation of Rebecca to be burned as a witch, with the detailed preparations for putting this doom into execution.

Several of the novels, one must admit, lack this alternation of the grave and the gay scenes. Thus the *Pirate, Fair Maid of Perth, Anne of Geierstein,* and *Quentin Durward* are the chief illustrations. In the stage descriptions of *Kenilworth* and *Old Mortality,* the humor is somewhat minimized, and in *Montrose* it alternates within the same scene, notably with reference to Dugald Dalgetty and his hesitation as to whether he will join the Scotch chiefs unless they offer him a larger stipend.

According to the custom in such productions, most of the operatic forms either abandoned altogether, or at least greatly minimized, the humorous elements.

SENTIMENTAL ENDINGS

Scott left the endings of his novels impressive enough, yet not always sufficiently theatrical for lovers of melodrama. The stories of Ivanhoe and Rebecca, the Earl and Amy, Ravenswood and Lucy of Lammermoor, had to undergo hazardous revisions. Some of the theatre-goers were pleased; many were repelled altogether. Not that audiences stickled over moot points of motivation and characterization. Niceties of dramatic art were not demanded, so long as ideas, theories, views of life, and sentiments especially, were reflected back to the audience from the stage.

Those jealous gods of melodrama who are appeased only by fortunate endings of plays often had to be recognized by dramatists. To the utter disregard of art, Amy had to be spared from death. To the utter disregard also of custom in the age of Ivanhoe, as Scott himself pointed out, Rebecca somehow had to be married to Ivanhoe, or else had to be transformed into some other person, like a long-lost daughter of Cedric's old friend. Though the current of tragedy in *Kenilworth* flows deep and swift, such was the rage for happy endings that the heroine had to be rescued. In the case of the lovers of Lammermoor, the tragic tide is too strong to be stayed, even though the ending, as told by Scott, proved unsuitable to the stage. Little changes had to be made along the way to tone down the awful doom, or to make the love of the two young persons even more romantic, though still tragic.

Dramatizations of his *Bride of Lammermoor* might be compared in detail to show the resultant modifications. Yet the common note of tragedy remains in all, while minor differences are not important enough to mark off one form from the rest. Does it make any real difference whether it is a coin or a ring that is broken between the two lovers? Whether it is a forged tale, or a false report of a foreign sweetheart of Edgar's, that turns the Bride away from her troth? Whether Edgar kills himself among the tombs of his ancestors, or is stabbed by a domestic, or is drowned in Kelpie's Flow, or goes down, bearing Lucy in his arms, in the quicksands near Wolf's Crag? Whether Lucy dies insane, or whether she stabs Bucklaw, or is stabbed by him? All these are relatively minor considerations of dramatic art.

Whatever changes were made in the main plot, the travesties enlarged them into a sort of *reductio ad absurdum*. So many melodramas ended to soft music that the makers of burlesques eventually laughed them off the stage. So great did the rage for scenes of mountains, forests, and Highland ballets at last become that Byron introduced exaggerated forms of these, along with a typical conservatory, into his version of *Lammermoor,* where none of these belongs by right of the novel itself.

The rage for introducing incidental music is admirably hit off by Byron in a scene, for which this is the descriptive announcement:

'A forest glade. How the head huntsman proves he is not

only a brick but a Norman arch, and how Alice presents a pretty appearance, though she shows a great fright at the appearance of Henry, who comes on, and, with Raymond, "discourses" anything but "eloquent music" concerning his sister's love for the enemy of his house, and how Edgar and Lucy sing a duet, and being about to have a parting, they naturally divide the air.'

Not only music, but pageantry and sentiment in large degree, marked the endings of some highly appreciated dramas. At the end of one, *Quentin Durward,* the Duke of Burgundy throws this nosegay to the hero and his countrymen:

'But why should I grudge this youth his preferment; since, after all, it is sense, firmness, and gallantry (which the Scots possess in ample degree) that have put him in possession of WEALTH; RANK; AND BEAUTY.' 'Picture formed—Curtain drops to music.'

We have noticed already that Janet Foster, in one *Kenilworth,* unlocked the mechanism of the trapdoor, while music was being softly played. One of the dramas treating of the tragic Scotch Queen ends thus:

'Douglas expires at Mary's feet; the latter swounds in the Abbot's arms. The chiefs and their clans form a characteristic group, and the curtain slowly descends to appropriate music.'

Perhaps the quintessence of melodramatic sentiment is distilled at the end of one of the Peveril adaptations. Fenella, posing as a deaf mute, has sacrificed her own life to save the man she loves, and her sovereign, from the dagger of the malignant Hudson, the agent of those who are conspiring against the King:

'Music—Fenella, lifting her eyes in silent prayer, joins the hands of Julian and Alice, who kneel. She then sinks back on the Countess of Derby's right arm; the Countess stretches her left hand toward Heaven, forming a fine picture of awe and devotion.   A striking group is formed, and the curtain slowly falls.'

Thus we observe that the dramatists followed the will of the major part of the audience: first, in making large or small changes in the endings of dramas for sensational and melodramatic reasons; secondly, in adding any musical, picturesque, or theatrical effects for the sake of deepening the impression.

Odd Characters and Star-Parts

'Hardly a single picturesque point of manners touched by Ben Jonson and his contemporaries,' says Lockhart of the *Fortunes of Nigel,* 'but has been dovetailed into this story.'[23]   King James in the novel and the plays shows some 'humor,' much in the old manner of Jonson, with his odd Scotch dialect, his superstition and fear, love of a joke, and profound aversion to paying his honest debts.   Nigel, too, has a great antipathy to being recognized in public places, a hot temper when it is stirred, and a way of getting himself into peculiar scrapes, all in the manner of some of the old plays.   It would almost seem that notes were taken from some old dramatist's book for Trapbois, Dick Monoplies, Jen Vincent, and some of the rest in *Nigel* and other romances.

Going back to one of the early novels, who could forget the lovable, but awkward and unpractical Dominie Sampson? Though he is a bundle of contradictions, even to the point of caricature at times, he has some prevailing traits like his ingrained forgetfulness, his love for scraps of Latin phrases, his devotion to the house of Ellangowan—all of which make him memorable in the novel and on the stage. In the play, the good man is skilled in all the dialects of India, though he has never been out of Scotland, a circum-

[23] 2. 274.

stance which makes Genest inquire as to how he could have thus mastered them?[24]

We picture the Dominie showing his amazement because the climate of Scotland seems to make his garments last a long time, whereas he is indeed arrayed in a new suit left at night in his room by solicitous friends in the home of Guy Mannering. We imagine the droll motions of Bailie Jarvie when he is rehearsing the consternation and humiliation he felt while waiting for some straggler to free him from the thorn-tree in which he was hanging by his coat-tails. We can verily hear the Rittmaster, Dugald Dalgetty, soldier of fortune, sounding the praises of his beloved steed, named Gustavus Adolphus, and like his master the hero of many battles. These three stand well toward the head of the column of notables that extends all the way from Fergus MacIvor of Scotland to Louis XI of France, and even to the learned lady of Constantinople, that vivid personage in one of Scott's last and poorest novels. Somewhere along the way, one might meet old Edie, the blind 'blue-gown'; Cuddie Headrigg, the droll countryman and his odd mother; old Caleb Balderstone, the resourceful and imaginative steward at Wolf's Crag; the hesitant and tight laird of Dumbiedikes; the morose Burleigh in his wayside lair; and even Jonathan Oldbuck himself, antiquary and humorsome Scot—and we have only begun to get well into the list.

Now, turning to the darker traits of human nature, we find that the list is undoubtedly much longer, though quite likely not so varied. Not a few of the creatures of Scott are moved by their peculiar 'weird,' as Allan MacAuley denotes the sense of gloom that envelops his soul. Here again the most startling of all such creations of the novelist is Meg Merrilies, with her 'imperious wilfulness,' her material care for the house of Ellangowan and its lost son, and, particularly, her mind both enlightened and disordered by prophetic insight.

[24] 8. 550.

Scott began to mould this type of character when he portrayed Flora MacIvor in his first novel. He found this variety of temperament, as shown in the successive novels of the series, not merely one that the public liked to see realized, but more especially one which he himself liked to portray. He enlarged the main details from time to time, making little changes here and there, until finally the sibyl type became a vogue of both the novel and the playhouse. So Mrs. Egerton, Charlotte Cushman, Mrs. Renaud, and a galaxy of lesser lights, having once achieved their own brilliancy, continued to shine undiminished in the dramatic houses of both continents.

Thus the varied favorites of the original story, and the modification for the stage, appealed to human interest in the odd, temperamental, and disorganized mind. For this reason, Helen Macgregor appears as the amazon who hurls defiance at a whole company of English recruits in the Highlands; Madge Wildfire, as the crazed body who fools the officers, braves the mob, and rescues the heroine of the play, a simple Scotch lassie who needs a guiding hand; old Elspeth, the informer and family historian of the Glenallen household; and Norna of Fitful Head, the queer prophetess who braves the moorland storm, and the dangers of the wreck at sea, for the sake of one whom she does not recognize as her own son.

Typical melodramas, then, modified traits of the original persons in the novels or exalted some parts to make them doubly impressive. The results vary from the most romantic melodramas to the drollest and most realistic. One can never forget characters like Allan MacAuley, the man of the mysterious 'weird' and the Highland gloom, the terrible creation that Beazley made for Macready out of the combined parts of Brian and Reginald of *Ivanhoe,* and Dugald Dalgetty, who stands out as one of Scott's most masterful creations, much improved over early sketches of the same kind, and worthy to be named beside Bailie Jarvie and Dominie Sampson. These are only a few of the many types of character that the dramatists drew with lifelike strokes, according to the original models of the romances.

Varied Turns in the Action

In previous chapters we have noticed how the chief scenes of the Waverley novels prompted many realistic and effective scenes of corresponding dramas. Many of the climaxes are most strongly set off. Let us call to mind the escape of Mary of Scotland from her virtual imprisonment at Loch Leven; the spirited duel between Hector and Lovel, with old Edie, the 'blue-gown,' refusing stoutly to leave the spot; the tragic moment when Edgar Ravenswood returns to find his betrothed has just agreed to wed another; the court-scene in which Jeanie Deans is enabled to secure the release of her accused sister; the discovery by Norna of Fitful Head that her former husband is indeed the father of the young man whom she has been protecting from her own son; the tense moments at Kenilworth and Cumnor Place; the visit of Henry Morton to the wayside lair of the morose Claverhouse; and the noble sacrifice of Fenella to protect the King and his friends from the malignant dwarf. Possibly the most intense of all is the scene in Beazley's *Ivanhoe* when the Castle of Torquilstone is shown aflame.

Contrasts in character are abundant and effective. Some that are called to mind at once are Dalgetty and Allan MacAuley; Brian and Ivanhoe; Leicester and Varney; Tressilian and Lambourne; Amy and Queen Elizabeth; Bucklaw and Edgar of Ravenswood; Louis XI of France and the Duke of Burgundy; Meg Merrilies and Dominie Sampson; Francis Osbaldistone and his cousin. Every novel has at least a pair of them.

The motive of the 'foundling'[25] is illustrated in many of the novels and the plays based on them. Some person

[25] William S. Dye, Jr., in *A Study of Melodrama in England,* informs us that these plays were numerous in the period between 1820 and 1840.

appears early in the romance, and later is shown to be different from what he has professed or seemed; or, as one travesty puts it, 'turns out to be somebody after all.' Vanbeest Brown becomes Henry Bertram, the lost heir of Ellangowan. Roland Graeme turns out to be the rightful heir to the estates held at first by Halbert Glendinning, and old Magdalen, another sibyl of the Meg Merrilies kind, proves to be his mother. Julian Avenel likewise finally takes possession of the estates that the steward has tried to appropriate. Often a second person of mystery comes into the foreground, to clear up the doubt as to the identity of the foundling. Besides Meg Merrilies and Mother Graeme, some of them are the White Lady of Avenel, or Anna who assumes the part in the *Monastery,* old Elspeth, Madge Wildfire, Norna, Annot Lyle, and Anne of Geierstein.

Other disguises are as confusing and elusive as they are plentiful in both the novels and the transcripts. Ivanhoe appears as the Palmer, and then as the Disinherited Knight, Richard as the Black Knight, the Soldan as Adonbec el Hakim, an Arab leech, Rob Roy at times as a mysterious Mr. Cawmil or Campbell, Sir George Staunton as George Robertson, Louis XI as a merchant when Quentin Durward first meets him, Prince David of Scotland as the Knight of the Couchant Leopard, Lord Geralin successively as William Lovel and as Major Neville, the Earl of Montrose as General Anderson, Magdalen Graeme as Mother Nicneven; and the list could be extended to more than twice this length. The use of the disguise is at once recognized as a favorite device of melodrama, and the adaptors of Scott certainly availed themselves of the material at hand in the novels.

We now conclude the consideration of the scores of dramas based on the prose romances of Sir Walter Scott. In number and influence they have had a marked effect on the history of melodrama. The vogue of Scott 'on the rebound' has been far greater than the dramatic historians, except one or two like J. C. Dibdin, have ever allowed themselves to intimate.

In every English-speaking land and on the continent of Europe, the immense fame of Scott has been mirrored accurately in the number and excellence of the melodramas and operas drawn from the various Waverley novels. When it comes to Scotland, one may speak in superlatives by saying that the adaptations stood in the front rank, as judged by original and subsequent popularity; they held their own with Shakespeare and the best of the older dramatists. Some of the actors in Scotland stood at the top of their class. Not a few also in England, at one time or another, helped produce a play or two from the Waverley list. The greatest American actress made Meg Merrilies one of her three principal parts for many years in both America and the British Isles. So we are confirmed in the impression that the Waverley plays are important in the history of drama in the nineteenth century.

XI. ADDITIONAL NOTES AND COMMENTS

Page 1. Scott's interest in drama. See the index to Lockhart's *Life of Scott* for suggestions of the relation of Scott to the drama of his country. Some of the page-numbers in the first American edition, which has been used throughout in this dissertation, are as follows: 1. 28, 59, 75, 79, 84, 122, 129, 144, 153, 171, 193, 224, 239, 266, 365, 404; 2. 301, 331, 360, 394.

Margaret Carhart, *Life and Work of Joanna Baillie,* refers to the interest that Scott took in Miss Baillie, whom he once called 'the best dramatic writer Britain has produced since the day of Shakespeare and Massinger.'

At the Edinburgh Theatre Fund Dinner of 1830, Charles Mackay alluded to Scott as 'the Shakespeare of our day,' asserting that the reading of the novels had brought about 'a wonderful revolution of opinion in Scotland in favor of the actors' art.' Odell, *Shakespeare from Betterton to Irving,* testifies that the dramatized novels of Scott raised the standards somewhat at Sadler's Wells between 1830 and 1840. J. C. Dibdin, *Annals of the Edinburgh Stage,* frequently speaks of Scott as a patron of the drama and of actors in Scotland.

Page 9. Scott and Daniel Terry. Scott stipulated with Campbell, editor of *Albyn's Anthology,* in which appeared the *Lullaby of an Indian Chief* written by Scott for Terry's *Guy Mannering,* that his name must not be divulged. Lockhart intimates that this was one detail of the plan to keep the public mystified in regard to the novels. See the *Life* 1. 404, 420, 444, 468; Scott's *Journal* (Harper edition), p. 379; Baker, *History of the London Stage,* p. 422; and *Dict. Nat. Biog.* 56. 84.

Page 43. Mackay in London. At least one London critic appreciated Mackay. In the *Times* for August, 1821, he said: 'He is the best comedian that we have ever seen make his debut in London. He is marvellously free from the coarseness and superfluous ornaments which mark the country performer. . . . There is no person who plays Bailie Jarvie or Dominie Sampson like him.'

Page 44. Actors in the Scott plays. For information as to the actors who appeared in the dramatizations of Scott, the *Dictionary of National Biography,* Adams' *Dictionary of the Drama* (of which unfortunately only one volume, A to G, was issued), *The Stage and its Stars,* Oxberry's *Dramatic Biographies,* and similar works are valuable.

Page 51. The Great Unknown. For several years Scott had

been mentioned as the Great Unknown, because of the rather widespread understanding that he was indeed the author of the Waverley novels. Critics now and then spoke of them as his children.

Eventually an anonymous dramatist tried to capitalize the idea by making a farce having this title. The piece ran for only a single night—or a part of it, since most of the action went off in dumb show at the Haymarket Theatre after the first act, even though both Liston and Terry were in the cast. This may have been a debased example of the 'Terry-fications'. One journal explained that the farce attempted to learn, by means of phrenology, whether Scott and the Great Unknown were indeed the same person. Another magazine pronounced it 'a contemptible piece,' 'justly condemned.'

See *Theatrical Pocket Magazine* 5. 89, and *Gentleman's Magazine,* 1828, part I, p. 269.

Page 58. Mrs. Egerton. This talented actress began her stage-career at Birmingham, but failed in heavy tragic parts. Later she attained the front rank in melodrama at Covent Garden, Drury Lane, the Surrey, and Sadler's Wells. Her notable rôles in dramatizations of Scott were Meg Merrilies, for which part she was the original at Covent Garden after John Emery had refused to undertake it, Helen Macgregor, and Madge Wildfire. Mrs. Egerton played the Queen to Charles Kean's Hamlet at Drury Lane, Young Norval in Home's *Douglas,* and also in Joanna Baillie's *De Montfort* and in *Jane Shore.* Oxberry remarked that Mrs. Egerton as Meg excelled Mrs. Bunn, Mrs. William West, Mrs. Yates, and Miss Kelly.

Page 62. Madame Vestris. Born of Italian parentage, Madame Vestris attained great fame as a singing actress. In 1832 the *London Tatler,* a dramatic magazine, pronounced her 'the best actress that ever sang and the best singer that ever acted.' In the adaptations from Scott, she is the best known for her Diana Vernon, Effie Deans, and parts in the *Pirate,* but her greatest was Pandora in an entertainment called *Olympic Revels.* During her own management of the Olympic Theatre, she did much to improve the scenery and staging of plays, having in her company such stars as Miss Murray, Farren, Bland, Liston, and Charles J. Mathews, whom she finally married. Her last appearance was in 1854 in a benefit for her husband. The *Dictionary of National Biography* has an excellent account of her life and many rôles.

Page 75. Thomas John Dibdin. Besides the songs, Dibdin is also credited with scores of dramatic compositions of all sorts. As an actor, he was introduced at the age of four as Cupid by Mrs.

Sarah Siddons. Dibdin was a beloved figure in the theatre for many years. In 1791 he appeared in Liverpool, then at Sadler's Wells in 1794, and next for seven years in many parts at Covent Garden. His *Mouth of the Nile,* commemorating Nelson's victory, won a great triumph. Under his management at the Surrey Theatre, he opened with his own *Humphrey Clinker* in 1816. Dibdin made a point of trying to bring out the best of melodrama at the Surrey, but his venture at last failed for want of successful opportunities.

Page 94. Fechter in America. The talented Fechter failed to .win the confidence of the audiences in America, largely because of his methods in business and elsewhere, which were arbitrary and high-handed. He retired from the stage, settled near Philadelphia, and lived for several years an embittered man, after suffering commercial and other misfortunes. He seems to have owned the manuscript of the Simpson play, or some other; for Kirby and Son of London, in advertising his effects to be sold at auction in 1880, mentioned among them 'the music and play of *Ravenswood.*' See Adams, pp. 204, 214; Brown 2. 156; *Drama Notes* for 1890, p. 119; and the *New York Tribune* for Dec. 11, 1866.

Page 107. Mr. and Mrs. Alfred Bunn. The Bunns were known in England and Scotland for their picturesque mountings of plays, for Mr. Bunn's literary and dramatic feuds, and for importing actors into London after they had made a name for themselves in provincial towns. Some of the players introduced thus by Bunn were Vandenhoff, W. Farren, Bartley, and Mathews. Edmund Yates, the actor, reported that Thackeray had Bunn in mind in his portrait of Mr. Dolphin, the manager, in *Pendennis.*

Bunn engaged Macready to act in various plays, but they never got along well together. Their ill-will toward each other culminated in 1836, when the great tragedian attacked Bunn in his room at Covent Garden. For this assault, Bunn obtained damages of one hundred and fifty pounds in a court of law. It has been asserted that Bunn wrote his *The Stage from Before and Behind the Curtain* largely to belittle Macready.

Page 108. Samuel Beazley. This dramatization of *Ivanhoe* is mentioned in the *History of the Theatre Royal, Dublin,* p. 28. Beazley, who was originally an architect specializing in theatrical buildings, designed certain alterations for Drury Lane in 1821, built the English Opera House (Lyceum), St. James and City of London Theatres, two others in India, two in Dublin (where he was popular as a reviser of plays), and one in Brazil. Some of his hundred or more dramatic compilations are *Lottery Ticket, Gretna Green,* and a translation of *La Sonnambula.*

Page 112. Mounting of Plays in Edinburgh. As an indication of the pains taken to mount plays in Edinburgh, one may cite the remarks of the critic in the *Drama Review* 6. 85. He said that Murray used about the same material as the 1822 version of *Ivanhoe,* but arranged it in a somewhat different manner. 'It has been got up with extraordinary magnificence, both as respects scenery and decorations; and we have the opportunity of knowing, were the facts doubtful, that a great deal of money has been expended upon it. There is one scene of Saxon architecture extremely well executed, though far too superb for the mansion of Cedric. The other scenes are mostly sylvan, some of them mere daubs, others imposing and beautiful.'

This reviewer also stated that the spectacle was the grandest he had seen at the Royal since he commenced to attend the play in this house.

Page 115. Operas mentioned by Towers. Besides the operas named before, Towers mentioned some sort of operatic works by A. Ciardi, John Parry, and T. Sari. No further information, however, has been found in other authorities. The same is true of some works other than the *Ivanhoe*. Likewise, the catalogue of the Library of Congress mentions amateur versions of most of the novels; but these are not here considered.

Page 115. Samuel Phelps and Miss Neilson. Samuel Phelps gave up a journalistic career to join the Corbett Ryder players in various northern towns, after which he came to Covent Garden, and for a time, especially in 1839-40, acted with Macready in various Shakespeare plays. Once, for a number of weeks, he alternated Iago and Othello with Macready.

Lilian Adelaide Neilson rose out of obscure and distressing circumstances to become one of the great tragic actors of all time. In commenting on her short life of only thirty-two years, the *Dictionary of National Biography* says of Miss Neilson: 'As a tragedian she had no rival during the latter half of the century.' Among many Shakespearean successes, her Juliet was 'perfect.' Yet she probably attained the summit of her fame as Amy Robsart and Rebecca of York in late dramatizations from Scott.

Speaking of Miss Neilson and Phelps, as they appeared in Drury Lane, Edward Stirling, manager of the playhouse then, reports as follows: 'Phelps played Isaac of York in a masterly style. Miss Neilson's Rebecca was a picture of the painter's pencil: her lovely features, foreign in cast, graceful bearing, and earnest acting, made the Jewish maiden the main feature of the piece. It was placed on the stage with careful study, real horses, and numerous auxiliaries.

. . . Rebecca realized a large sum—8000 pounds—more than Walter Scott received for his original romance.' (*Old Drury Lane* I. 290.)

Page 125. R. W. Elliston. This talented actor managed a number of playhouses, notably Drury Lane from 1819 to 1826, ending in bankruptcy. He was long remembered for his various escapades, humorous and otherwise, and for his dissipations, which robbed him of becoming an actor of the first rank. Charles Lamb, who had a fellow-feeling for the shortcomings of Elliston, pronounced him 'the best lover on the stage in both tragedy and comedy.' Lord Byron said of him: 'I can conceive of nothing better than Elliston is in gentleman's comedy or in some parts of tragedy.'

Page 126. Dibdin's *Kenilworth*. John Lowndes of London printed Dibdin's text, the preface to which explains that the shortness was demanded by the management because longer plays at Covent Garden had been said to be dull. According to this preface, Dibdin compiled the drama in two days.

Page 179. Imitation of Scott by Mély-Janin. One quotation from the *Figaro,* relative to Mély-Janin adaptation, shows the attitude of the French critics. 'It seems that when he composed it, the author used a pair of good scissors rather than a pen. What is good to take is also good to be kept, of course; but on the French stage it is not enough to take. One must disguise one's thefts; one must be original in one's imitation. The chief defects of the novels that are put on the stage are want of color and incoherence. The author took great liberties with the dramatic art. He has trodden upon (and quite in the English and Spanish way) the respectable rule of the unity of place. . . . The author has taken too much and too little from Scott; hence, the lengthy passages, lack of connection, improbabilities, historical misconceptions that swarm on every page.'

Page 183. Multiplicity of adaptations from Scott. After a time the theatres began to poke fun at the great number of plays drawn from English and American sources—notably, Byron, Scott, and Cooper. Thus, during a humorous sketch at the Gymnase, Paris, as early as 1824, one of the ladies was reported as suffering from an attack of Romanticism, 'that is, the art of speaking without making oneself understood.'

Then the following dialogue ensues, as quoted by Draper in his *Rise and Fall of French Romantic Drama,* p. 211:

'The Baron. My sister and nieces inhabit a chateau in the Department of Ille-et-Vilaine and pass their time in reading the novels of Lord Byron, Scott, and Company.

'Madelon.   Is this a business firm?

'The Baron.   Yes, and it exploits most profitably the craziness of the age.'

Page 185.   The versatility of Balfe.   Edward Ball, in his *Thirty-five Years of a Dramatic Author's Life,* page 119, says: 'Our popular operas are unquestionably excellent books, although Davidson declares that Balfe could make an opera out of an act of Parliament. See *Robert the Devil, Lucia di Lammermoor, Norma, The Bohemian Girl, Sonnambula,* etc.'

Page 203.   English borrowings from French plays.   Conditions did not wholly change in the next decades.   Percy Fitzgerald informs us that 225 plays were almost literally transferred across the Channel between 1850 and 1880.   In the year last named, no fewer than half of 40 plays running during the season in London were either direct translations or else imitations of the dramas of Paris.

XII. DRAMAS AND OPERAS RELATED TO THE NOVELS AND POEMS OF SCOTT

For convenience to the reader, the names of the dramatic productions drawn from the works of Sir Walter Scott are appended here in the alphabetical order of the names of the novels and poems. Though only the dramas adapted from the novels have been considered, a list of plays based on the poems is also included, for the sake of completeness. Yet there are a dozen or more casual mentions of other dramatic works which are not included, because the names of the authors and the time and conditions of acting have not been discovered.

A star placed before the title of a play indicates that the printed text in at least one form has been read; two stars indicate that the text was read by some one else, who submitted notes that are used in the discussion. Undoubtedly some of the later titles repeat in different words some older ones, for many plays may have been slightly changed or revamped, and then introduced under new names.

THE ABBOT

*1. The Abbot; or, Mary of Scotland. Henry Roxbury Beverley. Tottenham Street, London, 18 Sept., 1820.

*2. Mary of Scotland; or, The Heir of Avenel. Anonymous. Anthony Street Theatre, New York, 17 May, 1821.

**3. The Château de Loch-Leven; or, l'Evasion de Marie Stuart. R. C. Guilbert de Pixérécourt. Gaieté, Paris, 3 Dec., 1822. 30 times.

*4. Mary, Queen of Scots; or, The Escape from Loch Leven. William H. Murray. Royal Theatre, Edinburgh, 3 Oct., 1825.

ANNE OF GEIERSTEIN

1. 'New play,' elaborately staged. Anonymous. Bowery Theatre, New York, 3 March, 1834. Never printed.

THE ANTIQUARY

*1. The Antiquary. Isaac Pocock. Covent Garden, 1818. 1 night.

*2. The Antiquary. Revision of 1 by Daniel Terry; music by Henry R. Bishop. C. G., 25 Jan., 1820.

3. The Antiquary; or, The Heir of Glen Allen. Modification of 2 for Edinburgh by W. H. Murray. 20 Dec., 1820.

THE BLACK DWARF

1. The Wizard; or, The Brown Man of the Moor. Anonymous. Lyceum, 20 July, 1817.

THE BRIDAL OF TRIERMAIN

**1. Triermain. Operetta in five acts by J. L. Ellerton. 1831.

2. King Arthur and the Knights of the Round Table. Music by T. S. Cook. Drury Lane, 26 Dec., 1834.

**3. Bridal of Triermain. Scott words used; music by Frederick Corder. Wolverhampton Music Festival, 1886.

THE BRIDE OF LAMMERMOOR

1. The Bride of Lammermoor; or, The Spectre at the Fountain. Thomas John Dibdin. Surrey, London, 7 June, 1819.

*2. The Bride of Lammermoor. John William Calcraft (real name John William Cole). Royal, Edinburgh, 1 May, 1822.

**3. Le Caleb de Walter Scott. One act and songs. Achille d'Artois and Eugène de Planard; music by Adolphe Adam. Théâtre des Nouveautés, Paris, 17 Dec., 1827. 52 times.

4. Mermaiden's Well; or, The Fatal Prophecy. New Brunswick Theatre, London, 1828.

*5. La Fiancée de Lammermoor. Victor J. H. Brahain Ducange. Porte Sainte Martin, Paris, 25 March, 1828. 51 times.

6. La Fiancée de Lammermoor. A. Eugène Scribe and Daniel F. E. Auber. Opera Comique, Paris, 1829.

7. Le Nozze di Lammermoor. 'Opera demi-serio' in two acts by L. Balochi; music by Michel E. Carafa (di Colobrano). Théâtre Italien, Paris, 12 Dec., 1829.

**8. L'Irlandais; ou, L'esprit national. M. Benjamin. Gymnase, Paris, 6 Sept., 1831.

*9. Lucia di Lammermoor. Grand opera by Salvatore Cammarano; music by Gaetano Donizetti. Naples, 26 Sept., 1835.

*10. Lucie de Lammermoor. Alphonse Royer and Gustave Vaës (pseud.). Grand opera in four acts, using the Donizetti music. Renaissance, Paris, 10 Aug., 1839.

*11. Lucy of Lammermoor. Based on 10; by George Soane. Niblo's Garden, New York. Printed, 1854.

12. Lucia di Lammermoor. Parody; text by C. Helmerding; music by A. Conradi. Wallner Theatre, Berlin, 20 Oct., 1859.

13. Lucia de Lammermoor. Three acts, six tableaux; D. T. F. de Luna and D. V. de Lalama. Barcelona, Spain, 1864.

*14. Lucia de Lammermoor; or, The Laird, the Lover, and the

Lady. Burlesque of 6 and other operas. Henry J. Byron. Prince of Wales Theatre, London, 25 Sept., 1865.

15. Master of Ravenswood. J. Palgrave Simpson. English Opera House (Lyceum), London, 22 Dec., 1865.

16. Ravenswood play based on 10 and older one by George Almar. Olympic Theatre, New York, 10 Dec., 1865.

17. Ravenswood. Herman C. Merivale. Based on 15. English Opera House, 20 Sept., 1890. 100 times.

18. Lucy Did Sham Amour. Dr. Northall. Chatham Theatre, New York, 28 July, 1848.

*19. Ravenswood. F. S. Ganter and G. H. Braughan. New Orleans, 1873.

20. The Last Heir. Stephen Phillips. King's Theatre, Glasgow, 23 March, 1908.

The Fair Maid of Perth

*1. Fair Maid of Perth; or, The Battle of the Inch. Henry M. Milner and Thomas Hailes Lacy. Coburg Theatre, London, 23 June, 1828.

2. Fair Maid of Perth. Played by Charles Bass Company at Perth, 23 Sept., 1828. May be modification of 1 or original play.

3. Fair Maid of Perth. D. V. Bell. Bowery, New York, 17 June, 1829.

4. La Belle Drapière. Berthet. Paris, 1843.

*5. Le Jolie Fille de Perth. H. de Sainte George and J. Adenis; music by Georges Bizet. Opera, three acts, four scenes. Théâtre Lyrique, Paris, 26 Dec., 1867.

6. Hal o' the Wynd. Standard Theatre, London, 14 Sept., 1874.

The Fortunes of Nigel

1. The Fortunes of Nigel; or, King James First and his Times. Edward Fitzball (real name Edward Ball). Surrey, 25 June, 1822.

*2. Nigel; or, The Crown Jewels. Isaac Pocock. Covent Garden, 28 Jan., 1823.

*3. George Heriot; or, The Fortunes of Nigel. W. H. Murray. Royal, Edinburgh, 6 Feb., 1823.

4. King o' Scots. Andrew Halliday (Duff). Drury Lane, 26 Sept., 1868.

Guy Mannering

*1. Guy Mannering; or, The Gipsey's Prophecy. Daniel Terry (and Walter Scott). Covent Garden, 12 March, 1816. 18 times.

2. Guy Mannering; or, The Gipsey's Warning. Anonymous. Park Theatre, New York, 16 April, 1818. 'First on any stage.'

**3. Meg Merrilies, Die Ziguenerin. W. von Gersdorf. Printed, 1818.

*4. La Sorcière; ou, l'Orphelin Ecossais. Frédéric [Dupetit-Méré] and Victor [J. H. Brahain Ducange]. Gaieté, Paris, 3 May, 1821. 67 times.

5. The Witch of Derncleuch. J. Robinson Planché. English Opera House, 30 July, 1821.

**6. The Gipsey of Derncleuch. Douglas Jerrold. Based on 4. Sadler's Wells, 26 Aug., 1821.

**7. Dirk Hatteraick, the Dutch Smuggler; or, The Sorceress of Derncleuch. Version 5, with addition of parts of Lucy Bertram and Dandie Dinmont, and with touches from 4. Coburg, 4 Nov., 1821.

8. Guy Mannering. Abridgment of 1 for Hodgson's Juvenile Drama; printed about 1825.

*9. La Dame Blanche. A. Eugène Scribe; music by Adrien F. Boieldieu. Paris, 10 Dec., 1825. (Based also on the Monastery.) Ran for 1340 times up to 1875.

10. The White Maid. English version of 9. Covent Garden, 2 Jan., 1827.

11. Guy Mannering arranged as 'a popular burletta.' St. James, 13 Dec., 1838; also for the Marionettes, St. James, 13 Dec., 1851.

12. Spae Wife. Dion L. Boucicault. Elephant and Castle, London, 1866.

13. Guy Mannering in New Guise. Robert Reece. Royal, Edinburgh, Dec., 1866.

14. Version 1 with new scenic effect. Staged by William Wyndham. Royal, Edinburgh, 1 July, 1867.

15. Meg Merrilies. Henry Leslie. Glasgow, 10 Nov., 1873.

16. Meg Merrilies. Robert W. Chambers. Daly's, New York, 12 March, 1897.

THE HEART OF MIDLOTHIAN

*1. The Heart of Midlothian; or, The Lily of St. Leonard's. Thomas J. Dibdin. Surrey, 13 Jan., 1819. Ran 170 times.

*2. The Heart of Midlothian. Daniel Terry. Covent Garden, 17 April, 1819. 15 times.

3. Versions 1 and 2 combined by William Dimond. Bath, 3 Dec., 1819.

4. Modifications for Scotland. Royal, Edinburgh, 28 Nov., 1822. 38 times.

5. Heart of Midlothian. William H. Murray. Royal, Edinburgh, 5 March, 1824.

6. The Whistler. George Dibdin Pitt. Based on 'some unpublished chapters of the novel.' Victoria, 18 Jan., 1833.

7. La Prison d'Edimbourg. Opera by A. Eugène Scribe and Eugène de Planard; music by Michel E. Carafa. Opéra Comique, July 20, 1833. 22 times.

8. The Heart of Midlothian. Version 6 translated and modified by Capt. Rafter. London ed. is undated; probably acted at the Princess.

9. La Vendéenne. Paul Duport. Gymnase, Paris, 24 April, 1837, 60 times.

10. Jeanie Deans. Dion L. Boucicault. Laura Keene's Theatre, New York, 9 Jan., 1860. Ran 54 times. Same with slight modifications, Astley's Theatre, London, 26 Jan., 1863.

11. Effie Deans; or, The Lily of St. Leonard's. Version 1 probably, revised by Shepherd. Surrey, 7 Feb., 1863.

12. Heart of Midlothian. Colin H. Hazlewood. 1863.

13. Circumstantial Effie Deans. Travesty on version 10. Robert B. and William Brough. St. James, March, 1863.

*14. Jeanie Deans. Opera by Joseph Bennett; music by Hamish McCunn. Prince of Wales, Liverpool, 22 Feb., 1872.

15. Effie and Jeanie Deans. George Hamilton. Albion, 29 Oct., 1877.

THE HIGHLAND WIDOW

1. Dougal, the Piper; or, The Highland Widow. Adelphi, Edinburgh, 20 Sept., 1836. 9 times.

2. Sarah; ou, L'Orpheline de Glencoe. Two-act opera. Alexandre Mélesville; music by Albert Grisar. Opéra Comique, Paris, 26 April, 1840.

IVANHOE

*1. Ivanhoe; or, The Jew's Daughter. Thomas J. Dibdin. Surrey, 20 Jan., 1820.

*2. Ivanhoe; or, The Jewess. W. T. Moncrieff. Printed, 1820.

*3. Ivanhoe; or, The Knight Templar. Samuel Beazley. Covent Garden, 2 March, 1820. 18 times.

**4. The Hebrew. George Soane. Drury Lane, March 2, 1820. 8 times.

*5. Ivanhoe; or, Isaac of York. Printed in Birmingham, 1820.

*6. Ivanhoe; or, The Jew of York. Printed in London, 1820.

7. Ivanhoe. Hodgson's Juvenile Drama, 1822.

8. Ivanhoe. Probably modification of 1 by J. W. Calcraft. Royal, Edinburgh.

9. Ivanhoe. Made by William H. Murray from the other plays. Royal, Edinburgh, 24 Nov., 1823. Never printed. 17 times.

**10. Ivanhoé. Emile Deschamps and Gabriele Gustave de Wailly. Odéon, Paris, 15 Sept., 1826. Printed, 1829.

11. The Maid of Judah; or, The Knights Templars. M. Rophino Lacy; music selected by Rossini. Based on version 10. Covent Garden, 7 March, 1829.

12. Das Gericht der Templar. J. R. Lenz. Published at Mainz, 1826.

**13. Der Templar und die Jüden. W. A. Wohlbrüch, with assistance and music by Heinrich Marschner. Printed in Leipzig, 1829.

*14. The Templar and the Jewess. English version of 13 by John P. Jackson. Printed about 1833.

15. Ivanhoe. G. Rossi. Produced at the Scala Theatre, Milan. Published, 1834.

**16. Il Templaro. Opera by Gerolomo-Maria Marini; music by Ottone Nicolai. Turin Festival ,1839.

*17. Ivanhoe. Travesty by Brough Brothers. 1850.

*18. Ivanhoe. Travesty by Henry J. Byron. Strand, London, and Royal, Liverpool, 25 Dec., 1862.

19. Ivanhoe. Cantata by Victor Roussy; music by Charles Victor Sieg. Théâtre Imperial de l'Opéra, Paris, 18 Nov., 1864.

**20. Ivanhoe. Fox F. Cooper. Astley's, Easter Monday, 1869.

21. Rebecca. Andrew Halliday (Duff). Drury Lane, 23 Sept., 1871.

22. Ivanhoe; or, Rebecca of York. D. R. Edgar. Liverpool Amphitheatre, 27 Nov., 1871.

*23. Isaac of York; or, Normans and Saxons at Home. Travesty. Thomas F. Plowman; music by Sir Arthur Sullivan. Court, 29 Nov., 1871. 100 times.

24. Ivanhoe. R. Cowie. Royal, Dundee, 15 Feb., 1875.

25. Ivanhoe Abroad; or, Ivanhoe Settled and Rebecca Righted. A second travesty by Thomas F. Plowman. Oxford Theatre, Oxford, 15 Jan., 1878.

**26. Rebecca. Paroles et Musique de A. Castegnier. London, 1882; Les Normans, slightly different version, Trouville, 1886.

*27. Ivanhoe. Opera by Julian Sturgis; music by Sir Arthur Sullivan. English Opera House, 31 Jan., 1891. 106 times.

28. Ivanhoe. Version 18 modified by Benjamin Aymar and John R. Blake. Columbia Univ. Dramatic Club, Irving Place Theatre, New York, 8 May, 1893.

*29. Ivanhoe. Maud I. Findlay. School Drama. Oxford Press, 1917.

KENILWORTH

1. Kenilworth Castle; or, The Days of Good Queen Bess. J. Robinson Planché. Adelphi, 8 Feb., 1821.

*2. Kenilworth; or, The Countess of Leicester. Thomas J. Dibdin. Surrey, 14 Feb., 1821; Covent Garden, 8 March, 1821. 14, 5 times.

*3. Kenilworth; or, England's Golden Days. Version 2 with added pageantry. Probably revised by William Dimond. Bath, 15 Dec., 1821.

*4. Le Château de Kenilworth. J. B. E. Cantiran de Boirie, Frédéric [Dupetit-Méré?], and H. Lemaire. Porte Sainte Martin, Paris, 23 March, 1822. Ran 49 times in 1822, 18 in 1823.

*5. Kenilworth; or, The Merry Days of Old England. Printed by J. L. Huie, Edinburgh, 1822.

6. Le Château de Kenilworth; ou, Le Comte de Leicester. A. Eugène Scribe and Alexandre Mélesville; music by Daniel F. E. Auber. Opéra Comique, Paris, 25 Jan., 1823. 35 times; by 1828, 60 times.

*7. Kenilworth. Combination of other plays with parts of the novel by William Oxberry. Nearest like version 5. Published in Edinburgh, 1824.

8. Emilia. Alexandre Soumet. Comédie Française, 1 Sept., 1827. 19 times.

9. Amy Robsart. Victor Hugo, but credited with his permission to his brother-in-law, Paul Foucher. Odéon, Paris, 13 Feb., 1828.

10. Die Flucht nach Kenilworth. J. R. Lenz. Published in Mainz, 1826.

11. Tilbury Fort. Edward Sterling. Gravesend, 1829.

12. Kenilworth. Ballet by M. Deshayes; music by Michael Costa. King's, 3 March, 1831; Covent Garden, 9 Feb., 1833.

13. Le Comtesse de Leicester. Théâtre Madame, 10 Oct., 1840. Resumé of older plays in French.

*14. The Earl of Leicester. Historical play by Samuel Heath. Printed in London, 1843.

*15. Kenilworth; or, Ye Queene, Ye Earle, and Ye Maydenne. Travesty by Andrew Halliday (Duff) and Frederic Lawrence. Strand, 27 Dec., 1858.

16. Amy Robsart. Andrew Halliday (Duff). Drury Lane, 24 Sept., 1870.

17. Kenilworth; or, Gentle Amy Robsart. Royal Alfred, 12 Nov., 1870.

18. Kenilworth. Travesty by Mark Kingthorne. Norwich, 10 May, 1880.

19. Little Amy Robsart. Travesty by George L. Gordon and J. Mackay. Philharmonic, 28 Jan., 1882.

20. Leicester. J. A. Coupland. 1884.

21. Kenilworth. Travesty by Robert Reece and H. B. Fairnie. Avenue, 19 Dec., 1885.

22. Amy Robsart. French opera by Paul Milliet; music by Isidore de Lara; translated and adapted by Frederick Weatherley, and produced in English by Sir Augustus Harris. Covent Garden, 20 July, 1893.

23. Kenilworth. C. J. Archer and A. E. Aubert. Croyden, 1 April, 1893.

24. Kenilworth. Grand opera by William Müller; music by Bruno Oscar Klein. Printed in Leipzig, 1894, acted, 1895.

25. Kenilworth; or, Amy's Aims and Leicester's Lesson. Travesty by Clayton F. McMichael; music by Edmond D. Beale. Univ. of Pennsylvania Dramatic Club, Broad Street Theatre, Philadelphia, 15 April, 1895.

26. Kenilworth. Max Goldberg. Hammersmith Lyric, 25 Nov., 1895.

27. Kenilworth. J. S. Blythe. Glasgow, 5 June, 1899.

The Lady of the Lake

*1. The Lady of the Lake. Thomas J. Dibdin. Surrey, 1810.

*2. The Lady of the Lake. Edmund J. Eyre. Edinburgh, 15 Jan., 1811.

*3. The Knight of Snowdoun. Thomas Morton; music by Henry R. Bishop. Covent Garden, 5 Feb., 1811.

**4. La Donna del Lago. A. L. Tottola; music by G. A. Rossini. San Carlo, Naples, 4 Oct., 1819; King's, London, 18 Feb., 1823.

*5. La Dama del Lago. National Theatre, Mexico City, 1833. Printed in Mexico, 1833.

*6. Blanche of Devon; or, The Death of Roderick Dhu. In Dramas for Home Representation, ed. by S. S. Steele, undated.

*7. Lady of the Lake. Travesty by Mortimer Thomson. Niblo's Garden, New York, 21 June, 1860.

*8. Lady of the Lake. 'Ephemeral burlesque' by Robert Reece. Royalty, Sept., 1866.

*9. The Lady of the Lake. Major Joseph Barton. Printed in Elgin, Illinois, 1871.

10. Lady of the Lake. Andrew Halliday (Duff); music by W. C. Levey. Drury Lane, 21 Sept., 1872.

11. Lady of the Lake. Cantata by Sir George Macfarren. Glasgow Town-Hall, 15 Nov., 1877.

*12. The Cross of Fire. Cantata by Heinrich Bluthaupt; music by Max Bruch. Translated into English by Henry D. Chapman, and published in New York, 1905.

THE LAY OF THE LAST MINSTREL

*1. Border Feuds; or, The Lady of Buccleuch. Published in Dublin, 1811.

2. Lay of the Last Minstrel. Cantata by James McCunn; music by Hamish McCunn. Published in London, 1888.

THE LORD OF THE ISLES

1. Robert the Bruce. Perth, August, 1819.

*2. Lord of the Isles; or, Gathering of the Clans. Operetta by Edward Ball; music by G. H. B. Rodwell. Surrey, 2 Nov., 1834.

3. Lord of the Isles. Henry Gadsby. Brighton, 13 Feb., 1879.

MARMION

1. Marmion; or, The Battle of Flodden Field. Anonymous. Printed in New York and Edinburgh, 1812.

*2. Marmion. James N. Barker; but credited for advertising purposes to Thomas Morton. Park, New York, 13 April, 1812; published in New York, 1816.

*3. Flodden Field. Stephen and Henry Kemble. Drury Lane, 31 Dec., 1818.

*4. Marmion. Edward Ball (Fitzball). Astley's, June, 1848.

THE MONASTERY

**1. La Dame Blanche. A. Eugène Scribe; music by Adrien F. Boieldieu. Opéra Comique, Paris, 10 Dec., 1825. (Also based on Guy Mannering.) By 1864 had run 1000 times; by 1875, 1340 times.

2. The White Lady; or, The Spirit of Avenel. In part a translation of version 1; music by T. S. Cooke. Drury Lane, 9 Oct., 1826. 9 times.

3. The White Lady. Translated by J. Howard Payne. Park, New York, 1832.

THE LEGEND OF MONTROSE

1. The Legend of Montrose. Thomas J. Dibdin. Surrey, 3 July, 1819.

*2. Montrose. Anonymous. Glasgow, 1820.

*3. Montrose; or, The Children of the Mist. Isaac Pocock; music by Henry R. Bishop. Covent Garden, 14 Feb., 1822.

4. Montrose. Version 3 adapted for Edinburgh by W. H. Murray. Royal, Edinburgh, 3 May, 1823.

5. Montrose. Version 2 shortened for Hodgson's Juvenile Drama, 1825.

*6. Montrose; or, The Gathering of the Clans. 'By a Gentleman of Glasgow.' Resembles 2 at many points. Glasgow, 1847.

OLD MORTALITY

*1. The Battle of Bothwell Brig, a Scottish Romance. Charles Farley; music by Henry R. Bishop. Covent Garden, 22 May, 1820. 12 times.

2. Old Mortality; or, Burley and Morton. Thomas J. Dibdin. Surrey, June 20, 1820.

*3. Old Mortality; or, The Battle of Bothwell Brig. J. W. Calcraft (Cole). Edinburgh, 3 May, 1823.

**4. Le Exilé. Achille Dartois, Théodore Anne, and Jules H. de Tully. Vaudeville, Paris, 9 July, 1825. 31 times.

5. Têtes Rondes et Cavalieri. J. A. P. F. Ancelot and J. X. Boniface. Vaudeville, Paris, 25 Sept., 1833.

6. I Puritani di Scozia; also called I Puritani ed Cavalieri. Count C. Pepoli; music by Vincenzo Bellini. Italian Opera, Paris, 1835.

7. Cavaliers and Roundheads. Isaac Pocock. Drury Lane, 13 Oct., 1835.

8. Los Puritanos de Escocia. Spanish version with Bellini music. Cruz, 1836.

9. Old Mortality; or, The Heir of Milnwood. W. E. Sutter. Sadler's Wells, 13 Sept., 1869.

10. Drumclog; or, The Covenanters. Edinburgh, 5 Sept., 1871.

11. '1679.' Charles Webb. Edinburgh, summer of 1873.

PEVERIL OF THE PEAK

*1. Peveril of the Peak; or, The Days of King Charles the Second. Edward Fitzball (or Ball). Surrey, 6 Feb., 1823.

*2. Peveril of the Peak. Version 1 modified for the Royal, Edinburgh, 12 April, 1823.

*3. Peveril of the Peak. Opera by Isaac Pocock; music by C. E. Horn. Covent Garden, 21 Oct., 1826. 9 times.

4. England in the Days of Charles the Second. W. G. Wills. Drury Lane, 22 Sept., 1877.

THE PIRATE

*1. The Pirate; or, The Wild Woman of Zetland. Thomas J. Dibdin. Surrey, 7 Jan., 1822.

2. The Pirate. J. Robinson Planché. Olympic, 14 Jan., 1822.

3. The Pirate. Anonymous; music by William Rooke. Drury Lane, 15 Jan., 1822. Later revised. 9 times.

*4. The Pirate; or, The Reimkennar of Zetland. 'Not founded on any other play.' Probably by W. H. Murray. Royal, Edinburgh, 29 March, 1824.

QUENTIN DURWARD

*1. Quentin Durward. R. Haworth. Published in London, 1823.

2. Quentin Durward. John Thomas Haines. Coburg, 9 May, 1823.

3. Quentin Durward. American version by R. W. Ewing. No record of production.

*4. Quentin Durward. J. L. Huie. Caledonian, Edinburgh, 23 June, 1823.

5. Quentin Durward; or, The Wild Boar of the Ardennes. Hodgson's Juvenile Drama, published about 1825.

6. Louis XI à Peronne. Jean-Marie Mély-Janin. Théâtre Française, 15 Feb., 1827. 50 times.

7. Louis XI. Casimir Delavigne. 1832.

*8. Quentin Durward. Edward Fitzball (Ball); music by Henry R. Laurent, Jr. Covent Garden, 6 Dec., 1848.

9. Louis XI; or, The Wicksey Warrior and the Nicksey Monarch. Burlesque. West Hartepool, 9 July, 1859.

**10. Louis the Eleventh. John Arthur Coupland. Published, 1889.

**11. Quentin Durward. P. Brill. Published, 1894.

*12. Quentin Durward. Charles A. Merz and Frank W. Tuttle. Yale Dramatic Association, New Haven, 13 June, 1914.

REDGAUNTLET

1. Redgauntlet. Anonymous. Acted in 1824.

2. Redgauntlet. Edinburgh, 1825. Probably by W. H. Murray.

3. La Quittance du Diable. Alfred de Musset. Accepted by Théâtre des Nouveautés, Paris, but probably never acted. 1830.

4. Le Revenant. Anonymous; music by Gornis. Opéra Comique, Paris, 1 Jan., 1834. 33 times.

*5. Redgauntlet. French opera by Paul H. Foucher and Jules E. Alboise de Pujol. Anbigu-Comique, Paris, 18 Feb., 1843.

6. Redgauntlet. A. D. M'Neill. Royal, Dundee, May, 1872.

ROB ROY

1. Rob Roy. 'Entirely new spectacle.' Pantheon, Edinburgh, 17 Jan., 1818. 6 times.

*2. Rob Roy Macgregor; or, Auld Lang Syne. Isaac Pocock. Covent Garden, 12 March, 1818. 32 times in London; 41 times in Edinburgh, first run.

*3. Rob Roy, the Gregarch. George Soane. Drury Lane, 25 March, 1818.

4. New version played by Corbett Ryder Company. Caledonian, Edinburgh, 29 March, 1825.

5. Third version played by Ryder Company. Edinburgh, 3 May, 1825.

6. Gregarch, the Highland Watchword. Astley's, 13 May, 1831.

7. Rob Roy. Opera by Friedrich von Flotow; words by Paul Duport and de Forges.

*8. Robbing Roy; or, Scotched and Kilt. Travesty by Francis C. Burnand; music by H. C. Stephens. Gaiety, 11 Nov., 1879.

9. Rob Roy. J. R. Park. Wishaw, 6 Sept., 1905.

St. Ronan's Well

1. St. Ronan's Well. J. R. Planché (or R. Planché). Edinburgh, 5 June, 1824.

2. Le Comte de Sainte Ronan; ou, l'Ecole et le Château. A. Eugène Scribe and Dupin. Théâtre du Palais Royal, 21 June, 1831.

3. St. Ronan's Well. A. D. M'Neill. Princess, Edinburgh, 5 June, 1824.

4. St. Ronan's Well. D. D. Fisher. Belfast, 21 Jan., 1876.

5. St. Ronan's Well. Richard Davey and W. Herries Pollock. Trafalgar, 12 June, 1893.

The Talisman

*1. Knights of the Cross; or, The Hermit's Prophecy. Samuel Beazley; music by Henry R. Bishop. Drury Lane, 17 Feb., 1825.

2. The Talisman. By an Edinburgh author. Royal, 22 June, 1825. 16 times.

3. Il Talismano; ossia, La Terzio Crociato in Palestina. Opera by Giovanni Pacini, 1829.

4. Richard en Palestine. Opera in three acts by Paul Foucher; music by Adolphe Adam. Opéra, Paris, 7 Oct., 1844. 8 times.

5. The Talisman; or, King Richard Coeur de Lion and the Knight of the Couchant Leopard. Brough Brothers. Drury Lane, 28 March, 1853.

**6. The Talisman. Catherine Swanwick. Printed in London, 1864 and 1882.

7. Il Talismano; or, the Knight of the Leopard. Arthur Mattison; music by Michael W. Balfe, revised by Sir George Macfarren. Translated into Italian by Signor G. Zaffira. Drury Lane, 11 June, 1874.

8. Talisman. Travesty by J. F. McArdle. Royal, Liverpool, 10 Aug., 1874.

9. Richard Coeur de Lion. Andrew Halliday (Duff). Drury Lane, 26 Sept., 1874.

10. Talisman. School drama by Maud I. Findlay. Oxford Press, 1917.

11. Richard the Lion-Hearted. Motion-Picture by Allied Producers and Distributors. New York, 1923.

THE TWO DROVERS

1. Second Sight; or, Prediction. Henry Goff. Surrey, 6 Feb., 1828.

2. Two Drovers. William H. Murray. Royal, Edinburgh, 10 Nov., 1828.

WAVERLEY

1. Waverley. Version used by Corbett Ryder Còmpany. Perth, 18 Oct., 1822.

2. Waverley; or, The Forty-Five. Caledonian, Edinburgh, 19 July, 1823. Possibly the same as version 1.

*3. Waverley; or, Sixty Years After. Edward Fitzball (Ball). Coburg, 8 March, 1824.

*4. Version 3 revised by J. W. Calcraft. Royal, Edinburgh, 22 May, 1824.

5. Waverley. New version. Adelphi, Edinburgh, 18 Sept., 1852.

6. Waverley; or, A Rebel for Love. Royal, Edinburgh, 11 Sept., 1871.

WOODSTOCK

*1. Woodstock. Isaac Pocock. Covent Garden, 20 May, 1826. 6 times.

2. Woodstock; or, The Cavalier in Edinburgh, a Tale of the Year 1651. Edinburgh, 17 June, 1826. 7 times.

**3. Charles Stuart; ou, le Château de Woodstock. Paroles de M. Félix de Croisy et Antoine Béraud. Porte Sainte Martin, Paris, 8 Sept., 1826. 35 times.

4. Charles II; ou, Le Labyrinthe de Woodstock. Alexandre Duval. Odéon, Paris, 11 March, 1828. 22 times.

5. Le Page du Woodstock. Xavier de Maistre, Duvert, and Dupeuty. Vaudeville, Paris, 8 March, 1828.

XIII. BIBLIOGRAPHY

Many libraries and individuals have generously assisted by furnishing books or valuable references. Some of these are the university libraries of Harvard, Yale, Columbia, Chicago, Michigan, and Pennsylvania; the public libraries of Boston, New York, Baltimore, Chicago, Pittsburgh, New Orleans, and Syracuse, and the Library of Congress (especially the Division of Music and the director) ; the Peabody Institute of Baltimore, the Newberry Library of Chicago, the Advocates Library of Edinburgh, the Bodlein of Oxford, the libraries of the British Museum and Miss Joan Joshua, who has taken some notes of various plays, the library of Perth, and Hon. Peter Baxter, author of the *Drama in Perth,* Dublin University, the different libraries of Paris and Mlle. I. Poettecher, who has investigated some of the newspapers and texts with regard to the French dramatizations of Scott, the Strand Theatre of London and Arthur Shirley; Frank J. Wilstach, Robert W. Chambers, John Golden, Benjamin Aymar, and Mrs. Kate Gerry Alexander.

Below is given a partial list of all the works found to be relevant, except for a few that yielded only a stray note or two each. The list is divided into two parts for the sake merely of convenience. Certain works are frequently mentioned in the footnotes of various pages. Most of these are indicated by giving only the name of the author, after the title of the book appears once or twice. These are easily noticed or may be located by name of author and title of work in the bibliography below. Thus 'Dibdin' means *Annals of the Edinburgh Stage* by James C. Dibdin; 'Genest' means *Some Account of the English Stage* by Rev. John Genest; 'Brown' means *The New York Stage* by Col. T. Allston Brown, and so on.

I

Titles of Books and Pamphlets

Adams, W. Davenport. Dictionary of the Drama. Unfortunately only one volume, covering from A to G, was printed. London, 1904

Angus, J. Keith. A Scotch Playhouse (Marischal Street, Aberdeen). London, 1878

Anonymous. Actors by Daylight. London, 1838-9

Arvin, Neil Cole. Eugène Scribe and the French Theatre. Cambridge, Mass., 1924

Baker, Henry Barton. Our Old Actors. London, 1903

Ball (or Fitzball), Edward. Thirty-Five Years of a Dramatic Author's Life. London, 1859

Ball, Margaret. Sir Walter Scott as a Critic of Literature. New York, 1907

Bancroft, Marie and Squire. The Bancrofts. London, 1909

Banyham, Walter. The Glasgow Stage. Glasgow, 1892

Baxter, Counsellor Peter. The Drama in Perth. Perth, 1907

Bowen, C. M. Manzoni and Scott. Dublin Univ. Rev. April-June, 1925

Boyd, Frank. Records of the Dundee Stage. Dundee, 1887

Brawley, Brerton. A Short History of the English Drama. New York, 1921

Brerton, Austin. The Lyceum and Henry Irving. London, 1903

Broadbent, R. J. Annals of the Liverpool Stage. Liverpool, 1908

Brown, T. Allston. History of the New York Stage. New York, 1903

Bunn, Alfred. The Stage both Before and Behind the Curtain. London, 1840

Canning, Hon. A. S. G. Sir Walter Scott, Studied in Eight Novels. London, 1912

Carhart, Margaret S. The Life and Work of Joanna Baillie. New Haven, 1923

Chambers, Robert. Sketch of the Edinburgh Theatre Royal. Edinburgh, 1859

Clapp, Henry A. Reminiscences of a Dramatic Critic. Boston, 1902

Clapp, William W., Jr. A Record of the Boston Stage. Boston, 1853

Clement, Clara Erskine. Charlotte Cushman. Boston, 1882

Cole, John William. Life and Theatrical Times of Charles Kean. London, 1859

Coleman, John. Fifty Years of an Actor's Life. London, 1904

Cook, Edward Dutton. On the Stage. London, 1883

Cook, Edward Dutton. Hours with the Players. London, ed. of 1883

Davidson, Gladys. Two Hundred Opera Plots. Philadelphia, 1911

D. G., ed. [George Daniel] Dramatized Works of Sir Walter Scott. London [1835?]

Dibdin, James C. Annals of the Edinburgh Stage. Edinburgh, 1888

Dibdin, Thomas John. Reminiscences. London, 1827; New York, 1828

Dictionary of National Biography. New York, 1885-1900

Dramas from the Novels, Tales, and Romances of the Author of Waverley. Edinburgh, 1823

Draper, F. W. M. The Rise and Fall of French Romantic Drama. London, 1923

Dunlap, William. History of the American Theatre. New York, 1832

Dye, William S., Jr. Melodrama in England from 1800 to 1842. Philadelphia, 1913

Edwards, Henry S. History of Opera. London, 1862

Fitzgerald, Percy H. Operas of Gilbert and Sullivan. Philadelphia, 1894

Genest, Rev. John. Some Account of the English Stage. Bath, 1832

Greg, Henry. Key to the Waverley Novels. London, 1898

Grove, Sir George. Dictionary of Music and Musicians, ed. by J. A. Fuller-Maitland. New York, 1904

Hazlitt, William. Dramatic Essays, ed. by William Archer and Robert W. Love. London, 1893

Hutton, Laurence. Curiosities of the American Stage. New York, 1891

Hutton, Laurence. Plays and Players. New York, 1875

Ireland, Joseph N. Mrs. Duff. London, 1882

Ireland, Joseph N. Records of the New York Stage. New York, 1867

Klein, Herman. Thirty Years of Musical Life in London. New York, 1903

Knight, Joseph. Theatrical Notes. London, 1893

Larousee, Pierre. Grand Dictionnaire Universel. Paris, 1867

Lawson, Robb. The Story of the Scots Stage. Paisley, 1917

Levey, R. M. and O'Rorke, J. Annals of the Theatre Royal, Dublin. Dublin, 1903

Lockhart, John G. Life of Scott. Philadelphia, 1838

Lohee, Henry C. Annals of Music in America. New York, 1922

Ludlow, N. M. Dramatic Life as I Found It. St. Louis, 1880

Lowe, Robert W. Bibliographical Account of English Theatrical Literature.

Macready, William Charles. Reminiscences, Letters, and Diaries, ed. by Sir Frederick Pollock. New York, 1875

Macready, William Charles. Diaries, 1833-1851, ed. by William Tonybee. New York, 1912

Marston, Westland. Our Recent Actors. London, 1888

McSpadden, J. Walker. Waverley Synopses. New York, 1909

McSpadden, J. Walker. Opera Synopses. New York, 1911

Matthews, Brander. Studies of the Stage. New York, 1894

Matthews, Brander. A Book about the Theatre. New York, 1916

Matthews, Brander and Hutton, Laurence. Actors and Actresses of Great Britain and the United States. New York, 1886

Melitz, Leo. Opera-Goers Guide, trans. by Richard Salinger. New York, 1921

Merivale, Herman C. Bar, Stage, and Platform. London, 1902

Morley, Henry. Journal of a London Play-Goer. London, 1866

Morris, Mowbray. Theatrical Criticism. London, 1882

Murdock, James E. The Stage. Cincinnati, 1884

Murray, William H. Farewell and Occasional Addresses. Edinburgh, 1851

Odell, G. C. D. Shakespeare from Betterton to Irving. New York, 1920

Oxberry, William. Dramatic Biographies. London, 1825-6

Partridge, Eric. The French Romantics' Knowledge of English Literature. Paris, 1924

Pascoe, Charles E. The Dramatic List. London, 1879

Paul, G. H. H. and Gebbie, George, eds. The Stage and its Stars. Philadelphia [1895?]

Pemberton, T. Edgar. Charles Dickens and the Stage. London, 1888

Pemberton, T. Edgar. Ellen Terry and her Sisters. London, 1902

Penley, Belville S. The Bath Stage. London, 1892

Phelps, W. May and Forbes-Robertson, Johnston. Life of Samuel Phelps. London, 1886

Pitou, A. Les Origines du Mélodrame français. Paris, 1910

Planché, James Robinson. Recollections and Reflections. London, ed. of 1872

Plowman, Thomas F. Fifty Years of a Showman's Life. London, 1918; New York, 1919

Price, W. T. Technique of the Drama. New York, 1905

Raymond, George. Life and Enterprizes of William Elliston, Comedian. London, 1859

Reingolds-Winslow, Catherine M. Yesterdays with Actors. Boston, 1887

Rendle, T. McDonald. Swings and Roundabouts. London, 1919

Robins, Edward. Twelve Great Actresses. New York, 1900

Robson, William. The Old Play-Goer. London, 1846

Rogers, May. Waverley Dictionary. Chicago, 1879

Scott, Clement. The Drama of Yesterday and Today. London, 1898

Sharp, R. Farquharson. A Short History of the English Stage. London, 1909

Smythe, Arthur J. Life of William Terriss. Westminster, 1898

Stebbins, Emma. Charlotte Saunders Cushman, Letters and Memorials of her Life. New York, 1899

Stirling, Edward. Old Drury Lane. London, 1881

Stoker, Bram. Personal Recollections of Henry Irving. New York, 1906

Terry, Daniel. British Theatrical Gallery. London, 1825
Theatre Royal, Dublin, History of. Anonymous. Dublin, 1870
Tompkins, Eugene. History of the Boston Theatre. Boston, 1908
Toole, James L. Reminiscences. London, 1889
Towers, John. Dictionary Catalog of Operas and Operettas. Morgantown, West Virginia, 1910
Upton, George P. The Standard Cantatas. Chicago, 1888
Upton, George P. The Standard Light Operas. Chicago, 1907
Walsh, Townsend. The Career of Dion Boucicault. New York, 1915
Waverley Dramas. Edinburgh, 1872. Reprint by J. L. Huie of the 1823 ed., save that a Nigel play replaces a Peveril of the Peak.
Weglin, Oscar. Early American Plays. New York, 1900
Wills, Freeman. W. G. Wills. London, 1898
Wyndham, Henry Saxe. Annals of Covent Garden. London, 1905

II
REFERENCES TO PERIODICALS

Some of the periodicals consulted are mentioned in the list given below. Except where specified, the definite references by years are given in the footnotes in the main text.

Athenæum, London, after 1832.
Atlantic Monthly, Aug., 1869. Article on Fechter by Charles Dickens.
Bath Chronicle, Bath Herald.
Bookman. New York, April and May, 1902.
Caledonian Mercury, Edinburgh.
Daily Pennsylvania of Univ. of Pennsylvania, 1893.
Drama, The. A Daily Record of Plays. October 22 to December 10, 1821. Two Gentlemen of Dublin University.
Drama, The; or, Theatrical Pocket Magazine. London, 1821-4.
Dramatic Notes. London, 1879-80.
Drama Register. London, 1851-3.
Dramatic Review. Vols. I and II. Edinburgh, 1822.
European Magazine. London.
French Periodicals: Le Constitutionnel, Les Courriere des Théâtres, Le Figaro, Le Globe, Le National, La Pandore, Le Revue et Gazette des Théâtres, Le Temps, Miroir des Spectacles, Moniteur Universel.
Gentleman's Magazine, 1818-1839.
Glasgow Herald.
London Magazine.

London Times.

New York Evening Post, Herald, and Tribune.

Revue Française, 1823.

Revue Hispanique, 1925.

Theatre, The; or, Daily Miscellany of Fashion, Edinburgh, 1822.

Theatre, The. Dublin, 1821-1822.

Theatre, The. London, 1878-1897. Contains criticisms by E. Dutton Cook.

Theatrical Inquisitor. Vols. I-VIII. London, 1812-16.

Theatrical John Bull. Birmingham, 1824.

Theatrical Journal. London, 1829-30; 1842-6.

Theatrical Looker-on. Birmingham, 1822.

Theatrical Magazine. London, 1822-3.

Theatrical Observer. London.

Theatrical Pocket Magazine (also called the Drama). London, 1821-4.

Theatrical Times. London, 1847-8.

Wilstach, Paul. Dramatizations of Scott. Bookman, April and May, 1902.

INDEX OF CHIEF NAMES AND TITLES

Below are given only the names of authors, plays, and theatres that are important in the history of Waverley dramas. It seems unnecessary to include the names of characters in the novels and plays themselves, or of those who have borne but a small part in the preparation and acting of the various transcripts from the novels of Sir Walter Scott.